The Cheapskate's Guide to
CRUISES

The Cheapskate's Guide to
CRUISES

The Very Best Trips for the Lowest Cost

Steve and Patty Tanenbaum

A Citadel Press Book
Published by Carol Publishing Group

Copyright © 1999 Steve and Patty Tanenbaum

All rights reserved. No part of this book may be reproduced in any form, except by a newspaper or magazine reviewer who wishes to quote brief passages in connection with a review.

A Citadel Press Book
Published by Carol Publishing Group
Citadel Press is a registered trademark of Carol Communications, Inc.

Editorial, sales and distribution, rights and permissions inquiries should be addressed to Carol Publishing Group, 120 Enterprise Avenue, Secaucus, N.J. 07094

In Canada: Canadian Manda Group, One Atlantic Avenue, Suite 105, Toronto, Ontario M6K 3E7

Carol Publishing books may be purchased in bulk at special discounts for sales promotion, fund-raising, or educational purposes. Special editions can be created to specifications. For details, contact Special Sales Department, 120 Enterprise Avenue, Secaucus, N.J. 07094.

Manufactured in the United States of America
10 9 8 7 6 5 4 3 2 1

Library of Congress Cataloging-in-Publication Data

Tanenbaum, Steve.
    The cheapskate's guide to cruises : the very best trips for the lowest cost / Steve and Patty Tanenbaum.
      p.   cm.
   ISBN 0-8065-2044-2 (pbk.)
    1. Ocean travel—Guidebooks.   I. Tanenbaum, Patricia. II. Title.
   G.550.T36   1998
   910'.2'02—dc21
                                                         98-39568
                                                                CIP

Dedicated to our parents,
for encouraging and sharing
our travels around the world

Contents

Preface   ix

Part I: Principles of Bargain Cruising

1. Stretching Vacation Dollars to the Limit:
   Four-Star Cruise Vacations at a One-Star Price   3
2. Free Travel to Your Cruise Ship: Frequent Flying
   on Terra Firma   28
3. Free Travel Cash: The Best Helping Hand   45
4. Take Another 5 to 20 Percent Off: Legitimate
   Discount and Rebate Travel Clubs and Agencies   56
5. Shopping and Booking Discount Cruises:
   The *New York Times* and *L.A. Times* Connection   63

Part II: Bargain Cruising: Selection to Bon Voyage

6. Selecting Ideal Cruises: Knowing Vacation
   Objectives and Destination   95
7. Be Savvy: Predeparture Essentials   124
8. Anchors Aweigh! Finding Your Ship and Cabin   146

Part III: A Smorgasbord of the Best Bargain Cruises

9.	Cruising Alaska: America's Last Frontier	179
10.	The Caribbean: A Tropical Delight	205
11.	Bermuda: Fun in the Sun	239
12.	The Mexican Riviera: South of the Border	249
13.	The Greek Isles, Turkey, and the Mediterranean: A Shimmering Necklace of Pearls	263
14.	The Yangtze River and Three Gorges Cruise: An Ultimate Adventure	289
15.	More World-Class Bargain Cruises	299
	Appendix A: Steve and Pat's Essential Contacts	319
	Appendix B: Cyberspace—Great Web Sites	323
	Index	329

Preface

We admit it—we love to travel and we love travel bargains of every kind, shape, and description. Steve's companion book, *The Cheapskate's Guide to Vacations*, highlights dirt-cheap global destinations like Moorea (Tahiti), Africa (for photo safaris), China, Israel, Paris, and London. Now our joint efforts have created this unique guide dedicated to discount cruising.

Cruising has truly become America's newest and favorite travel pastime. Consequently, many cruise books offer a variety of information. All too often this takes the shape of hundreds of pages of cold facts, figures, and perhaps small black-and-white photos of every cruise ship sailing the seven seas. Choosing a cruise vacation can be quite daunting.

We lead readers down a money-saving travel path. If the phrase "four-star cruising at a one-star price" is near and dear to your heart, then this is the book for you. We invite readers to enjoy our entertaining approach. Together we will explore the rewarding, fascinating, and many-faceted world of bargain cruise vacations.

Rest assured that, wherever possible, this guide is based on our personal experiences, which include America's favorite cruise itineraries, from Alaska and the Caribbean to our recent exotic cruise on the Yangtze River and beyond. From beginning to end, we offer money-saving advice on virtually every aspect of cruising. Readers also find an array of toll-free telephone contacts that will save hundreds of dollars on the cost of cruise vacations. Special travel contacts (one is a full-service discount travel agency) are ready to help "cheapskate" readers lock in those once-in-a-lifetime cruise deals before they are sold out. Both novice and veteran cruisers are welcome to our world of pampered cruise vacations.

This guide is user friendly. Part I deals with principles of bargain cruising, including free travel, free travel cash, and discount strategies galore. Part II explores the world of bargain cruising. A few of the topics include selecting the right cruise, predeparture essentials, and how to avoid shipboard expenses. Part III offers an array of the world's most fabulous cruise itineraries available at incredible cheapskate prices.

For novices, we demystify cruise jargon and peculiar customs associated with the wonderful and sometimes wacky world of cruising. (We will remember forever a human-sized penguin greeting passengers as they boarded their Alaska cruise ship!) Cruise veterans will find new and effective money-saving advice. Throughout our guide, readers will find "Steve and Pat's Tips," emphasizing savings, safety, comfort, and convenience. These special money-saving tips insure a dream cruise and a lifetime of fond memories. We sincerely wish all readers to live their dreams on a fabulous cruise!

PART I

Principles of Bargain Cruising

1

Stretching Vacation Dollars to the Limit: Four-Star Cruise Vacations at a One-Star Price

You deserve to vacation like royalty at an easily affordable price, right? This has been our travel philosophy and way of life for many years. What do we mean by a four-star cruise vacation at a one-star price? The following example tells it best.

Not long ago we embarked on a spectacular one-week Alaska cruise. A short time later we found ourselves on a journey back in time to the glacial age! This four-star cruise vacation, including round-trip air fare from San Francisco to Fairbanks, Alaska, was cheapskate-priced at $799 each! Then we received a cabin credit of $100! With today's fierce competition among cruise lines, there seems no limit to the low-priced cruise deals available. In 1998, the Holland America Line offered several spring and fall Alaska Inside Passage cruises for the low price of $755, with free round-trip airfare from selected cities. The cruises sold out within several days.

Is it any wonder that cruising is America's fastest-growing travel industry? In recent years the number of newly commissioned cruise ships has soared. Cruise companies have launched scores of new ships, adding approximately 35,000 new berths.

The seniors-only crowds have given way to younger passengers and families.

This competition due to all the new luxury ships caused some cruise lines to fail, while others survived by consolidating. Carnival's recently purchased Cunard and Celebrity Cruises merged with Royal Caribbean International. The result is a thriving industry that finds cruise lines battling for the billions of dollars annually spent. The competition will bring all of us the best cruise deals ever!

A one-week, seven-night cruise is the most common of seagoing vacations, and coincides perfectly with Americans' one-week vacation habit. We want readers to enjoy fabulous one-week cruise vacations to exotic destinations such as Alaska, the Caribbean, and Mexico at prices so low everyone can easily afford them. Just how low? Our targeted cheapskate price range, including round-trip airfare and the one-week cruise vacation, is $450 to $850 per person, while fellow passengers are paying hundreds and even thousands of dollars more. No matter what price is paid, everyone visits the same incredible, exotic ports of call, uses the same amenities, delights in the same gourmet meals, and wallows in the same pampered twenty-four-hour room service. Except for the very, very rich and famous, who enjoy spending their cruise vacation in their expensive suites, all passengers will have the same cruise experience. Will our cabins be smaller than those of passengers paying thousands of dollars more? Sure. But except for cabin size and location, little differs.

So how do our cheapskate prices compare with a land-based vacation? Consider any major hotel found in New York, Las Vegas, or Maui. The average hotel room is priced at $175 per night. The following applies to a land-based vacation at such a first-class hotel:

- Three meals per day, including gourmet dinners and exotic flaming desserts—*not included*
- Free twenty-four-hour room service—*not included*
- Free evening Las Vegas–style nightclub acts—*not included*
- Still hungry? Midnight buffet?—*neither available nor included*
- Free transportation from city to city or country to country—*not included* (Sorry, land-based hotels rarely move off their foundations.)

These extras are easily valued at $100 or more per person, per day, or $600 per week! Yet everything listed, and more, is included in the price of every cruise. There is no better vacation value, considering the ambience, comfort, and downright luxury than a fabulous cruise vacation.

Cruises, compared to land-based, all-inclusive resorts, have advantages and disadvantages. Most land-based resorts charge at least $1,000 per person, per week. Cruise ships offer many more features. Newer ships sport such four-star amenities as outdoor Jacuzzis, masterpiece atrium lobbies, exotic water slides, and even caviar bars. Today, modern ships offer unparalleled value and amenities for our hard-earned dollars.

Consider a recent example. Carnival's newest luxury ship, the *Elation*, weighs 70,000 tons and holds 2,040 passengers. The ship's amenities include a six-story atrium lobby, ten "theme" bars, an Olympic outdoor jogging track, a fully-equipped spa and fitness center, and an elegant "lap" swimming pool with an elaborate water slide. Do you think such new ships charge full brochure prices? In mid-1998, Costco Travel, one of our many recommended discount travel agencies, offered a seven-night Mexican Riviera cruise on the *Elation*, priced at $813. Other money-saving strategies, like free travel cash, may reduce prices further. Whether choosing an older, more intimate ship or the newest luxury liner, our goal is to help stretch travel dollars so that cost is never a barrier to a dream cruise vacation.

Two Beautiful Words: *All-Inclusive*

If any two words justify America's infatuation with cruising, they are *all-inclusive*. Let's expand the idea with more words. *All-inclusive at a cheapskate's price.*

Club Med gets the credit for popularizing and promoting the value of an all-inclusive resort vacation. This is a major reason for the skyrocketing popularity of all-inclusive cruise vacations. Many believe the all-inclusive idea is the very heart and soul of today's cruise industry, and that is a major reason people are flocking, in record numbers, to book and enjoy fabulous cruise vacations.

For those readers who have yet to experience a cruise vacation, here are words that Rod Serling might utter: You are about to enter a world like no other where normal habits and conventions are suspended and where your nearby "servant" awaits, twenty-four hours a day, to grant your every wish and command. It is a place where culinary fantasies are fulfilled, any time day or night, and where a floating palace of gleaming chrome, wood, and steel becomes a home away from home, a place where a front door opens on exotic ports of call that fulfill wild travel fantasies. Climb the gangway: You are about to enter 'the cruise zone.'

All-inclusive means that the price paid for the cruise includes almost every aspect of service, facilities, and amenities at no extra charge, including all the extras normally paid for on a standard land-based vacation. Consider our list of the most common, all-inclusive cruise amenities:

- Lodging (cabin) on a luxurious floating hotel
- All the incredible gourmet meals one could possibly want, i.e., breakfast, lunch, dinner, snack bars, a midnight buffet, room service, and snacks
- High-caliber Las Vegas–style shows and variety entertainment every evening
- Twenty-four-hour room service provided by dedicated floor stewards
- Breakfast in bed
- Most cruise lines include port charges in the advertised prices
- Dance instructions
- Guided tours of the bridge and kitchens
- Miscellaneous shipboard activities such as lectures and demonstrations
- Tour advice for shore excursions
- Bridge tournaments
- Special culinary shows, like the march of the flaming baked Alaska and flaming desserts cooked at your table
- Special teens' and kids' programs, meals, and menus
- Free aerobics and other assorted exercise and tone-up classes

- Unlimited use of the cruise ship's free facilities, such as: pools, lounge chairs, and sundecks; Ping-Pong, shuffleboard, and handball, basketball, paddle, and tennis courts; outdoor Jacuzzis; shopping arcades; public areas such as libraries and lounges; a fitness center with the latest electronic exercise equipment and free weights; first-run movies in a full-sized theater or piped directly to cabins' TVs; evening dancing in disco lounges or nightclubs; free boat tender service to and from many ports of call; casino gambling to your heart's content and daily bingo games; and outdoor jogging tracks.

On more exotic cruises, like our journey on the Yangtze River, all shore excursions and sightseeing are escorted and included in the cruise price. This fact gives greater meaning to *all-inclusive.*

Gourmet Dining and Never a Check

Imagine! While relaxing in bed in your "hotel" room, the doorbell rings. You jump to your feet, throw on a bathrobe, and open the door. A waiter delivers two deluxe continental breakfasts. The day gets off to a fine start, except one thing is missing. . . .

You enjoy a marvelous five-course lunch at a fine restaurant. The service is impeccable. You enjoy an appetizer, soup, salad, a gourmet entree, and a superb dessert. Everything is perfect but one thing is missing. . . .

Dinnertime has arrived and your gourmet five-course meal, including flaming desserts prepared at your table, is downright scrumptious. Again the service is impeccable, and yet one thing is missing. . . .

You have a snack attack at 11:55 P.M. You are in luck. Your "hotel" has a superb daily midnight buffet. You snack to your heart's content. But one thing is missing. . . .

During the vacation week you enjoy using twenty-four-hour room service to order bowls of fruit, continental breakfasts, and club sandwiches. But each time one thing is missing. . . .

You are seated at a poolside table taking in the warming rays of the tropical sun. You stroll to a nearby gourmet buffet or lunchtime grill and return with a four-course lunch fit for a vacationing king. Again, you have it all, but one thing is missing. . . .

If you have not guessed it, the one thing missing from each of these meals is *the check!* Outside a cruise vacation, few Americans ever experience such an incredible array of nonstop affordable culinary delights.

At a land-based vacation hotel, how much per week, per person, would such pampering and gourmet dining cost? Six gourmet meals would total at least $450 over six days. The buffet, assuming three visits per week, would add another $40. One room-service order per day for a snack or sandwich would add at least $60 per week. The reasonable total cost per person, per week, would be $550. *This food bill alone is equal to the cost of many cruise vacations!*

Let us compare the food and related service on cruise ships to meals offered at most all-inclusive resorts such as those found in Jamaica, Mexico, or even Tahiti. If you expect to enjoy five-course gourmet meals featuring lobster, Kansas prime rib of beef, and flaming desserts you should be heading to Fantasy Island! Even Club Med with all its French ambience settles primarily for buffet dining. Forget finding twenty-four-hour room service at most land-based, all-inclusive resorts. In all these respects, cruise vacations win hands down.

Five Vacations for the Price of One

Land-based vacations have their proper place in the travel universe. We have enjoyed fabulous dream vacations to the tropical paradises of Maui and Tahiti. In these world-class destinations, we never found ourselves sitting on the beach reminiscing about the gourmet cruise ship meals or ports of call we were missing. Fortunately, we take several vacations per year, which allow us to enjoy pampered cruises *and* exotic land vacations.

We wish this was the case for more Americans. Most working people look forward to one vacation per year. With this in mind, it is not surprising that more Americans are realizing that cruise vacations can deliver five vacations in one, something a land vacation cannot!

Imagine a vacation where one is transported each evening, while asleep, to a new exotic Caribbean island. On one such island, a calypso band and barbeque await vacationers. Another port of call might be the distinctly French island of Martinique, with its Parisian-style cafes and shops. Still other islands might be St. Maarten/St. Martin, a former half-Dutch and half-French colony, and Barbados, a former British colony. Envision this magical journey from one exotic port of call to another without constantly packing and unpacking and changing hotels. Only a cruise ship, a floating luxury hotel, makes such vacation dreams come true.

Each port of call offers exciting shore excursions such as scuba diving and snorkeling adventures or a leisurely drive through a tropical rain forest. Do not forget the shop till you drop trips that "go for the gold" (and gems) in jewelry-laden duty-free shops.

Only a cruise offers, in luxurious and effortless fashion, three, four, or five new and different ports of call during a one-week vacation. And cruising the gentle waters of the Caribbean between ports of call provides time to kick back, relax, and take it all in.

What Is Free Cruise-Ship Transportation?

Let us backtrack just a bit. Not long ago we were again visiting Maui. This time we decided to visit Hawaii's active volcano, Kilauea, at Hawaii at Hawaii Volcanoes National Park on the nearby "Big Island" of Hawaii. Unfortunately, the usual cost for such a one day getaway was $270 per couple for round-trip airfare on Aloha Airlines. While on a scuba-diving vacation in Cozumel, a large island off Mexico's Yucatán peninsula, we paid big bucks for a day trip to Cancun on Mexico's mainland. On another visit to Cozumel, we took a day off from scuba diving and flew to the mainland to visit the Mayan ruins at Chichen Itza, deep in the lush Mexican jungle. (Actually, we would have happily paid more had there been a real landing strip rather than a bumpy clearing in the jungle.) On each of these excursions we spent hundreds of dollars for one-day getaways. But do not overlook the best free perk of cruise travel—ships that not only provide lodging but also double as floating luxury hotels, transporting passengers from one exciting port of call to the next.

This is a good time to emphasize the importance of cruise itineraries: the "five vacations in one" are all the better when the cruise ship follows your dream itinerary.

Vacationing Like the Rich and Famous

In May 1998 the *Grand Princess* became the word's largest and most costly cruise ship to set sail. The ship has a price tag of $300 million! The brochure rate for a premium suite plus balcony is $4,305 for a one-week Caribbean cruise. However, do not despair over such extravagant prices. This is where the magic of cruising kicks in. The *Grand Princess* has eight categories of inside cabins ranging in brochure price from $1,838 to $2,118. By following our advice, a *Grand Princess* cruise can become a reality for less than $1,000 per person!

Do not forget that except for cabin selection, every inch of this floating palace, with all its amenities, is available to all her passengers. Exactly what type of amenities does today's megaluxury cruise ship offer? Here is our short list for Princess Lines's *Grand Princess:*

- Three elegant dining rooms
- A glass-walled nightclub and disco suspended fifteen decks above the sea
- A nine-hole putting green
- A wedding chapel
- Nightclub shows in three lounges nightly
- The Horizon Court restaurant, open twenty-four hours with panoramic ocean views
- Four pools and six outdoor Jacuzzi-type spas—Calypso Reef and Pool with bar, whirlpool, spas, and retractable dome
- Neptune's Reef, a lavish pool and spa
- A burger grill, pizzeria, and ice cream sundae bar
- The Plantation Spa, with suspended swim "against the current" pool, spas, sauna, a state-of-the-art exercise and aerobics room, jogging track, and juice bar

- Voyage of Discovery, a virtual-reality entertainment center
- The largest (13,500 square feet) floating casino in the world
- A children's center and pool, plus a teens-only spa
- Center Court, offering paddle tennis, volleyball, basketball, spectator seating, and the Center Court Bar.

Not all cruise ships are fifteen-deck, 2,600-passenger giants like the *Grand Princess*, yet most ships have their own special charm, ambience, and luxuries. All major cruise ships offer elements of lavish extravagance few of us experience in our normal lives. Is it any wonder then that cruise vacationing like the rich and famous is becoming America's favorite holiday adventure?

Dispelling the Myth: "We're Too Young or Too Old to Cruise"

We freely admit it. When our first thoughts of cruising surfaced, we chalked it up to a midlife vacation crisis. After all, we have enjoyed more than 175 tropical scuba dives such as world-class diving in Cozumel, swimming with sea turtles in Maui, and filming an underwater video of shark feeding in Moorea (Tahiti).

As our first cruise vacation beckoned, a decision had to be made. Would we finally depart from our decades-old custom of independent travel when there was no compelling reason to do so? Could we ignore an incredible cruise bargain? After all, the full-page newspaper advertisement by Princess Cruises described a seven-night, Inside Passage and Gulf of Alaska cruise, including round-trip airfare from San Francisco to Anchorage, Alaska, for $849. Then a local discount agency added a $100 cabin credit. As we noted earlier, final net price, if we booked, was $799 each!

What about our genuine, "We love independent travel and we are too young to cruise" concerns? We had heard about the "older crowd" on cruise vacations. Even more worrisome, we heard that Alaska cruises attract older crowds than other cruise itineraries. How were we to decide? What level of concern did the age of fellow passengers warrant? The question was: Would the forced confinement on a luxury cruise ship equal a visit to America's magnificent last frontier? Whether tablemates were young or young at heart was simply not the main consideration in our final decision. The same was true of evening entertainment, which we assumed would be geared to the older crowd. With all this in mind, the scale quickly tipped in favor of the only logical decision, but we knew Alaska offered tons of fun and adventurous land excursions. The die was cast and we were soon off to Alaska! This decision changed our future travel lives forever, and for the better.

Our Alaska decision is worth sharing because it addresses a major concern—age. There we were, in our early forties, sharing a dinner table with six "older" passengers. We immediately hit it off with a sixtyish couple from Boston. Not only were they young at heart but also looked fifteen years younger than their ages. In the end we hung out with them on the ship, explored Alaskan towns together, and took the same small seaplane trip to a remote fjord. We had a ball! This and other cruise experiences have given us a lifetime of fantastic memories.

➥ **Steve and Pat's Tip:** *Many cruise ships assign dinner seats according to the general age of the passengers. If the age of tablemates is important, discuss it with the travel agent or the cruise line* before *booking a cruise or before they assign tables on the cruise ship.*

"We're Too Young to Cruise" Participation Quiz

We aim our quiz at the twenty- to forty-five-year-old crowd. Count the yes answers to find out whether a cruise vacation should be in your future travel plans.

Are you aware that bingo is the most exciting daytime cruise activity? Just kidding! This was our test question to see if you are awake! Here are the real questions:

Are you too young to:

- enjoy disco dancing into the wee hours of the morning?
- lounge poolside while sipping piña coladas?
- enjoy excellent scuba diving in tropical waters?

- go rafting on a glacial river?
- experience great snorkeling and white Caribbean beaches?
- enjoy invigorating aerobic classes at sea?
- order breakfast in bed at no charge?
- savor gourmet meals with fabulous flaming desserts?
- relish romantic "alternative dining" available on many ships?
- play basketball or paddle tennis at sea?
- enjoy glitzy Las Vegas–style revues?
- soak in outdoor Jacuzzis under the stars at sea?
- save 66 percent off the cost of a similar land-based vacation?
- cruise with passengers ranging in age from kids to grand parents?

➥ **Steve and Pat's Tip:** *Carnival's "Fun Ships" cater to all age groups but* **definitely** *cater to a younger crowd. Recent statistics show 40 percent of Carnival's passengers are in the thirty-five-to-fifty-four age group; 20 percent in the twenty-five-to-thirty-four age group; and 10 percent are under twenty. Carnival also offers a second midnight cabaret show nightly. This pleases the younger night-owl passengers. Commodore Cruise Line has a no formal dining policy and embarks from New Orleans, both of which beckon a younger crowd. Most Princess Line cabin beds (all on its newest ships) convert to queen size. The new* **Grand Princess** *offers three live shows, in different locations, each evening. Norwegian Cruise Line offers sports bars with twelve TV sets and satellite reception on many of its ships. Most new cruise ships offer outdoor Jacuzzis under the stars.*

Remember—make your own party! Before booking a cruise, know the age group of the passengers. Caribbean cruises draw younger crowds and families. Lower-priced cruises draw more families. If a younger crowd is a *must*, then choose a singles-only cruise or opt for land-based resorts such as adults-only Club Med or Hedonism II. We can only offer our experience and encouragement to at least try that first cruise. There is so much to gain and so little to lose when younger passengers board their first cruise ship with the right frame of mind. Are young couples and singles too young to cruise? Absolutely not!

Too Old to Cruise? Hah!

Does a cruise book need to convince seniors and retirees that a cruise vacation is right up their alley? The answer to this question seems obvious enough, right? So why discuss the matter at all?

Not long ago, there was a notion that the "golden years" are the prime time to enjoy the proverbial rocking chair on the porch. Today, seniors only need to board a jet and within hours they are transported to the cruise ship's departure city, such as Anchorage, Los Angeles, Fort Lauderdale, or Athens. For some time, retired seniors with available time and money recognized the incredible values and opportunities afforded by cruise vacations, so seniors are the best source of repeat business for cruise lines. Who, then, exactly are we trying to convince and why are we trying to convince them?

Our message is aimed at seniors and retirees who, because of limited income, poor health, or both, feel that their time to live new dream vacations has past. For some, this is true. For many others, this need not be the case. If you are a senior or know one, consider the following reasons why a dream cruise vacation should be part of your life or theirs:

- All-time, low prices for one-week cruises starting at about $450!
- All-inclusive cruises save money.
- Connecting airfares are cheap or free for those following our advice.
- Transportation to and from a cruise ship to airports can be arranged.
- Minimum baggage handling
- No packing or unpacking while traveling from one exotic port to another
- Special diets are available with advance notice.
- Every ship has a doctor onboard for emergency treatment.

- No language problems onboard most ships
- Need a break? Enjoy twenty-four-hour room service in the quiet of your own cabin.
- Health spas with soothing mineral baths
- All ships have elevators.
- Passengers may choose a cabin close to the elevator.
- Great sightseeing is often enjoyed from a cruise ship's deck, as in Alaska.

➥ **Steve and Pat's Tip:** *Seniors should obtain trip cancellation insurance that waives all preexisting medical conditions. Then, a full refund for the entire package is available if a sudden worsened condition results in cancellation of the cruise. Travel Guard International offers this insurance with a full waiver of preexisting medical conditions if its policy is purchased within seven days from the date of the cruise deposit. Call (800) 826-1300 for a brochure or purchase the policy by phone. Cruise lines offer similar policies if purchased at the time the vacation is booked. See Chapter 5 for more details.*

What about seniors who are eighty-five or even ninety years old? Consider our recent fifteen-day trip to Mainland China visiting four cities and then cruising the Yangtze River for six days. Our large group of eighty included two gentlemen aged eight-three and ninety-two! They not only kept up with the group but often did better than some younger sixty-five- to seventy-five-year-olds! Of course they took risks on such an arduous vacation, but they did it, including climbing the Great Wall. Compared to travel in China, luxury cruising is a piece of cake.

Are we encouraging all seniors, despite their physical condition, to consider a cruise vacation? We would like to but we cannot. Not all seniors and for that matter not all forty- or fifty-year-olds, are fit to head out to sea. Cruise ships rightly refuse to accept passengers who require active and ongoing medical treatment. Onboard, cruise physicians are not equipped to provide care for preexisting medical problems. If you are concerned, we encourage you to take the first step and talk with your doctors. Find out if your medical conditions are manageable and do not require active care for the length of a cruise vacation.

In the end, it is one thing to dwell on a lifetime of wonderful memories, but another to realize that at any age new memories await at the next port of call.

Your Cruise May Be Free If You Are Lucky: Gambling at Sea

At the time of publication, Princess Cruises was touting the virtues of its new megaship, the *Grand Princess,* and proudly announced the ship's largest casino afloat.

It may be called Las Vegas–style "adult" entertainment, casino entertainment, or gaming. Regardless of the name, we are talking about gambling on the high seas. One cruise brochure put it best: "All you need to enjoy our casino is luck!" If and when luck strikes, your cruise may just turn out to be free! Do cruise brochures mention that you can lose a bundle? No way! We urge moderation when it comes to gambling on the high seas.

Shipboard casinos mimic but are never identical to their Las Vegas cousins. Games include a variety of slots, craps, roulette, and blackjack. Other milder forms of gambling include daily bingo games and the customary "horse race."

➥ **Steve and Pat's Tip:** *All casinos are open evenings through early morning. However, not all casinos are open daytime hours; casinos are closed while ships are in port. If you must know exact hours of day-to-day operation, check with the cruise line before booking.*

To those who view gambling on the high seas as great adult entertainment, we offer these words: Good luck and break the bank!

Taking the Fear out of Formal Dining

The idea of an incredible all-inclusive cruise vacation at a spectacular price sounds wonderful. The informality of daytime cruise activities is perfect. While lounging at poolside, playing paddle tennis, or attending cooking demonstrations, we expect to dress appropriately for all such casual activities. However, evening dress codes at sea are quite another thing on most cruise ships.

> ↪ **Steve and Pat's Tip:** *Absolutely* abhor *dressing up? Try alternative dining, if available, or don clean jeans, shirt, and tie, head for the dining room, avoid the maître d', and cross all fingers. Most ships will allow such a passenger into the dining room, though fellow passengers may frown. Such errant passengers are defiantly ducks out of water.*

One-week cruises schedule two formal dinners. Traditional dress for these occasions is evening gowns for women and tuxedos for men. However, such formal wear is never required and is rarely seen on mass-market cruise ships. The most common rule at sea for formal nights is a dark suit for men and a cocktail dress for women. The Captain's Gala Dinner, a formal affair, is common to all cruises. Another two dinners are informal, and only require a jacket and tie as opposed to a tuxedo for men and casual dresses for women. The remaining evenings are casual, permitting slacks and dress shirts for men and pants suits or casual dress for women.

The vast majority of passengers enjoy the change of pace from casual to the occasional formal and informal dinners. This is the perfect time for couples to strut their evening stuff.

> ↪ **Steve and Pat's Tip:** *What if a passenger absolutely refuses to participate in formal dress evenings? There is hope! Royal Caribbean International and Commodore Cruise Line offer the best room-service menus. Passengers may order main dining room menu items for delivery to their cabin. Also, many ships have alternative dining options so that passengers may avoid all formal and even informal dining. We encourage readers to ignore this tip and enjoy all their meals in the elegant splendor of their ship's main dining room!*

You Do Know Where Your Kids Are: The Perfect Family Vacation

Today, family cruises have exploded onto the cruising scene. Carnival Cruise Line, the leader in family cruising, has experienced a 60 percent increase in the number of children participating in their year-round kids' program. In 1995 the line carried more than 100,000 children and 1997 saw this number hit a new record of 160,000. Because family cruises are an important moneymaker, nearly all the major cruise lines have decided to go after the family market. This is especially true during the summer vacation months and major holiday vacations such as Thanksgiving, Christmas, and Easter. Suddenly, major cruise lines are announcing new programs tailored for children ranging in age from two to seventeen and filled with nonstop activities. What does this new marketing attitude mean for time-pressed and value-conscious families looking for a unique family adventure that fits everyone's needs?

First, the biggest blessing of a family cruise is an opportunity to vacation as a family and enjoy a thrilling adventure. All-inclusive cruising provides a floating luxury hotel that visits new and exotic ports daily. It is the most efficient and relaxing way for families to travel to new horizons. No tiring transfers from hotel to hotel, no dragging luggage or screaming, tired kids, no relentless packing and unpacking, no shopping for restaurants that serve children, no searching for swimming pools with lifeguards, no screening of baby sitters, no endless planning kids' activities. Is this your definition of heaven? We hope you agree that family cruising offers unique opportunities for fun and a "together" vacation experience. Having decided to do it, now is the time for serious homework to pick the perfect cruise for your family.

Since kids have a short attention span, select a cruise that schedules a port visit nearly every day. Everyone can stretch their legs and see a new place and different culture. This alone guarantees that no child will be bored and whining that they are stuck on the ship with nothing to do! Plan onshore excursions, i.e., field trips, with the kids in mind. After an exhausting day of fun in the sun with lots of other youngsters, even the most difficult child will have little to complain about or any energy left.

> **Steve and Pat's Tip:** *For first-time family cruisers, check out Caribbean itineraries. Nearly 50 percent of all cruise passengers sign on for vacations in the warm and wonderful Caribbean. Most of the major lines that cruise these routes, eastern, western, and southern, have extensive kid's programs, and more importantly—lots of children. Carnival sometimes carries up to five hundred youngsters per cruise. If your children are particularly antsy, try a three- to four-day cruise in combination with a stop at Disney World. Select the route that is best for your family and then discuss the amenities each line offers specific age groups. If the youngsters are part of the ship decision, they will feel included and those hours spent cruising will be even more enjoyable to all.*

Remember—on a cruise ship you do know where your children are! Cruise ships provide a natural boundary for kids, if they do not play leapfrog with the railing! All jokes aside, parents can rest assured that their offspring are somewhere on the ship. Most important, children can enjoy the company of their own peers in well-supervised programs. Trained counselors keep them occupied and happy from morning to night. Most ships offer a variety of activities designed for children of all ages. Swimming pools with fun water slides, game rooms, Ping Pong, arts and crafts, toy-stocked playrooms, movies, shuffleboard, deck tennis, ice cream parlors, junior Olympics, exercise groups, bingo, dancing classes, and karaoke parties are examples of the many fun opportunities available.

Cruise lines have not overlooked family activities. Many ships offer onboard activities that the entire family can enjoy. Adult-oriented events are available, so adults can spend time together during the day participating in skeet shooting, bingo, golf instruction, basketball, deck tennis, exotic cooking lessons, planning port shopping, first-run movies, and in the evening there are Las Vegas shows for teens. Children will often surprise a parent by their levels of maturity when allowed to plan their own activities.

Onboard Kids' Programs and Activities

Carnival Cruise Lines

All ships have a year-round kids' program, Camp Carnival, operating from 9:00 A.M. to 10:00 P.M. Carnival's trained youth staff conducts the program. It offers a variety of age-appropriate activities geared toward the program's four age groups: toddlers (two to four), intermediate (five to eight), juniors (nine to twelve), and teens (thirteen to seventeen). Entertainment designed especially for children is offered—plus backstage tours.

All the Fun Ships have well-stocked playrooms, ice cream parlors, teen discos, and video arcades. On the line's six Fantasy-class vessels, a second playroom was added featuring a vast array of toys, games, and activities designed for kids aged five to twelve. The *Destiny* has a two-level, 1,300-square-foot children's play area and has expanded activities for all four groups. The new *Elation* will feature a greatly expanded children's play facility and a high-tech Virtual World game center, which includes sixty video and arcade games. The larger vessels have accentuated kid's programs and developed more activities than are offered on the smaller ships. Pick a larger Carnival ship for the best program, activities, and entertainment for children.

No one forgets parents. Multi-generational activities like family arts-and-crafts sessions to photography workshops are available. All Carnival vessels feature at least three swimming pools, including a kid's wading pool with a water slide.

Celebrity Cruises

Celebrity is a more upscale cruise line that does have an excellent program for kids, especially during the summer months. Like the Carnival program, they divide the children into four interest groups with appropriate activities, each supervised by trained counselors. A clubhouse is on every ship, and most hold activities in special areas strictly for children.

Costa Cruises

This Italian line dotes on family groups, places little emphasis on separating children from adults, and promotes an atmosphere of *familia*. During the day, the Costa Kids Club keeps the children happy so parents can rest and relax. They design its programs to turn all the youngsters into one big happy Italian family by the end of the cruise.

Disney Magic

The *Disney Magic* was scheduled to begin cruising in March 1998. However, the cruise line postponed that date to July 30, and hopefully by the time you are reading this book the *Disney Magic* is plying its vacation trade to the Bahamas. This ship is touted as providing the most comprehensive children's programs ever. It is designed with a separate family pool, special family lounge, designated teen club, video arcade, and supervised children's center open until 1:00 P.M. Check with any travel agent for the status of the *Disney Magic,* or check the Internet for the most current information. Be warned that many families had their vacations canceled by unforeseen delays.

Holland America Line (HAL)

Because Holland America is a mass-marketed cruise line and sails everywhere, programs for children have become a priority. Club HAL is a supervised children's program designed for three age groups: five- to eight-year-olds, nine- to twelve-year-olds and thirteen and up. Various activities are available, such as arts and crafts, movies, ice cream parlors, golf lessons, games, disco parties, and ship tours. The cruise line advertises that Club HAL is not simply a sitting service. Parents are not allowed to merely drop the kids off and leave them for the day. Excursions just for kids are available on many cruise ships. Check with the excursion reservation desk for a list.

Norwegian Cruise Line (NCL)

The Kids Crew program is available all year and, like Carnival, NCL divides the kids into four age groups: Junior Sailors (ages three to five), First Mates (ages six to eight), Navigators (ages nine to twelve), and Teens (ages thirteen to seventeen). The Junior Sailor Program takes place in the morning for one to three hours during holiday weeks and summer months only. The other three programs are available all day and year-round. During time in port, activities are offered in the afternoon and early evening for the oldest three groups. Youth coordinators are college students who attend classes in communication, safety, confidence building, and taking care of children with special needs. A variety of supervised arts and crafts, contests, games, sports, parties, dances, ship tours, talent shows, movies, and adventures are scheduled on each ship. Every ship has a kid's playroom. Families are not excluded and can join in the activities. The best all-year program is on the *Norway*, which has more facilities for kids than any other ship.

Premier Cruises

The *Big Red Boat* is a symbol of the Premier line and offers a combined three-day Disney World visit and a three-day cruise packages ideal for a family's first cruising experience. The line has the most extensive child and teen programs in the industry. Each ship has at least fifteen counselors trained in child care, education, first aid, and so forth. Kids are separated into five age groups for participation in all-day activities until 10:00 P.M. Supervised on-shore excursions for kids are available. This allows parents the rare freedom to explore new cultures and ports without the kids. Most other cruise ships do not offer children's programs when the ship is in port, but times are changing.

Princess Cruises

Primarily, Princess is a cruise line for adults and not generally marketed for children. Children under eighteen months are not allowed. However, the Caribbean cruises in the warm summer months have made Princess's itineraries more child-oriented. All ships have trained counselors and special areas, or "fun zones," dedicated to kids' activities.

The Princess program is called Love Boat Kids. Two distinct age-specific programs are available. They divide children into either the Princess Pelicans (ages two to twelve) or the Princess Teen Club (ages thirteen to sixteen). Activities include movies, swimming lessons, arts and crafts, pool games, scavenger hunts, deck parties, ship tours, videos, and cartoons. Teen entertainment involves theme parties, murder-mystery games, karaoke, shows, pizza feasts, teen disco, and educational classes. State-of-the-art facilities will debut on the *Grand Princess*, *Sea Princess*, and *Ocean Princess* in the future.

When the ships reach a port of call, Princess's Adventures Ashore program offers excursions and tours designed for youngsters of all ages. At the Princess Cays, the line's private island in the Bahamas, a special area has been set aside where children can play while supervised by the ship's counselors. Parents can then spend an afternoon on the beach by themselves.

Royal Caribbean International (RCI)

The Kids, Tweens, and Teens programs are available year-round on *Sovereign of the Seas*, *Majesty of the Seas*, *Monarch of the Seas*, *Nordic Empress*, and *Viking Serenade*, and during the summer, Easter, and the winter holiday season on the other ships. Their programs are some of the most extensive afloat. Trained counselors are available to supervise activities such as sea-cruise investigation, scavenger hunts, tournaments, freeze dancing, human bingo games, Masquerade Parade, T-shirt contests, and pajama parties.

Kids' Meals Onboard

All parents need time to themselves. With this in mind, consider mealtimes. Occasionally, parents and kids alike want to enjoy their favorite foods in peace. For kids, this means eating their "gourmet" meals, such as pizza, hot dogs, hamburgers, Cokes, and ice cream, with other children. Most ships have special kids' menus with food items especially for young people. Some ships have separate dining areas for kids, which affords parents time to rest and relax with an adult-only meal. Other ships offer family dining with an extensive child's menu. Again, check out the meal and dining plans before making a decision.

➥ **Steve and Pat's Tip:** *Carnival Cruise Line offers fast-food throughout the ship. The Lido provides hot dogs and hamburgers for lunch, a Mexican bar for tacos and burritos, and a pasta bar for Italian favorites. The pizzeria is open all hours. Yogurt and ice cream are available from machines. For parents and older teens, the late-night buffets have a wide selection of snack food items. Do not forget twenty-four-hour room service.*

Discount Rates for Children

At first glance, value-conscious parents may consider a family cruise to be a total extravagance. Do not be fooled. The cruise lines know about vacation budgets, so significant family discounts and incentives are available. For a seven-day cruise, additional family members under the age of twelve who share the same cabin with two adults can cruise for as little as $100 to a maximum of one-half the full fare. Generally, babies under the age of two sail free. Request a crib when booking your cruise.

Carnival Fun Ships Keep track of Carnival's promotions during the year. Special rates are occasionally advertised for third and fourth passengers to sail for free. Carnival boasts some of the largest staterooms in the industry, so they can easily accommodate a fifth berth or crib. *Destiny* has the first-ever family staterooms, as well as a large number of connecting cabins. Caribbean seven-night cruises start at $669 per person.

Celebrity Cruises Special discounts are offered to single parents except during peak vacation periods. The newer ships have cabins with connecting doors especially designed for families. Seven-night cruises and special sailings start from $799 per person, with discounted prices for kids under twelve.

Holland America Line (HAL)   Discounts between $60 to $100 per day are available for third and fourth passengers sharing the same cabin. Children from the ages of two to seven pay a weekly rate of $350 for a one-week cruise when staying in their parents' cabin.

Norwegian Cruise Line (NCL) and the Royal Caribbean International (RCI)   Both of these lines can accommodate six passengers in a cabin at an incredible discount. Ready for that snug family feeling? NCL offers seven-night Caribbean cruises starting at $663 − $100 onboard credit = $563 per person. RCI has seven-night Caribbean cruises starting at $699 per person.

Premier Cruises   One or two kids vacation free when accompanied by one paying adult per child on the seven-night Big Red Boat Cruise and Orlando Land Vacation. Free admission to all theme parks, a rental car, and port charges are included, and the total cost is only $898 per adult.

Princess Cruises   Children are always discounted when sharing a cabin with two adults. Charges are 50 percent of the minimum rate despite the price of the individual cabin so the rate can drop to $85 to $150 a day. Discounts are available for early booking. If two cruises are booked back to back, significant discounts are available on the second cruise.

Regal Cruises   For third and fourth passengers, Regal always offers discounts ranging from $200 to $350 per person, per week. Check on low-season discounts, when the rate can drop as low as $100 for a third or fourth person for one week. However, Regal is not geared to entertain children like some of the other ships are.

Royal Caribbean International (RCI)   Children as third and fourth passengers in a cabin pay as little as $65 to $100 per day. Early bookings can reduce the brochure price by as much as 40 to 50 percent.

Baby-sitting Services

All ships with children's programs provide sitting services, although the prices and hours vary per cruise line. They screen all sitters before hiring them. Parents can arrange in-cabin sitting (if available) or deliver their children to the kids' activity center.

Carnival Cruise Line Twenty-four-hour sitting is available at the Playroom, day or night. All sitting is in the form of a slumber party. Just drop your child off: pillow, blankets, and cribs are provided.

Celebrity Cruises Twenty-four-hour sitting is available on all ships. Group baby-sitting and pajama parties are available in the various playrooms until 1:00 A.M. In-cabin sitters can be arranged by the cabin steward. Sitting is often offered at ports of call.

Costa Cruises Group sitting is available from 9:30 A.M. until 1:30 P.M.

Holland America Line Sitters may be available from the ship's regular staff, but this is not guaranteed. Principally, the cruise line only offers kids' programs according to demand. According to the cruise line, children's programs are not baby-sitting substitutes nor a day care center.

Norwegian Cruise Line The line is now offering guaranteed sitting. Cabin baby-sitting is available from noon until 2:00 A.M. for $8 per hour. Group sitting is available in the playroom from 10:00 P.M. until 1:00 A.M. for $4.00 an hour.

Premier Cruises Group sitting is a cross between a slumber party and a day-care center and available twenty-four hours a day. Children up to twelve can spend an overnight at the Playhouse for a small charge. In-cabin sitting is available.

Princess Cruises All Princess ships with children's centers offer group sitting while the ship is in port, available from 9:00 A.M. to 5:00 P.M. for a separate charge. Late evening sitting is available from 10:00 P.M. to 1:00 A.M., also for an additional charge. Private in-cabin sitting is available.

Regal Cruises Sitters are unavailable for children under five and during meal times.

Royal Caribbean International Group sitting is available at the children's areas. Like HAL, they recruit in-cabin sitters from the ship's staff members during their off hours. Services cannot be charged to a shipboard account.

Get answers to all of your questions before booking a cruise. Read the cruise brochures for our recommended cruise lines, or call the cruise lines directly for the latest information. Better yet, contact Pearson Travel, our favorite all-service, discount travel agency, at (800) 336-1066 or (401) 274-2900 and talk to a friendly, knowledgeable representative. See Appendixes A and B for cruise line toll-free numbers and Web sites.

A wonderful first cruise will give new meaning to the idea of a satisfying, fun, and memorable family vacation. We predict that upon returning home, parents and their offspring will be eager to plan the family's next cruise outing!

2

Free Travel to Your Cruise Ship: Frequent Flying on Terra Firma

Our battle cry is: "Free airline travel for *everyone!*" We have enjoyed free travel to world-class destinations such as Africa, Israel, and the Caribbean.

This brings us to one of the very few negative realities of cruise life. Most cruise vacationers must travel long distances to reach the cruise ships' departure cities. For Caribbean cruises, ships depart from the Miami–Fort Lauderdale area in Florida, San Juan, Puerto Rico, and New Orleans, Louisiana. Mexican cruises depart from Los Angeles, California, while Alaska cruises depart from Anchorage, San Francisco, Seattle, and Vancouver. There are many other cruise itineraries and departure cities. New York City is the departure point for cruises to New England, Canada, and Bermuda.

One way or another, most passengers will be paying hundreds of dollars or more to cover the cost of plane transportation to their cruise ship's departure city. Cruise lines often help to reduce, but never eliminate, these expenses by offering lower-cost airline fares. On rare occasions, a cruise line will offer the best of all-inclusive cruise packages—one that includes round-trip airfare—though usually from a select group of U.S. cities.

Our goal is a lofty one. It goes far beyond merely reducing the major cost of such necessary airline travel. We seek to eliminate the cost entirely by pointing the way to free travel to virtually any cruise-ship departure city, whether that city is Miami, Los Angeles, or Copenhagen, Denmark! We offer alternate strategies, such as free companion tickets, for those occasions when free travel may not be available. This permits one person of each couple to fly free, thereby reducing the cost of air travel to departure cities by 50 percent.

In the old days they called them frequent-flyer programs. Today they call them free travel airline programs. Our highest recommendation is for the American Airlines AAdvantage program.

➥ **Steve and Pat's Tip:** *Call the American Airlines AAdvantage desk at (800) 882-8880. Request a free AAdvantage (frequent-flyer) account for each ticket-purchasing member of the family or travel companion. Free accounts will be set up on the spot. This is the first step to free domestic and global travel. Children who travel as passengers will receive the same miles as adults for each flight. Of course, kids are not able to participate in our following second strategy for banking more megamiles.*

The second, final step is equally simple. Obtain a Citibank AAdvantage Visa or MasterCard that works in partnership with the American AAdvantage program. This Visa or MasterCard allows cardholders to bank one mile for each dollar charged through purchases. Cardholders will soon receive a myriad of free-miles promotions.

In less time than one can imagine, American Airlines will be issuing free travel awards based on banked program miles. As in the past, program miles are also earned for each mile actually flown on American Airlines flights. Okay, at this point you may be muttering something like, "How does this help me when I take a flight maybe once every couple of years? How in the world can I ever accumulate the thousands of miles needed for free travel?"

Fear not. We are perfect examples of how this exciting program works for all of us! We fly free to exotic global destinations like Israel and Africa even though we rarely fly on American Airlines. The plain fact is that fully 90 percent of our American AAdvantage program miles are obtained from sources other than flying! These sources are available to all of us each and every day. Let us make this absolutely clear: even those who rarely or never fly on American Airlines (or any other airline for that matter) will soon qualify to fly free anywhere in the world, including cruise ships' departure cities.

Though we do not believe in paying annual fees on credit cards, the Citibank AAdvantage card is a winning exception to this rule. Because the payback is so great, we are willing to pay the $50 annual fee. In fact, most years American Airlines and Citibank offer special promotions that more than pay for the yearly fee.

➡ **Steve and Pat's Tip:** *Do not be confused. There are different types of Citibank cards. Make sure to request and obtain the Citibank AAdvantage Visa or MasterCard that is connected to the American Airlines AAdvantage program. American Airlines gives a bonus of 3,000 miles to every new cardholder. These bonus miles more than cover the first year $50 cost of the card. To obtain a Citibank AAdvantage card, call (800) 359-4444 and apply for either the Citibank AAdvantage Visa or MasterCard. Be sure to request the 3,000-mile bonus. Congratulations! You are now a bona fide member of the best free travel program in America.*

It is equally important to emphasize that compared with other bank cards, Citibank offers superior customer service. Whenever we had problems with a merchant or questioned a bill or an erroneous finance charge, Citibank has courteous humanoids (live operators) available twenty-four hours a day, seven days a week. And upon request, Citibank will issue an additional card, at no extra cost, to a second authorized user.

Want to avoid all finance charges? Simply (or perhaps with some difficulty) pay off the bill in full, each month. Because this

Free Travel to Your Cruise Ship

is our monthly practice, we are not concerned with Citibank's interest-finance rate. For those interested, Citibank's current yearly interest rate is about 17.9 percent.

Here are proven strategies for gathering thousands upon thousands of miles at lightning speed. Keep in mind that members need only 25,000 miles to obtain the first-level award, a free round-trip domestic ticket to any destination in the continental United States.

To amass the necessary miles for free travel, use the Citibank AAdvantage cards for *all possible purchases*! Forget writing checks whenever possible. Charge everything that would usually be paid in cash or by check. Here are some examples of the best ways to use the Citibank AAdvantage Visa or MasterCard:

- For all purchases and services—not sure Visa or MasterCard is accepted? Ask!
- For all recurring monthly bills such as utilities, cable TV, and cellular phone.
- Monthly medical plans often accept credit card payment. This can add up to thousands of miles per year.
- Charitable donations.
- Big-ticket items. A friend recently purchased a $14,000 time-share property from Marriott and charged it to his Citibank AAdvantage card.
- A $10,000 Jet-Ski can be purchased with a Visa card.
- Whenever buying a car, van, truck, or RV, determine whether the deposit or purchase price can be charged.
- Automobile repairs, maintenance costs, and gasoline purchases
- Home repairs, household equipment, appliances, and hot tubs
- Textbooks and tuition expenses at private schools and colleges
- Membership costs for athletic clubs and other organizations
- Vacation costs, including air-and-land packages, plus all expenses incurred during vacations.
- Jewelry purchases. Nineteen ninety-seven was a banner year for us. We charged a glittering diamond wedding ring! Chalk up thousands of miles!

➦ **Steve and Pat's Tip:** *When it comes to big-ticket items, such as major jewelry purchases, two principles come into play. Each adult member of the family should obtain their own Citibank AAdvantage card. This gives cardholders a chance to double their credit limit. Since the total price of Pat's ring exceeded the available credit on one card, we charged half the price to each of our cards. Another good strategy is to call Citibank and request an instant increase in your credit limit.*

See our following section on the monthly American AAdvantage newsletter-flyer, which offers scores more opportunities to obtain hundreds to thousands of bonus miles.

Here is an example that still "hurts." For years, Steve's dentist, Norm, refused to accept credit card payments. During a recent visit, his bill was more than $400. This time Steve noticed a Visa sign on the counter. Norm was finally catching up with modern times. As the nitrous oxide took effect, Steve was tantalized by images of our next tropical vacation paid for, in some small part, by these dreaded dental visits.

➦ **Steve and Pat's Tip:** *You will see mention of free travel cash. We can only ask you to wait until you have read Chapter 3, which is aptly titled "Free Travel Cash: The Best Helping Hand." You will be amazed to learn of a world where American corporate icons give away hundreds to thousands of dollars of free travel cash for the asking!*

Want to bank even more miles? A few years ago we booked an incredible cheapskate package to London on American Airlines. The "London on Your Own" package included eight days' lodging, round-trip air travel from the West Coast, and daily breakfast. The cost using free travel cash (from Nabisco) was just $517 each. We charged the trip on our Citibank card, received 1,034 miles for the vacation package, and each of us also received 11,000 frequent-flyer miles because we flew on American

Airlines. This vacation accumulated almost one-half of a free domestic ticket for each of us on American Airlines, worth $300.

➥ **Steve and Pat's Tip:** *Why should you pay for two Citibank Visa cards with two $50 annual fees? Because in the end, you come out ahead. On our American Airline flight, to London, we each banked 11,000 miles in our American AAdvantage accounts. By having individual Citibank cards, we quickly rounded off both accounts to 25,000 miles, the first plateau that qualified each account for a free round-trip U.S. ticket. Also, as we noted, two cards may be used to split a purchase when the credit limit on one card is not sufficient.*

Whenever vacationing in a foreign country, be certain to charge all purchases on Citibank AAdvantage cards. This usually results in the most favorable exchange rate while also gathering additional hundreds to thousands of miles. In November 1997 we again returned to London. This time we used our free cash (from Zostrix) on a British Airways package. The eight-day air-and-land package was net priced at just $595 from the West Coast. Before leaving we opened free airline accounts with British Airways. Later we received 11,000 miles each with a 5,000-mile bonus for obtaining a British Airways–related Visa card with Chase Bank. Because British Airways allows the pooling of miles into a single family account, we returned from our London vacation with about 27,000 miles.

When it rains, sometimes it pours. More good news: American Airlines is the sister airline of British Airways. Consequently, the addition of the British miles instantly qualified us for a free round-trip airline ticket on American Airlines to any destination in the continental United States. Once we accumulate 3,000 more miles on our Chase Visa card, our 30,000 British Airways miles will qualify for a round-trip ticket from the West Coast to San Juan, Puerto Rico. Free airfare is a valuable asset if we decide to book a southern Caribbean cruise departing from San Juan.

> **Steve and Pat's Tip:** *The joy of a dream vacation is worthless if bankruptcy waits around the corner.* Never *charge frivolously to accumulate miles. Keep track of the charges, perhaps in a check register. Always earmark sufficient funds to pay off the entire balance each month to avoid costly finance charges.*

Each month American Airlines sends an American AAdvantage newsletter to all program members. This newsletter is a good source of new promotions that generate additional hundreds or even thousands of free miles. Here are some samples:

- Chains of hotels such as Sheraton and Forte offer hundreds of free miles for each day of lodging in the hotel.
- Rental car companies offer up to 1,000 free miles per day of use.
- Holiday Inn offered a 1,000-mile bonus for staying one night or more in the hotel.
- The number of miles needed to qualify for a free ticket can be reduced, such as the usual 80,000 miles to 60,000 miles for a ticket to Australia, a 25 percent discount.
- American AAdvantage Dining Club offers three miles for each dollar spent at selected restaurants. New members receive a 5,000-mile bonus for purchasing ten meals over a two-month period. The club includes low-priced restaurants such as Pizzeria Uno, a well-known national chain.
- Hundreds to thousands of bonus miles can be earned when using a partner security brokerage firm, certain charities, and selected real estate firms to purchase or refinance a home.

The list truly goes on and on!

Not long ago an associate, Nancy, who participates in the American AAdvantage program, reported that she received a valuable piece of "junk" mail. Nancy was on a limited and randomly selected AAdvantage mailing list that controls the number of promotion participants. This deal offered Nancy up to 15,000 free program miles. She deposited $6,000 in a new

Citibank checking account and agreed to use the bank's free electronic banking service. In return she received 12,500 free program miles! If she agreed to the direct deposit of her paycheck, Citibank would have given her an additional 2,000 miles.

➥ **Steve and Pat's Tip:** *When Citibank would not mail us a promotion certificate similar to the one Nancy randomly received, Steve called a local Citibank office. The manager indicated that his branch had a limited number of certificates in stock. He eagerly invited us to his branch and allowed us to use one of "his" certificates so that we, too, could participate in the promotion. A few minutes later we collected our 12,500 free program miles.*

Two years ago we were on the winning end of a random mailing. We received a free companion ticket, randomly mailed by American Airlines, good for a flight anywhere in the continental United States. They generously mailed this free ticket in appreciation of our long-standing American AAdvantage membership.

By participating in several of these incredible offers over a period of just eight weeks, we accumulated about 20,000 free miles. This is almost one free round-trip ticket anywhere American flies in the United States, or half the amount needed for a free round-trip ticket to Paris, London, Tel Aviv, or Moscow!

As a rule, we only apply for free (no annual fee) credit cards. Offers for such free cards arrive in our mail weekly. On the other hand, we happily pay the yearly fee for our Citibank AAdvantage Visa cards. Occasionally, there are deals that beckon us to obtain yet another Visa card even though it carries a yearly fee. One example is the free companion ticket offered by United Airlines to those who obtain their Mileage Plus First Visa or Mastercard card. After we pay the first year's fee and receive the promised perk, we cancel the card to avoid any further annual fees.

The Diners Club Connection

Enter another piece of "junk" mail we truly loved. The envelope contained a solicitation for a costly $80-per-year Diners Club card. Why did we accept the offer? First, Diners Club offered us 12,000 frequent-flyer miles if we used the card just once each month of the year. There was no minimum charge required. We could charge $5 in gas at our local Shell station each month to qualify for the 12,000 free miles. This alone is worth far more than the $80 fee.

The second reason may just cause us to keep the card despite its hefty fee. The Diners Club program offers Club Rewards. Members obtain two points equal to one frequent flyer mile for each dollar spent, similar to the mile per dollar we obtain with our Citibank AAdvantage Visa card. Now comes the twist. At a later time and at a member's request, the banked, Diners Club miles can be sent to any one of the twenty-two frequent flyer accounts, including American AAdvantages. Consider the incredible flexibility of the following example.

Let's say an American AAdvantage member's account contains 35,000 miles. The member also has a smaller United Airlines account that contains 20,000 miles. The member also has a Diners Club account that contains 5,000 miles. Later, if the member wants a free round-trip ticket to Paris, Diners Club will transfer its 5,000 miles into the member's American AAdvantage account. This meets the 40,000-mile criteria for a free round-trip ticket to Paris. If the same member needs a free ticket from New York to Los Angeles or San Francisco, they could transfer the 5,000 miles from Diners Club to the United Airlines account. This meets the 25,000-mile requirement to qualify for a free round-trip ticket to the West Coast.

The idea of such super flexibility is golden, but there is a downside. Since Diners Club is not a Visa or a MasterCard, it is not universally accepted for retail purchases other than restaurant charges, meals, and lodging at most hotels. It is gradually being accepted at ever more retail outlets, such as the following:

- Shell and many other gas stations
- For newspaper and magazine subscriptions

- Most telephone services
- Major retailers of computer equipment and software, such as CompUSA and Egghead Software
- Major stores from Gucci and Montgomery Ward to Oshman's Sporting Goods and the Sharper Image.
- Allied, United, and North American Van Lines

➥ **Steve and Pat's Tip:** *During our first membership year Diners Club offered valuable and ongoing incentives for its members. We justified our continued membership at the hefty $80 per year fee when Diners Club offered a 5,000 mile renewal bonus. To find out current new member incentives, call Diners Club at (800) 234-6377.*

The key is getting into the free-travel game. Join Citibank AAdvantage and become a player. This is one game that is winnable by all. If we had a dollar for each person who plays the lottery and yet ignores the corporate handout of free global travel and free travel cash, we would indeed become wealthy.

Let us leave this section with a brief description of American AAdvantage's free round-trip ticket awards to the most popular cruise departure cities in the world:

- **25,000 miles**   Continental U.S. locations such as Los Angeles, Miami, New Orleans, New York, and San Francisco
- **25,000 miles**   Vancouver, B.C., and Alaska
- **30,000 miles**   San Juan, Puerto Rico
- **35,000 miles**   Hawaii
- **40,000 miles**   Venice, Italy, and St. Petersburg, Russia

➥ **Steve and Pat's Tip:** *What about the expensive airfares for cruises that embark from Los Angeles or Vancouver but then disembark in Honolulu? For 35,000 program miles, American Airlines will issue a two-city ticket from almost any U.S. city to either Vancouver or Los Angeles, and then a return flight home from Honolulu. Another wonderful option from American AAdvantage!*

Welcome to a new world of free U.S. and global travel to cruise-departure cities and noncruise vacation destinations alike. Nothing beats free travel!

Competing Programs

In recent years, several new types of programs have hit the marketplace. In one new program, a local bank promotion awarded 5,000 airline miles to new customers. Thereafter, miles accumulated by using the bank's noncredit debit card. When the bank mentioned that their miles could be used on any airline, we checked further and learned that the program was exclusive to the bank. What does this mean? Many such programs use their own exclusive accounts so that accumulated miles may not be combined with the miles we have been saving in our favorite American AAdvantage accounts, that is to say, the bank has no relationship whatever with American's official free-travel program. We recommend against such programs. When in doubt, ask, "Can the miles be transferred to my American AAdvantage account?" If the answer is yes, ask to see this in writing.

We also received a promotion flier from Worldlink, the company that offers an excellent discount telephone calling card. The flyer read: "Call and Fly." The program's flyer asserted that participants may use program points to fly on any airline. As with the above bank program, Worldlink's flyers' small print confirmed that its points "cannot be transferred to any other awards program."

Always be a good travel consumer and read before leaping into a new program. Compare them all. Those mentioned above are opposites of the Diners Club program, which allows miles to be transferred into any airline program account.

Whenever a new program appears, do the necessary homework and determine whether it offers benefits equal to or better than the American AAdvantage program. We continue to highly recommend the American AAdvantage program. Simply put, it continues to offer greater value than its competitors.

Free Companion Airline Tickets

When free travel is not an option, a free airline companion ticket may do the money-saving trick. What exactly is a free companion ticket? One person buys a plane ticket at the low advertised price and the spouse or travel companion flies absolutely free!

As in the case of free travel cash, free companion tickets involve three parties, all of whom come out winners. First and foremost are the airlines issuing the free companion tickets; next is the flying public; and third are the banks who issue airline-program related Visa and MasterCards. How common are these give aways? Banner years for for free companion tickets were 1997 and 1998. At one time or another, and sometimes simultaneously, American Airlines, United Airlines, and Delta Airlines were busy giving away free companion tickets pretty much for the asking.

Delta Airlines' Sky Mile Program

Once again we received junk mail that we truly loved when a letter arrived concerning our American Express Optima card. It offered a free companion ticket deal if we would exchange our current card for a Delta Airlines Sky Mile American Express card. The bonus was a free Delta Airlines companion ticket. Even better, the free Delta companion ticket, unlike most issued by other airlines, is good not only in the continental United States but also on any Delta flight worldwide.

➡ **Steve and Pat's Tip:** *Always scrutinize such programs. Call the airline and confirm that their free companion tickets can be used on the airline's lowest published and/or advertised fares. The value of a free companion ticket is lost if the purchased ticket costs double or triple the price of the lowest economy fare. We gladly report that most companion tickets can be used with the lowest advertised economy prices.*

Delta's international, free companion ticket can be used with Delta's advertised economy fares. In a money-saving flash, we signed on and paid the $50 fee for the new Delta Sky Mile Visa card. We now have a full year to use our free Delta companion ticket, which will conservatively save us $300 to $1,000!

➥ **Steve and Pat's Tip:**   *Always be a savvy consumer. Our free Delta companion ticket failed to arrive in the promised four to six weeks. Steve made an appropriate inquiry with no luck. Then, when the card was six months overdue, Steve wrote to the president of American Express. The ticket arrived within the month. As an apology for the delay, American Express gave us a $50 credit toward any meal charged on the card.*

Here is a fantastic deal issued by American Airlines in 1997 and again in mid-1998. Once again, these were random mailings to AAdvantage members. In fact, when this promotion likely surfaces again in 1999 it will appear in our newsletter so that readers may participate in the program and reap its rewards.

We were asked to solicit four people who would apply for new Citibank AAdvantage Visa cards. When four friends and associates applied for the Citibank cards, we received 10,000 free program miles and our friends received an American Airlines free companion ticket good for one round-trip ticket anywhere in the continental United States. The paid ticket must be priced at $358 or more. This certainly covers all coast-to-coast flights as well as most other flights over reasonably long distances. The ticket is usable on American's lowest advertised fares, making this a fabulous, money-saving deal for the four new cardholders. The free companion ticket is in lieu of the usual 3,000 bonus miles given to all new cardholders.

A somewhat different American Airlines giveaway, announced in their monthly newsletter, offered a free companion ticket to those purchasing a one-night stay at any of several listed hotels. While the listed upscale hotels often charge through-the-roof prices of $200 or more per night, the list included the San Jose

Fairmont Hotel. Its lowest one-night rate qualifying for the free companion ticket was just $89.

Are all these programs open to the general public? The answer is a resounding *no*! Many times such offers are advertised by random mailings, such as the American Airlines and American Express Optima card deals. Also, American Airlines often issues its offers in its monthly newsletter, sent to members of the American AAdvantage program.

Want a United Airlines free companion ticket right now? A little-advertised United Airlines free companion ticket program has been ongoing for the past two years.

➥ **Steve's Instant Free Companion Ticket Tip:** *To obtain a United Airlines free companion ticket, call (800) 592-6700 and confirm that the promotion is ongoing. Then, apply for a United Airlines Mileage Plus First card (Visa or MasterCard). Pay the first year fee of $60 and receive a United Airlines free companion ticket, good for a round-trip ticket to any continental U.S. destination. Once the companion ticket is received, the Visa card may be canceled prior to the year-end renewal date to avoid a second-year $60 fee. We flew to New York using our United Airlines free companion ticket, paying $455 for one ticket and receiving a second ticket absolutely free!*

Singles and Companion Tickets

How can singles enjoy the 50 percent savings of free companion tickets? Finding a travel companion who will share the cost of one paid ticket. There is absolutely no rule barring singles from traveling with a "friend" so that both may share the companion ticket savings of 50 percent off the regular price. Be creative. Spread the word to friends and associates. Place free and low-priced advertisements whereever they are available. Often local flea-market papers offer such free or low-priced personal ads. Place index-card advertisements on bulletin boards at work or at local supermarkets.

➥ **Steve and Pat's Cyber Tip:** *Place an ad on the Internet. For just $15, an ad may be placed in AOL's classified travel section under the subtopic, "Tickets and Events." It is amazing how many people are ready to pick up on such a money-saving deal, especially if the travel destination is a popular one.*

When it comes to cruising, these deals offer a solid opportunity to cut the cost of flying to the cruise ship's city of embarkation by 50 percent. The shelf life of such tickets is usually one year, giving all of us ample time to put them to good use. But what about new offers? Perhaps little advertised deals similar to the United Airlines giveaway? We are always at the ready to share current bargains and deals with anyone and everyone within earshot. And now, for those who want to learn of new deals as they happen, our efforts will continue even after your purchase of this book.

➥ **Steve and Pat's Tip:** *Consider subscribing to* Steve and Pat's Cheap Travel Newsletter! *Learn about all the latest deals, many of which are here today and gone tomorrow. For a bargain one-year subscription, send $10 plus four self-addressed, stamped envelopes to* Steve and Pat's Cheap Travel Newsletter, *Box 1956, Lafayette, CA 94549. See Chapter 3 for further details.*

Other Freebie Perks: First-Class Upgrade Freebie

We are always interested in options aimed at improving our comfort during all phases of a cruise vacation. Why travel to a cruise ship's departure city in economy class when a free first-class seat is available? Our favorite Citibank AAdvantage program that awards a free round-trip flight anywhere in the continental United States for 25,000 miles will throw in a free first-class seat for an additional 15,000 miles (40,000 miles total) for each passenger. The upgrade to first class on American Airlines flights to San Juan, Puerto Rico, is an additional 30,000 miles, for total of 60,000 miles each from any mainland U.S. city.

Junk Mail We Love

Another motto is: Do not judge junk mail by its cover! Fully half of our junk mail deserves and receives an immediate toss into the "circular file." However, we always make certain whether or not the remaining mail is equally useless.

Worldlink

A 1998 example is the insert that arrived with our Worldlink telephone calling-card bill. Worldlink announced its new *Call and Fly* free-travel promotion. We have already discussed the problem with such exclusive programs that do not permit their miles to be combined with other airline free-travel accounts. Scrutinize all such programs. Some who use their Worldlink card often may accumulate miles quickly. If the program works and the card provides a needed service, use it. Worldlink offers ten points for every dollar spent on phone calls and give a 5,000-mile bonus for first-time use. Get a 250-point bonus whenever a monthly bill exceeds $50, and 500 points for a bill that exceeds $100. Want more? Worldlink offers a free round-trip ticket to any continental U.S. destination, including Alaska, for just 20,000 points. If we only made more monthly calls.

> ➥ **Steve and Pat's Tip:** *The minimum monthly charge for a Worldlink card is just one dollar. To obtain information on obtaining a Worldlink card, as well as their super-low rates for domestic and international calls, contact the Call and Fly program customer service center at (888) 556-5191.*

MCI

Not long ago we spotted a full-page MCI advertisement, obviously part of the current telephone wars. MCI was offering a free domestic round-trip airline ticket to new members. The simple condition was that new members' monthly bills must be at least $25. We took immediate exception to the new-member requirement. After all, why punish loyal MCI customers such as us? We called MCI and were quickly told that we, too, could become part of the promotion even though their full-page newspaper advertisement was clearly limited to new members. We promptly signed on. Twelve months later we received a free companion ticket worth up to $600 on domestic travel. Another great freebie!

Southwest Airlines

On another occasion we received a letter from Southwest Airlines, our favorite commuter airline. For us, Southwest provides connecting flights to both Los Angeles and New Orleans, the departure cities for Mexican Riviera and Caribbean cruises, respectively. This time the "junk mail" included an application for a Southwest Visa card. The fee was waived for the first year, and Southwest offered a bonus of four free segments toward a free flight. This equaled the credit received for two round-trip flights. Southwest is very generous with its free-travel program; only sixteen segments or eight round-trips are required to qualify for a free round-trip ticket anywhere Southwest flies from the West Coast to New Orleans or to the East Coast.

3

Free Travel Cash: The Best Helping Hand

Do you recall the cliches, "Nothing is for nothing" and "You get only what you pay for"? Forget them. They no longer apply to you. During the past thirteen years, we have received thousands of dollars in free travel cash from corporate vacation giveaways. Since 1994 alone, we received $6,700 from such American icon companies as Kraft foods, Nabisco, and most recently the Jonny Cat Litter Company. Use free travel cash like travel script, and use it to help pay for dream cruise vacations.

Before we dive into this new world, a few definitions are in order:

Free vacation cash giveaways   Major advertising promotions sponsored by American icons like Kraft and Nabisco
Sponsoring or issuing company   Major companies wanting to reward customers who purchase their product. The past list of companies includes Kodak, Nabisco, Kraft, Country Time Lemonade, Penzoil, and Jonny Cat.
Original mail-in certificates   Original certificates (not copies) found in the program's announcement advertisements and later mailed to the sponsoring company with receipts or UPC labels to obtain free travel cash.

A window of opportunity to participate A short time span during which participants must submit their mail-in certificates with receipts or Universal Product Code (UPC) labels to get the free vacation cash from the sponsoring company. The Jonny Cat promotion allowed only ninety days to submit receipts and UPC labels.

Free travel cash or vacation cash Colorful travel script issued in $25 or $50 denominations by the sponsoring company and available in unlimited amounts.

Longevity The period during which free travel cash can be used toward a vacation. Once obtained, free travel cash can be used for eighteen months to two years from the date of the program's release.

Program's travel agency One travel agency is selected for each promotion and must be used to book all vacations with free travel cash. Simply dial the travel agency's toll-free number.

ITH (International Travel House) A New Jersey company that creates, markets, and administers these promotions for the sponsoring companies.

Future programs ITH has released one or more promotions annually during the past fourteen years! They plan to continue in the future.

In the 1990s, we used free travel cash to help pay for our global cheapskate vacations, including cruise vacations. We took eight-day vacations that included airfare from the West Coast, hotels, and most breakfasts. Our total vacation package prices, using available free travel cash, was: Tahiti, $499 each; London, $517 each; Paris, $565 each; and a Carnival Mexican Riviera cruise, $499 each.

In the newest vacation cash giveaway, which started in 1998, we requested and received $3,000 in free Jonny Cat travel cash. How long did we wait to use it? Within several weeks of receiving $3,000 worth of colorful script in $25 denominations, we reserved a summer 1998 Greece and Turkey cruise vacation. Because the vacation was fourteen nights, we used $500 of the free vacation cash to help pay for the already low-priced, vacation package. When was the last time a corporate "friend" donated $500 in "cash" toward the cost of your dream vacation? No matter! Soon you will be saying, "Only in America!"

Of course, you must buy the company's product and then send the mail-in certificate with purchase receipts and UPC proofs of purchase to the sponsoring company. The free travel cash, or script, issued by the sponsoring companies usually arrives by mail in four to six weeks. As fun and picturesque as the script is, it is even more fun to use!

In 1995, we spent $38 purchasing Nabisco cookies. In return we received $1,700 in Nabisco free travel cash script. Sounds unbelievable? Remember, we are talking about Nabisco's Oreo cookies!

The script is used like cash. It is redeemable as a cash credit toward vacations booked through the travel agency chosen by the sponsoring company. Keep in mind that the promoting companies have no say concerning one's choice of vacations or cruises. Nor can they affect the price of a vacation or cruise. When we use travel cash, we simply shop for the best air-and-cruise package or air-and-land vacation package with the lowest price. We call the promotion's selected travel agency, have them book it, and let some corporate benefactor pay hundreds of dollars toward our vacation bill.

Let us emphasize the wonderful longevity feature of these programs. When a new program starts in 1999, its free vacation cash will most likely be usable until the year 2001!

Are Travel Dollars Available Now?

The honest answer is yes, no, and maybe. Let us explain. Free vacation cash giveaways have offered free travel cash continuously for the past fourteen years! Depending on when you read this book, free travel cash is either available or you and we are waiting for the next promotion. There is no better place and time to learn of these promotions than right now.

ITH released the 1998 Jonny Cat $600 Vacation Cash Rebate program with a full-page newspaper advertisement that appeared in forty-eight million Sunday newspapers. Read on and learn our best strategies on how to find the next of these incredible programs.

Are Travel Dollars Really Free?

Based on years of experience with these promotions, our answer is a resounding *yes*! In the recent 1998 promotion, we spent $105 to purchase thirty bags of cat litter. However, we happen to have not one, not two, but *four* cats! Assuredly, all thirty bags of litter will be used. We also purchased Jonny Cat Litter "on sale" and received $100 of free travel cash for each bag we bought! That is $3,000 of free Jonny Cat cash.

We are often purchasing products that we would buy without the promotion. In other cases, the cost of the product that we must purchase is trivial when compared to the free cash return. The $1,700 of Nabisco travel cash we received was truly free, considering it only cost $38 at a local flea market to buy the Nabisco crackers and cookies. Is there any doubt that we gleefully devoured the Oreos?

Be smart program participants by following in our foot steps. Spend only nominal dollars to purchase the products needed to obtain large amounts of free travel cash. Be creative. Luckily for us, the Nabisco program did not require submission of cash register receipts, so that flea market purchase worked well. The Nabisco program only required submission of UPC proofs of purchase found on each box of cookies. Using Nabisco's "special doubling" offer, for every three boxes we received $100 in travel cash, so we considered this travel cash absolutely free! Shop for discounted or sale prices. Often, when a program is first released, local dealers will offer special sale prices. Use any and all strategies to save on the purchase price of the program's product. Where there is a will, there is usually a money-saving way!

Are some promotions more expensive than others? Unfortunately, yes. A 1997 giveaway involved Zostrix, a popular ointment used for the topical relief of arthritic pain. We can assure you that Zostrix was neither as tasty as Nabisco cookies nor as cost-effective as previous program-related products. The lowest price per purchase of Zostrix was $10. Making things worse, each $10 purchase qualified for only $50 in free vacation cash, and only $200 in free cash could be used on a seven-night vacation. Compare this with the more typical Jonny Cat promotion, in which we received $100 for each $3.50 purchase. Did we ignore the Zostrix promotion? No way. We still received an instant return of $200 for $40 in purchases. How many of your investments pay that kind of dividend?

When a product offered is not useful to us, we skip it and wait for the release of the next program. This was the case some years ago when Carlton cigarettes announced their travel cash giveaway. Fortunately for us, the far more "appetizing" Kraft and Nabisco programs started simultaneously with the Carlton promotion. Easy choice!

A Typical Free-Vacation-Cash Promotion

First, participants submit the UPC proofs of purchase and original cash register receipts by mail to the listed address. In four to six weeks participants receive their free travel cash in colorful $25 script denominations.

Next is the fun part. Participants shop for the vacation of their choice at the lowest available price. After choosing their vacation, participants simply complete a brief booking form and submit it with a $100-per-person deposit and the proper amount of free travel cash. The booking request is forwarded to the participating travel agency, which makes the booking and quickly confirms it with the participant. About two weeks before departure the travel agency will mail all necessary travel documents. That's it!

> ➡ **Steve and Pat's Tip:** *In the case of an urgent booking, the selected travel agency may agree to accept the script, proofs of purchase, and booking form directly. Simply give them a call. We have done this occasionally.*

Free-vacation-cash giveaways typically provide $100 to $500 in travel cash per couple, or one-half this amount for singles. The cash may be used to help pay for vacations of four to fourteen nights. Participants can use their free travel cash for eighteen months to two years from the date they receive the script. A few basic rules describing how to use the free travel cash follow:

- $100 per couple toward a minimum four-night cruise or vacation that includes the purchase of round-trip noncharter airfare
- $300 per couple toward a minimum seven-night cruise or vacation that includes the purchase of round-trip noncharter airfare
- $500 per couple for a minimum fourteen-night cruise or vacation that includes the purchase of round-trip noncharter airfare
- All the above applies to combination cruise-and-land vacations.

➥ **Steve and Pat's Tip:** *Ask the post office for a proof of mailing certificate when making a submission of cash register receipts and UPC proofs of purchase. Also make a photo copy of the entire submission. Once our submission was "lost in the mail." Fortunately, after we submitted our copies, we received the requested $1,700 of Nabisco free vacation cash.*

Using Your Free Travel Cash

The competition among cruise lines is intense. We find incredible cruise bargains advertised regularly in the travel sections of Sunday newspapers. We repeat the value of periodically reading the nation's best travel sections in both the *New York Times* and *Los Angeles Times*.

➥ **Steve and Pat's Tip:** *Cruise lines often advertise seven-day cruises that usually mean seven nights as well. Planning to use free vacation cash on an air-and-cruise package? Then make certain that a "seven-day" cruise does include* seven nights *aboard a ship or the cruise will not qualify for free travel cash.*

We should also mention that prior giveaways allowed free cash on any four-, seven-, or fourteen-night cruises whether or not they included round-trip airfare. This was wonderful for people who live near departure cities like Los Angeles and Miami. The 1998 promotion added a new rule that requires round-trip airfare be included with all cruises.

➡ **Steve and Pat's Tip:** *We did a "hybrid" of sorts when it came to our summer 1998 Greece and Turkey land-and-cruise vacation. Since the vacation package included fourteen nights and round-trip airfare from New York to Athens, we could use the maximum—$500 of Jonny Cat vacation cash. We simultaneously used our American AAdvantage miles to fly free from San Francisco to New York.*

Frequently, cruise lines advertise incredible bargain prices for "cruise only" and indicate, usually in micro-print, that "low-priced airfares are available from most cities." In the case of the 1998 promotion, any cruise-and-airfare combination works. We could submit an advertised air-and-cruise package to Four Seasons Travel, or we could submit a cruise-only booking and have Four Seasons book the round-trip airfare to the ship's departure city. The uses of free vacation cash are endless, since we, and not someone else, select the vacation of our choice. Imagine an exotic Russian cruise from Moscow to St. Petersburg that includes round-trip airfare from New York City?

How to Find Future Free-Travel-Cash Giveaways!

This is where we reveal our best strategies and tips for finding future promotions. Full or half-page advertisements in the shiny coupon or insert section of major Sunday newspapers announce most earlier programs. In fact, the president of Jonny Cat informed me that their full-page announcement advertisement appeared only once, on the first Sunday of January 1998. So why do 99 percent of people we meet show glazed looks when we discuss this subject? Our best guess is that most people simply ignore the coupon sections of their Sunday newspaper, and others are so busy clipping fifty-cent coupons they don't realize how legitimate and valuable these programs really are.

Make it a habit to scan each Sunday newspaper's coupon-insert and travel sections, where such announcements are usually found. Check with friends and family who live in distant areas, since some programs have limited geographical distribution. Be good travel consumers and keep a constant vigil for such programs from other sources. In one case, my associate found a travel cash giveaway announcement in a flyer distributed by a major local supermarket chain. In other cases, companies use "rip-off" pads, found on dealers' counters, to announce their new program. Sheets from these pads also act as the original mail-in certificates.

Mail-In Certificates

We emphasize that an original mail-in certificate, which appears in the program's announcement advertisement, is usually necessary to participate in these programs. In January 1998, the full-page newspaper announcement included the mail-in certificate. When Steve heard that some of his readers missed this one-time advertisement, he contacted Jonny Cat's customer service people. They kindly sent Steve a pad of fifty mail-in certificates that he distributed to loyal readers. Other savvy readers contacted the company directly and received the original certificates.

One strategy, recommended to readers of Steve's *Cheapskate's Guide to Vacations,* failed miserably for reasons beyond his control. Our following tip describes the problem.

➡ **Steve and Pat's Tip:** *Do not waste time and money (for stamps, calls, and faxes) contacting ITH. While ITH creates great free vacation cash programs for its clients, it is quite another story when is comes to dealing with the public.*

Many of Steve's readers complained that ITH ignored their many inquiries. Perhaps they say it best:

- "I have sent a letter to this company . . . I have tried to call . . . I have faxed . . . and have [had] no response." (Chuck L.)
- "I faxed . . . I got no response . . . I cannot find a telephone number." (Robert F.)
- " . . . not been able to obtain any information . . . from ITH . . ." (Lauren S.)

For the record, Steve sent a copy of Chuck L.'s letter to the president of ITH and received no reply. Follow our self-help advice on how to discover new promotions and consider our following announcement.

Intent on ignoring our advice? The ITH contact follows:

International Travel House (ITH)
Thomas Reddington, president
789 Route 202 North
Bridgewater, NJ 08807
(908) 685-7644; fax: (908) 429-1022

Next is a sure-fire strategy for staying on top of new travel cash promotions and other super money-saving programs.

Steve and Pat's Cheap Travel Newsletter

In 1997, and again in mid-1998, a major problem became obvious. We received valuable pieces of identical junk mail we truly loved. The Citibank promotions authorized us to distribute American Airlines AAdvantage program certificates entitling each holder to a free companion ticket. Each companion ticket, worth up to $700, was good for a free flight anywhere in the continental United States. Of course, we gave certificates to friends and associates, but our inability to distribute them to loyal readers frustrated us.

In early January 1998, the great Johnny Cat Litter free-travel-cash giveaway started. We spotted the full-page announcement advertisement in our Sunday newspaper, as did most of Steve's readers, but what about the others? There was no way of getting the word out to Steve's loyal readers who may have missed the program's announcement advertisement.

Almost weekly we learn of one or another super deal or short-term promotion. How do we share them with our deserving readers? How can readers who discover amazing and valuable promotions share them with others? Why should all these money-saving opportunities be lost? The answer is one word: communication!

We have decided to build a better mousetrap in the guise of *Steve and Pat's Cheap Travel Newsletter,* which debuts in January 1999! Those who enjoy our *Cheapskate's Guide* approach to money-saving deals, ideas, and tips, plus advice on travel comfort, safety, and convenience will enjoy our four-issue-per-year newsletter. It will cover both cruises and world-class air-and-land vacation packages. All readers are simultaneously encouraged to share their own bargain discoveries with us! Whenever we accept a reader tip for publication, the reader will receive a free lifetime subscription to the newsletter.

Our high-tech approach will find us using multiple means of communication, including "snail mail" (our P.O. Box address), e-mail, and our modest Web site, at cheaptravel.net, that will feature periodic updates and announcements.

➡ **Steve and Pat's Ironclad Guarantee:** *There is nothing to lose and much to gain. Read all four of our first year's issues. Be amazed and entertained by our ongoing publication. If not satisfied, return the four issues for a full refund. Better yet, share the issues with friends, and encourage them to join in the money-saving fun!*

Subscribing to *Steve and Pat's Cheap Travel Newsletter*

Our first-year introductory price is just $10, plus four self-addressed stamped envelopes! That's *it*! Mail your envelopes and a $10 check, payable to Steve Tanenbaum, to the following address:

Steve and Pat's CTN
P.O. Box 1956
Lafayette, CA 94549

As always, our goal is to inspire readers to live their dreams and enjoy world-class cruise-and-land vacations at dirt-cheap prices. With your support and participation, we will deliver "hot off the press" money-saving deals, plus comfort, convenience, and safety advice that can save your vacation, so we will all continue to be travel winners!

4

Take Another 5 to 20 Percent Off: Legitimate Discount and Rebate Travel Clubs and Agencies

When all else fails, take another 5 to 20 percent off! What exactly does this mean? There are some who have yet to obtain free vacation cash or a free companion ticket, and who have not yet set up their American AAdvantage free travel account. Do not give up! When it comes time to book a dirt-cheap cruise advertised by a major cruise line, there is still an opportunity for further savings. Simply book the cruise and any necessary airline tickets with one of the following discount or rebate travel agencies.

Pearson's "Cash-in-Your-Pocket" Promotions

Pearson Travel of Providence, Rhode Island, is an American Express full-service travel agency that offers exciting money-in-your-pocket promotions and gives special attention to clients identifying themselves as *Cheapskate's Guide* readers. *Cheapskate's Guide* readers from Phoenix, Los Angeles, Orlando, Iowa, and Chicago have already received added benefits by booking with

Pearson Travel. The company's vice president has impressive references, and Pearson's history dates back to 1929. Check out these great cash-in-hand deals.

➥ **Steve and Pat's Exclusive Pearson Deal:** *Pearson's Cruise Savings: Book any one-week cruise and identify yourself as a* Cheapskate's Guide *reader and receive $100 in American Express travelers checks. Bargain-priced Caribbean and Mexican Riviera cruises selling for $549 to $599 will be net priced at $499 to $549 per person.*

Pearson's Vacation-Package Savings Pearson will guarantee $100 per couple in American Express travelers checks for any one-week, air-and-land vacation package booked with them. This reduces our favorite one-week Moorea package to just $709.

Miscellaneous Pearson's Savings Pearson's Last-Minute Club specializes in last-minute travel discounts. Pearson Travel does not charge a fee to join. Be sure to call Pearson for their latest deals for 1998 and 1999!

As a convenience for West Coast readers, Pearson's offices are open until 6:00 P.M. on weekdays. Contact Pearson at the following address and phone number, or by e-mail:

Pearson Travel
93 Dyer Street
Providence, RI 02903
(800) 336-1066 or (401) 274-2900 fax: (401) 831-5328
pearsontravel@edgenet.net

Travelers Advantage

Travelers Advantage has many years of success as a national discount and rebate travel program. Its major advantage is a 5 percent rebate available to all members on all travel arrangements. The annual membership fee is $59. Members book their vacations using a special toll-free number.

> **Steve and Pat's Tip:** *Five percent seems like no big deal. We were not impressed until we booked our first African safari. Although our airfare to Nairobi was free, the two-week, land-and-photo safari package cost $4,000 for both of us. Upon returning home, a $200 Traveler's check was in the mailbox. Now we appreciate the Travelers Advantage rebate program.*

Travelers offers a three-month trial membership, with valuable new member incentives, for only one dollar. To induce new memberships, Travelers offers a no-strings-attached, one-night-free hotel voucher, valued at $100. Use it at popular national hotel chains such as Days Inn, Ramada, and Howard Johnson. This voucher is good for one night of lodging, absolutely free. It is not a two-for-one voucher that requires the purchase of a one-night stay to receive the second night free.

Travelers also sends to new members a major-airline voucher that can save a family up to $240 on a single flight. Want still more? Travelers also includes a national hotel directory good for 50 percent off the list or "rack" rates. Since the parent company, CUC, owns Entertainment Publications, the hotel directory is a clone of the one in Entertainment editions. Even better, Travelers sends members their magazine *Excursions*, which contains great tips and special low-priced cruise and vacation packages. The current issue announces a seven-night Royal Caribbean cruise for $699 and a Holland America Alaska cruise for $993, which includes a cabin upgrade. Both include port charges. Call (800) 877-8786 to hear their current hot-line offerings.

If a member chooses to cancel the membership during the year, Travelers will fully refund that year's fee, no matter whether the free hotel voucher was used. Also, keep in mind that they automatically charge the annual renewal fee to the member's Citibank Visa or other credit card account unless the company receives a cancellation request. All of us are big winners with the options this program provides. To obtain further information or to join Travelers Advantage, call (800) 843-7777 or (800) 482-2964, or write:

Travelers Advantage
Box C32123
Richmond, VA 23261

➥ **Steve and Pat's Tip:** *Problems with Travelers Advantage's service? Call the number above and request cancellation of your membership. The company will most likely offer a variety of new incentives and discounts so you will drop the request.*

The Sears Discount Travel Club

When we received confirmation of a recent travel reservation with Travelers Advantage, the return address read, "Sears Travel Club." We learned that CUC runs both the Travelers Advantage and Sears Travel Club programs. Though the programs are almost identical, the incentives may differ. Joining a Sears discount travel club may be more comforting to some. We encourage readers to compare the incentives of both clubs. To join or request information, call the Sears Discount Travel Club or Travelers Advantage at (800) 835-8747.

Costco Travel

Costco Travel's program began in 1994. Presently, the ever-changing program runs a cruise reservation center in San Diego, California. Their program offers a 5 percent discount or rebate on cruises priced at less than $3,500 and 10 percent on cruises priced at more than $3,500. They also provide bonus upgrades on selected sailings. Remember, only Costco members may use this discount service.

How does the program work? Call Costco Travel at (800) 800-8505 and request their brochure. Cruise lines currently appearing in Costco's brochure include Disney, Radisson Seven Seas, Holland America Lines, (HAL), Princess, Carnival, and Royal Caribbean International (RCI). Check out their deals and call the Costco Travel Center for current prices, availability, and to book a cruise. Big on the plus side, the prices include port charges and taxes.

Some examples of Costco's cruise rates follow:

- HAL's seven-night Alaska cruise for $951, with two-category cabin upgrade
- Carnival's seven-night Mexican Riviera cruise for $603
- Carnival's seven-night western Caribbean cruise for $694
- RCI's seven-night southern Caribbean cruise for $966

National Variable Rebate Travel Agencies

We love savings options, so here is another one for readers to seriously consider. These national agencies rebate their commission, usually 10 percent. They differ from the above clubs and agencies because they require booking fees to qualify for their rebates. Simply compare the services and discounts each provides and decide which offers the greatest savings. These agencies also offer discounts on air-only and land-only bookings.

Pennsylvania Travel

This independent discount travel retailer has fine credentials. Pennsylvania rebates its commission, usually 10 percent, to its customers, and charges a booking fee scaled to the total cost of the booking. We called Pennsylvania Travel and they immediately faxed us their brochure that provided all necessary details. Call Pennsylvania Travel at (800) 331-0947 or (610) 251-9444, or fax (610) 644-2150.

Travel Avenue (Chicago)

This discount retail travel agency offers a 7 percent rebate on vacation packages and cruises. Unlike similar agencies, the agency charges a flat booking fee of $25 if full payment is made immediately, or $35 for a deposit when final payment comes later. Travel Avenue will fax their brochure. Call Travel Avenue at (800) 333-3335, or fax (312) 876-1254.

Entertainment Publications' Travel-Related Savings

Domestic Savings   Many readers are familiar with Entertainment Publications's incredible two-for-one discount books, which offer hundreds of dollars in real savings. In 1998, there were 137 U.S. city editions covering most of the nation. These books function primarily as fund-raising tools for charities, schools, and other qualifying organizations. The selling organization retains most of the money raised by book sales. U.S. Entertainment Publications editions cost about $40 each. Most users find that their books quickly pay for themselves.

Our local San Francisco Bay Area edition contains several hundred pages with two-for-one coupons that cover most aspects of dining and recreation. They include hundreds of fine-dining restaurants, casual restaurants, and informal fast-food take-out restaurants. Other coupons offer similar savings on local parks, museums, sporting events, movies, theater, and much more. Anyone want to pay daytime bargain matinee prices whenever going to a favorite movie theater in the evening?

Travel Savings   The Hawaii Entertainment Publications edition has savings opportunities for cruising the islands. It offers valuable sightseeing, recreation, and restaurant coupons that are usually two-for-one so that one person obtains the service or meal absolutely free. Did we say food? Amazingly, there are times during a lengthy Hawaiian Islands cruise vacation when passengers may just need to give up a cruise ship meal and grab lunch while touring the islands. The edition covers all the major Hawaiian Islands one will visit when cruising or vacationing interisland. We often recoup the price of the book with one coupon. For example, the most recent Hawaiian edition included a free $45 parasailing ride off the historic whaling town of Lahaina. Buy a full-priced ticket for a half-day Zodiac rafting trip around the island of Lanai, get the second ticket free, and save $120! Again, purchase a regular-priced ticket for a half-day sail and snorkeling trip to the crescent-shaped, Molokini Crater Marine Preserve and receive a second ticket free. Everyone who plans to visit Hawaii by cruise ship or on a more traditional land vacation should purchase this money-saving edition.

There are also fun, money-saving International Entertainment Publications editions for cities like London, Paris, Sydney, and many more. Of course, these editions find their greatest use during land-based rather than cruise vacations. However, we would be remiss if we failed to plug you into this valuable domestic and international resource.

One element that is common to all the Entertainment Publications are airline, cruise, car rental, and hotel discounts. The 1998 editions contain $100-per-couple coupons for Holland America Line, Norwegian Cruise Line, Celebrity Cruises, and Carnival. The Entertainment coupons are usable only on higher-priced outside cabins and suites. We recommend the far more versatile and valuable Pearson Travel discount.

The Entertainment editions also include discount and upgrade vouchers for car rentals including National, Budget, and Alamo. These are great for independent exploration during a day in port. For example, a Hawaiia cruise will leave passengers with a full day on Maui, and wheels are a necessity for private sightseeing. On Oahu, a car is necessary to escape the densely crowded downtown Waikiki Beach area. Renting a car enables you to explore the island for the day and enjoy its quiet, serene, beauty. Of course, cruise ships can always arrange for exciting shore excursions at each port of call.

Should you have trouble finding a local distributor, called Entertainment Publications at (800) 374-4464. We guarantee that your Entertainment book will pay for itself many times over, unless you ignore it. With that said, we want you to promise us just one thing and one thing only: that you will use it!

➥ **Steve and Pat's Tip:** *Want another big way to save? Move right on to Chapter 5 and our discussion of cruise-only travel agencies. These companies specialize in cruises and often create exclusive cruise deals, many of which include airfare, not found elsewhere. The savings offered by these specialty agencies is often 20 to 50 percent off the regular advertised prices.*

5

Shopping and Booking Discount Cruises: The *N.Y. Times* and *L.A. Times* Connection

Often in life, bigger is by far better. At movie theaters, a small bag of popcorn is enough for us, but only through the opening credits! That is why we and most others go for the large or even refillable "challenge" size. You may love, hate, or never spend a moment thinking about the *New York Times* or *Los Angeles Times*. Regardless, their Sunday travel sections are indispensable resources for our *Cheapskate* travel efforts. Consider our nonscientific comparison.

Spread out before us, as we write these very words, are the Sunday travel sections from these newspapers and our two local papers, the *San Francisco Chronicle* and the *Contra Costa Times*. The *New York Times* Travel Section is forty-eight pages long and the *Los Angeles Times* section contains thirty-six pages. The *San Francisco Chronicle*'s Travel Section consists of twenty-four pages, and the *Contra Costa Times*'s is eight pages long. The *New York Times* and *Los Angeles Times* travel sections together include approximately eighty pages of Sunday travel material. This translates to the absolute best selection of current vacation bargains and travel news. Their articles and reader adviseries provide helpful and often invaluable information on travel comfort and safety topics. Their papers carry advertisements for major cruise itineraries in Alaska, the Caribbean, on the Mississippi River, or on a Russian River cruise from Moscow to St. Peterburg!

> ➥ **Steve and Pat's Tip:** *Home delivery of the weekend* New York Times *is the best travel investment. The* Times *has a national home-delivery option. To subscribe, call (800) 455-8273. Questions? Call the* New York Times *customer service at (800) NY-TIMES.*

No home delivery? Find a local source of out-of-town newspapers. Try the telephone yellow pages under "Newspapers—Out of Town," "Newspapers—Foreign" or "Newsstand—All-Night." Whatever it takes, we can assure you it will be worth your effort. Did we mention that these newspapers also have the best arts and leisure sections in the United States?

Cruise-Only Travel Agencies

America's infatuation with cruising has produced many cruise-only travel agencies. Their names always include the word *cruise* in their company logo. Cruise-only travel agencies range from small, single offices to nationwide chains and franchises. These agencies offer a greater level of cruise experience and expertise than general travel agencies. Still, beware: This does not mean that you will always receive the best advice; the employee could be a trainee.

> ➥ **Steve and Pat's Tip:** *Do not be bashful when your vacation is at stake. Always ask a travel agent about their background, credentials, and experience. If it turns out that the agent is in training, ask the agency's owner for a more experienced person.*

Shopping and Booking Discount Cruises

Due to their high volume of business, cruise-only travel agencies often have special relationships with cruise lines. This in turn permits them to advertise special incentives and deals. Many of these agencies find super-low cruises and create extraordinary air-and-cruise packages. Although not a cruise-only agency, we include The Whole World of Travel since most of its business is dedicated to cruise vacations. Whole World does its homework and specializes in creating exclusive, bargain-priced cruise-and-air packages.

Of course, the higher-priced cruises do increase an agency's profits. All agencies prefer to sell $5,000 to $10,000 per person deluxe cruises rather than a $649 bargain.

What do cruise-only agencies fail to deliver? Our short list follows:

- No participation in free-travel-cash promotions
- No advice on free-travel and free-companion-travel certificates
- They promote higher-priced cruises
- They are commission-based, so cruise prices may be higher than discount and rebate travel agencies
- They promote volume sales, not personal service

However, cruise-only agencies do deserve serious consideration because they are specializing in cruises and have close ties to the cruise industry. They may just come up with an incredible low-priced, air-and-cruise package for you.

Consider the following list of local and national, cruise-only travel agencies when planning a cruise vacation:

Whole World of Travel

We recommend this agency because it is dedicated to cruising and dirt-cheap prices. The agency hunts down special low airfares and creates exclusive air-and-cruise packages. Because we cannot book these packages through other travel agencies, we cannot use free travel cash or other rebates.

Whole World of Travel's recent offerings include a nine-night, Celebrity Alaska Inside Passage–Only cruise embarking from San

Francisco and disembarking in Vancouver. They priced the air-and-cruise package, including taxes and port charges, at $1,007. Other packages included an eleven-day RCI cruise from Ensenada, Mexico, to the Hawaiian Islands for $1,591. This package included round-trip airfare from the West Coast. Also, RCI had a one-week Mexican Riviera cruise on RCI's older ship, *Song of America*, priced at just $577, which included port fees and taxes. Contact Whole World of Travel at (800) 458-3636 or (916) 488-8000.

Cruise World

This nationwide chain of specialty agencies advertises in major newspapers, including the *New York Times*. Their ads are a wealth of information. A typical *New York Times* advertisement lists the bargain sailings of *twelve* cruise lines! And we mean *bargain* prices, like seven-night cruises which include port charges for $678 (eastern Caribbean—Holland America Line), $649 (Caribbean—Norwegian Cruise Line), $727 (Caribbean—Princess Cruises), and $775 (western Caribbean—Celebrity Cruises). For information on current offerings, check the *New York Times, Los Angeles Times,* and local newspapers. For a free *Cruise World* magazine, call (800) 442-9278.

CruiseMasters

This specialty cruise company started in 1974. In 1998, it merged with Travel Services International and has several sister cruise-specialty companies. This means clout. For a free thirty-page cruise magazine, *Captain's Log,* call (800) 242-9000. Check the terms and conditions on the back page. Remember: Sale prices apply only to the boldface sailing dates listed in their advertisements. Also, small print at the bottom of many ads refers to nasty add-ons such as taxes and port charges.

How good are some of their prices? Does $699 for a full one-week Mexican Riviera cruise on Carnival's new megaship the *Elation* sound interesting? However, this low price only applies to a single September 1998 sailing. The magazine states that other "also available" dates listed in the ads "are subject to a higher price."

CruiseOne

This is a home-based franchise. The home-based franchise owner may or may not have lots of experience. One owner was curt when he realized we were not calling to book a cruise. Another owner, Harry, in Valley Stream, New York, was courteous, helpful, and immediately detailed his five-years of experience in booking cruises—and we had called Harry on a Sunday!

This is important to know in the race to lock in a fantastic deal the same day it appears in a Sunday newspaper. Ask for a free *CruiseOne* magazine. Call owner Harry at his Valley Stream franchise at (888) 703-7245 or (516) 872-1466.

Ambassador Tours

This cruise-specialty agency is celebrating its forty-third year in business. Their catalogue is the *Vacation Discounter,* with thirty-one pages of cruise values. Call Ambassador at (800) 989-9000 and ask to be on their mailing list.

Travel of America (TOA)

Call TOA and ask to be placed on their mailing list to receive a thirty-one-page, *Cruise and Tours* catalogue. Call (800) 228-8843.

Costco Travel

If you are not a Costco member, call Costco Travel's Cruise Center at (800) 800-8505 and request a copy of their travel discount catalogue.

Cruise Travel Center

Their eight-page flyer has hundreds of deals. At present, their low prices do not include port fees and taxes. Call (800) 231-7447 to request a flyer.

Time to Travel

Their recent merger with Golden Bear Travel makes them one of the largest of the nation's cruise providers. The subscription for their sixteen-page, "Cruise Net Collection" catalogue costs $9.99 per year. Nevertheless, call (800) 524-3300 and request a free sample copy.

Cyberspace: The Travel Resource for the Year 2000

You have heard about it, read about, talked about it, and perhaps spend your life dabbling in it. The Internet, also known as the World Wide Web, or the Net, is a great place to look for travel bargains.

Assume one Sunday morning several inviting cruise advertisements are in the *New York Times* Travel Section, each offering a similar Caribbean itinerary. Which cruise line and ship is right for you? Helpful information beyond that found in brochures may often be found on the Web. For example, most brochures do not directly compare the amenities between ships. This information and more are only key strokes away when "surfing" the Web.

➥ **Steve and Pat's Tip:** *No computer? Do not skip this chapter. Ask friends, family, or acquaintances who surf the Web to help check these valuable Web sites. Or try your local libraries with friendly librarians to teach you how to find these Web sites. Do not let this incredible resource pass you by!*

Want a good example of Web surfing? While planning a vacation to Rome, Florence, and Venice, we cruised the Web and started looking up restaurants in the various cities. We found a Venetian restaurant and studied its delicious-looking menu. Already, we were learning menu items and prices. Then we looked in amazement at the reservation form for the restaurant on our computer screen. If we filled in a date and time, with a single keystroke the reservation would be transmitted instantly to the restaurant in Venice.

We are talking computer power! Just several months ago we purchased our London theater tickets on the Web. Or find a train schedule, including best routes and prices, for almost any train system on earth! We could go on and on. On the other hand, when I attempted to purchase low-priced plane tickets to Hawaii, we found 90 percent of related Web sites referring us to their offices usually by way of a toll-free number. By the year 2005, only 5 percent of travelers will be purchasing their vacations on the Web.

Helpful Categories

Exhaustive Information   The amount of valuable current available information is limitless. Ever heard of the small English town of Bingley? We visited friends living in this British hamlet, several hours north of London, and had no difficulty finding Bingley by surfing the Web.

A New Window to Recreation   Regardless of the port of call, the Web provides instant access to all available recreational activities. Want to book a jet-boat excursion in Queenstown, New Zealand? Or learn about shopping at the Grand Bazaar in Istanbul? No problem! There is no end to the power of this new medium. We recently purchased two sixth-row center seats for London's smash hit *Beauty and the Beast* on the Web.

Maps   You can locate a color map of any city in the world and print it in minutes. The same is true for subway or underground metro systems.

Transportation   Most passengers need transportation to their cruise ship's departure city and from the airport to their cruise ships. Details on all facets of transportation are found on the Web.

Sightseeing at Ports of Call   Want information on shopping, recreation, museums, flea markets, castles, beaches, or any of a hundred other topics? All this and more is easily available on the Web. During its Hawaiian Islands cruise, one ship stops at Christmas Island in the republic of Kiribati. Surely you know about Kiribati? No? Within minutes, we printed everything we needed to know about this tiny South Pacific island nation, once known as the Gilbert Islands.

Cruise-Line Web Sites

"Steve and Pat's Great Web Sites" is found in Appendix B in the back of the book. It contains Web sites for all major cruise lines, and that is just the beginning. Want to check out the latest deals from cruise-specialty agencies? Ready to purchase a camcorder from a New York discount camera shop? Need to track different airlines' frequent-flyer miles? Require information on converting U.S. dollars to foreign currency? All this and more is on our special list of cruise and money-saving travel-related Web sites. Those that are boldfaced carry our special recommendation.

Deciphering Cruise-Ad Jargon

Entering the cruise marketplace requires effort and diligence. When shopping for a cruise bargain, remember the phrase "Let the buyer beware!" The following glossary will help explain confusing cruise ad jargon and double-talk:

Tipping double-talk? Holland America Line advertises its "no tipping required" policy. What does this mean in the real world? See "Tipping on the Seventh Day" in Chapter 7 to find out.

Cruise vacation guarantees See our special section "Too Good to Be True—Cruise Guarantees" in Chapter 6.

You don't know what you can't see As certified members of the baby-boomer club, magnifying reading glasses have invaded every room of our home. Every cruise advertisement contains a block of microscopic print. Skip the fine print and disappointment or disaster may follow. Read it all!

Restricted sailings Most cruise sale prices apply to limited or dated sailings often described in the microscopic print portion of an ad. When sailings are limited and no dates are listed, contact the cruise line or a local travel agent for the necessary details. Some sale cruises are restricted to certain state residents. Then again, we have seen the same Alaska cruise limited to New York residents in a *New York Times* ad and limited to California residents in a *San Francisco Chronicle* ad. Be aware, scrutinize, and ask questions, especially when an ad's micro-print seems a bit unfriendly.

Best available cabins   This wonderful term means that within one or more categories of cabins, the best locations are given out on a first-come, first-served basis at the time of booking. It is the best of cruise worlds when this applies to a bargain cruise cabin.

Limited cabin selection   In most sale ads the micro-print shows the cabin category(s), such as K or L, to which the sale price applies. We immediately confirm that the sale price meets our minimum cabin standard, i.e., an inside cabin with two lower beds. Check the cruise line's brochure or contact a travel agent as soon as possible. The cruise line's Web site often has the ship's schematic or a list of cabin categories. Not all cruise Web sites include these details. Fortunately, most "sale" advertisements apply to inside cabins with two lower beds.

Port fees and taxes   Search each advertisement for the beautiful words "port charges included" or "port charges and taxes included." Other ads phrase it as "port fees included." Most, but not all, cruise lines include port charges and taxes in their advertised and brochure prices. A reference to port charges will be somewhere in most cruise ads. Always confirm that "included" means all port charges. We are not as concerned about governmental taxes, which are usually between $12 and $25.

Nights versus days   Many popular cruise ads read, "a seven-night cruise" or "one-week cruise." Most seven-day cruises are also seven-night cruises. Check this if you are planning to use free travel cash that requires seven nights.

What is the name of that ship?   Read the cruise advertisement from top to bottom and determine whether it names the ship making the bargain sailing(s). Call the cruise line for this essential information.

Departure or embarkation city   A recent advertisement stated, "one-week Caribbean cruises, $665–$895 from Miami, San Juan, and New Orleans." Call the cruise line to learn if the lowest bargain price includes the departure city of your choice.

Cruise-only versus "includes air" Ninety percent of bargain cruise advertisements say that the sale price applies to "cruise-only." On the other hand, 10 percent of the bargain cruises are sold as air-and-cruise packages. In the latter case, free airfare usually applies only to "selected" cities. When an additional flight is needed to reach a "selected" city, airlines offer low add-on fares.

Add-on airfare Let us define *add-on fares* by the following example: Shortly we head out to Greece and Turkey. The Homeric package includes round-trip airfare from New York to Athens. Homeric offers airfares from other U.S. cities to New York. Their West Coast add-on fare is $410. We opted to use 50,000 American AAdvantage program miles for two free tickets to New York that saved us $820! Occasionally, an add-on fare may be so low that it is not cost-effective to use a free-travel award. Simply buy the add-on airfare.

Two-for-one specials Give us a collective break! This advertising gimmick does *not* assure that the total price of the cruise with one person traveling "free" will be the best price. If the micro-print states the paying passenger must pay "full brochure price," you may begin to smell a small rodent. Always compare actual costs regardless of the advertising hype.

➥ **Steve and Pat's Tip:** *Did you find an advertisement that seems perfect for you? Want to move like lightning and nail down the reservation before the time limit is up and the offer is gone? And you do not have free travel cash? Call Pearson Travel at (800) 336-1066 or (401) 274-2900. Pearson is a full-service American Express–related agency that offers great deals and the necessary full service for help and instant booking. Check Chapter 4 for additional discounts.*

Itineraries A recent Premier cruise advertisement included four boxes, each showing a different itinerary and price. Other cruise ads may read Southern, Western, or Eastern Caribbean. Call the cruise line to find out the exact itinerary for the advertised cruise.

Time limitations Most bargain cruise advertisements offer special sale prices if booked immediately or by a certain date. The summer 1998 cruise magazine *Captain's Log* states that their lowest "value prices" apply only to cruises booked by July 31. Always dissect cruise advertisements from top to bottom microprint. When in doubt, call the cruise line's toll-free number.

How Many Days in a One-Week Cruise?

Forget calculators. We can easily count fingers on this one. Let us say first that seven-day cruises are the most common, and the most popular cruise destinations are Alaska, Mexico, and Caribbean. Planning to use free travel cash? The cruise must include seven nights. Most advertised seven-day cruises are seven-night cruises. For example, Carnival's Mexican Riviera cruises leave from Los Angeles at 4:30 P.M. Sunday and sail for seven nights, returning to Los Angeles at 9:00 A.M. the following Sunday. So the cruise lines are honestly advertising seven *full* days on the ship.

Vacation advertisements can be very confusing. Take a look at the following example. Although this advertisement applies to a noncruise vacation, the principle is the same. In 1998, Pleasant Tahitian Holidays' advertisements for a Cooks Bay Resort package read, "Moorea and Tahiti Nine Days...." The package included six nights' lodging at Cooks Bay Resort and one night's lodging on the island of Tahiti. The total was seven nights' lodging in French Polynesia. Other major Tahiti tour operators call the same vacation a "seven-night" or an "eight-day and seven-night" package.

Homeric Tours advertises our recent cruise-and-land vacation extravaganza to Greece and Turkey as a sixteen-day "Grecian Voyager" vacation. The ad says sixteen days, but quickly points out that it is fourteen nights of actual vacation. The remaining days are travel days to and from Greece. Once we confirmed the fourteen nights in Greece, we rejoiced that our fourteen-night vacation qualified for $500 in free travel cash.

Paying for Your Cruise—the Frequent-Flyer Connection

Let's face it. It hurts to lay out big bucks for most items we purchase in our day-to-day lives. Perhaps a dream cruise has been reserved at a cheapskate price. What happens next? Within a matter of days of reserving a cruise, it is time to book the cruise and pay a hefty deposit of $200 to $500. The balance of the total cruise vacation price is due within forty-five to ninety days before departure. Whether the price per person is $599 or more, charge it on a Citibank AAdvantage Visa or MasterCard and earn more than 1,000 American Aadvantage miles, and earn more miles by paying for all shipboard expenses, tips, specialty services, and shopping sprees with a Citibank or other airline-related credit card. Next, collect miles by charging the cost of shore excursions. And do not forget gold and diamond purchases at the Caribbean wholesale jewelry emporiums! Some passengers will chalk up thousands more miles—and huge Visa bills!

Cabin Selection—Pick the Best Location

Without a doubt, cabin selection and location is the key to cheapskate cruising. By "key," we refer to the one major concession we are prepared to make in exchange for an incredible bargain vacation price. We accept the fact that most advertised cruise bargains are limited to one or several lower categories of inside staterooms.

> ➥ **Steve and Pat's Tip:** *Let us repeat our refusal to consider the lowest of low-end categories—inside staterooms with upper and lower bunk beds. The good news is that cabins on newer ships do not have this configuration. Older ships usually advertise inside cabins with two lower beds at bargain prices.*

Inside Versus Outside Staterooms

Outside staterooms have a window and may cost $400 to $800 or more per couple! This is the obvious and major difference between inside and outside cabins. However, there is more to consider.

The square footage of the inside and outside cabins are most often exactly or roughly the same. Take top-rated Celebrity Cruises's spanking new ship, the *Mercury*. This state-of-the-art ship's inside and outside cabins are the same size—a spacious 172 square feet. Outside low-end cabins on other ships may be larger, but only slightly, so size is not a major consideration. Without further ado, let us give you our take, which may just put the window factor into proper perceptive:

- The ship's inside and outside cabins are roughly the same size.
- All amenities are usually the same.
- Twenty-four-hour room service is the same for all cabins.
- The lowest categories of inside and outside cabins usually face one another on the same deck.
- Some outside cabins have obstructed views due to lifeboats or deck supports.
- During days at sea, the view is ocean, ocean, and more ocean.
- Major sightseeing is often best from the upper decks. The best 360-degree viewing is from the upper promenade decks.
- Unlike land-based hotels, the upper decks have spectacular outdoor amenities, such as pools, hot tubs, and other recreational facilities.
- Outside cabins offer status and are usually brighter with great ocean views.
- The restaurants, spas, lounges, movie theater, disco dancing, and nightclub shows draw passengers from their cabins.
- Exciting ports of call also draw passengers from their cabins.
- Romance! Just think, intimate romantic interludes at anytime of day are always best in a naturally darkened windowless cabin.

What if an outside cabin is offered as a free upgrade or for a nominal extra charge? Go for it!

Snob Control We are seated at our dining room table when a snooty-looking fellow passenger looks us in the face and says, "We have a beautiful outside cabin with a great view," and then adds, "How is your cabin?" We might just answer, in less-than-serious fashion, "Inside cabins are the only way to go. Our cabin is in the dead center of the ship, so we never feel the ship's rocking motion. And of course, and we hate to say this, but if there is ever a collision, outside cabins are the first to go!"

In the end, cabin categories are a consideration but not the end-all when it comes to enjoying a fabulous cruise vacation at a cheapskate price. We are satisfied with a two-lower-bed, inside cabin in the best location available. If we can wrangle an upgrade at almost no cost, so much the better.

Meal Seating Selection—Make the Right Choice

Let us cut to the chase on this one. For our money, taste, prejudice, and inclination, we opt and recommend the late rather than the early seating. Does this work for everyone? Of course not. However, those who are undecided or who lack experience need to know more before making this most critical of all cruise decisions. First, we will define what is early and late seating. Read slowly and carefully. It may affect the very success of your cruise vacation. (Most cruise lines serve the main meals daily in the dining room.)

Early Seating Breakfast at 7:30 A.M., lunch at 12:00 noon, and dinner at 6:00 P.M.

Late Seating Breakfast at 8:45 A.M., lunch at 1:30 P.M., and dinner at 8:30 P.M.

First, we admit it—when we are on vacation we are not ready to wake up every day at the crack of dawn. It is not as if one can jump into a bathrobe and simply mosey to the dining room for breakfast. Dining-room meals, whether breakfast, lunch, or dinner, are major events. Consider the RCI's breakfast menu items: eggs Benedict, minced lox and onion omelette, broiled Scottish kippers with lemon butter and steamed potato, and banana pancakes with real maple syrup. We are talking serious meals to get the day started, as one expects on a cruise.

Exactly when must early diners set their alarm clocks to insure prompt arrival at their table for the 7:30 A.M. breakfast? We shudder thinking of the obvious answer. It means waking daily by at least 6:30 A.M. This is not our idea of a leisurely start to each vacation day. We did say we were totally prejudiced on this one, right?

Also, we see a problem at day's end. On our Mexican Riviera cruise we spent the day using the pool and related facilities at the luxurious Crystal Hotel. We truly enjoyed every moment. At 3:00 P.M., we were parasailing, swimming, resting and—relaxing! In Alaska, our ship stopped at Juneau, the state's capital. We headed toward Mendenhall Glacier and enjoyed a half-day rafting trip down the less-than-treacherous river. Afterwards, we headed back to town and spent hours exploring this unique Alaskan outpost.

So what is wrong with these snapshots of exciting and fun ports of call? A full day in port allows passengers to spend the entire day at their leisure. Passengers may return to the ship as late as 6:00 P.M. Remember early seating time is 6:30 P.M. Also, one or two of the dinners will require formal dress. We could be sexist and dare ask how much time a woman needs, after a day of shore excursion, to relax and dress for a formal dinner. A couple of hours? If it takes thirty minutes to return to the ship, early diners must head back to the ship at 3:30 P.M.! On the flip side, the late-dinner seating is at 8:30 or 9:00 P.M. This permits a full afternoon visit in every port of call and a return time of 6:00 P.M. Ample time remains to rest and relax before dressing for dinner.

Yes, those having breakfast at 7:30 A.M. may head to each port of call earlier in the day, by about 10:00 A.M., but for us the prime sightseeing time is late morning until that final ship's bell rings at 6:00 P.M.!

There is one obvious downside for the late seating. Late diners must attend the second 10:30 P.M. evening show. For many this is too late, and hence sufficient reason to book the early seating and then enjoy the earlier 8:30 P.M. evening shows.

Confirm Your Dining Hour Selection

Once made, it is often quite difficult to change one's dining selection. Think of a filled-to-capacity ship packed with 2,000 or more passengers. Once the more popular late seating is fully booked, remaining passengers, even those preferring the late seating, are usually required to accept the early seating. Just imagine the chaos if passengers could board their ship and then expect to change their seating.

➦ **Steve and Pat's Tip:** *When your travel documents arrive, immediately check the time listed for dining—early or late? Does it confirm what you selected when your cruise was booked? If it is at all unclear, contact your travel agent or cruise line—fast! Have written confirmation of your* correct *seating selection* before *leaving home!*

Safety of Life at Sea (SOLAS)—No Titanics Today

Basically, the cruise industry has an excellent safety record. Cruising is the safest method of transportation today. It is estimated that thirty-five million people have traveled over the seas in a cruise ship. The cruise industry complies with all the standards of the International Maritime Organization (IMO), a specialized agency of the United Nations started in 1958. The IMO governs the operation of cruise ships around the world. These regulations are monitored by both the country that registers the ship and the port-of-call countries. Each country is responsible for certifying that ships bearing its flag meet the requirements of the Safety of Life at Sea (SOLAS) Convention and its amendments.

In the United States, the Coast Guard examines each new vessel when it first enters service at an American port. Thereafter, all ships are subject to quarterly Coast Guard inspections. The Coast Guard has the authority to require correction of any deficiencies before allowing a ship to take on passengers at any U.S. port.

Current requirements state that a passenger ship must be capable of being abandoned thirty minutes after a warning is sounded. There should be twice as many lifeboat seats as passengers and life jackets for 125 percent of the ship's capacity. The lifeboats should be covered to protect the passenger. Additionally, in 1992 SOLAS passed an amendment, which became effective in 1997, requiring that all fire protection and life saving equipment be updated, including low-location lighting, smoke detectors, and automatic sprinklers. Starting in 1994, all ships had to be built with sprinklers, fire detection systems, smoke alarms, and self-closing doors. Retrofitting rules contain a grandfather clause allowing older ships built before 1994 to postpone installation of automatic sprinklers until 2005 or 2009 if the ships are built of noncombustible materials and meet other standards.

Cruise lines using these ships are required to apply to their country of registry for an exemption and receive certification that their ship meets the necessary criteria. If the exemption is granted, then the Coast Guard can only verify that the certification standards have been met and that sprinklers are not required at this time.

➡ **Steve and Pat's Tip:** *Ask your travel agent or cruise line if their ship has an automatic sprinkler system everywhere, including laundry rooms, the most common fire hazard location onboard ship. Second, check the age of the ship. If it was built before 1994, ask if it received an exemption from the sprinkler requirement of 1997. Carnival Cruises has been building sprinkler systems on its ships since 1982. Premier Cruises and Princess Cruises state that their ships meet and exceed the 1992 Amendment to Safety of Life at Sea.*

Travel Insurance—the Absolute Best Policy

Personal Belongings Coverage

Vacations are precious to us. We wish to lie on the deck of our cruise ship, savoring beautiful sunsets and contemplating our exotic, forthcoming ports of call. The last thing we want to do is worry about thousands of dollars of camera equipment and other valuable personal belongings.

Before leaving on our cruise vacations, we customarily purchase personal belongings insurance coverage, technically called travel baggage insurance. The policy covers not only luggage but virtually everything we bring with us on vacation, including sporting equipment, camcorders, cameras, jewelry and even such items when borrowed from another for the trip. The cheapskate price for this peace of mind, for a typical one-week cruise vacation, is $20 for the required minimum $500 of coverage for baggage and personal belongings. The cost for $1,000 worth of coverage is $30, and a hefty $50 buys the maximum coverage of $2,000.

How much coverage should you buy? We consider several factors: What equipment do we need to cover? Are we traveling with our lower-priced 35mm cameras or a more expensive Hi-Band 8mm camcorder? Is the cruise vacation going to be a high-risk venture with tropical beach exposure to sun, sand, and water? A rule of thumb is calculating the replacement cost of the most expensive camera or camcorder and then adding another $250 to $500 to cover the replacement value of miscellaneous clothing, belongings, and luggage. This usually translates to $1,500 for the camera bug (Steve) and the minimum $500 for Patty. Remember, never overinsure.

Travel Pak (short for Travelers Travel Insurance Pak) This coverage is a very travel consumer-friendly insurance product. It has few exclusions and none that affect most vacationers. The excluded items are autos, boats, commercial equipment, and bicycles, except during transit. More important, it covers most everything we take on vacation.

Theft of Personal Belongings

Some years ago, we arrived at San Diego Airport en route to a sailing and scuba-diving vacation in the Sea of Cortez and were horrified to learn that one of our bags was missing. It just happened to be our major equipment bag, which contained $1,400 in mostly new scuba-diving gear. It seems one or another airport employee stole the bag. The maximum legal liability of domestic airlines for lost or damaged luggage and contents is $1,250 per passenger.

Approximately two weeks after the loss, the airline offered to settle our claim for a paltry $700. We summarily rejected the offer for being far too low. We informed both the airline and Travelers Insurance Company that we expected to be fully reimbursed and suggested they pay us the full value of our loss and share the payment between themselves. Our trusty Travel Pak policy provided $1,000 per person coverage for our luggage and possessions on this vacation. Within two weeks we received a check from Travelers for $1,350, virtually full reimbursement!

Carelessness—the Human Trait We Hate to Admit

In late 1994, just before departing for Moorea in French Polynesia, we learned that our Nikonos V 35mm underwater camera was severely damaged. The repair estimate was an astounding $500! The cause of the "problem" was an accidental buildup of salt near the shutter mechanism that caused it to freeze up. It seems we neglected to have the camera professionally cleaned, as suggested by the manufacturer, after our previous trip to Moorea just three months earlier. We retrieved the policy and filed a claim.

To its credit, the Travel Pak policy is "no-fault." Consequently, it does not exclude damage resulting from accidents even when the policyholder is negligent. This is the best type of all-risk coverage one can buy. Within a few weeks we received Travelers' $500 check.

➥ **Steve and Pat's Tip:** *Keep those old Travel Pak policies. Sometimes the damage, like that to our Nikonos V camera, is not known until months later. For at least one year after a vacation, Travelers will accept valid claims made under the Travel Pak policy.*

Lost Items (How to Lose Without Being a Loser!)

During our recent cruise on China's famed Yangtze River a member of our group, a hip young guy from Los Angeles, leaned over the railing. In an instant his $125 designer sunglasses fell into the Yangtze, never to be seen again. The young man was both embarrassed and horrified. We turned to one another and smiled knowingly. Our vacation days are never ruined by this type of occurrence because Travel Pak covers such losses.

Camera Coverage (Did You Hear Something Drop?)

Most passengers bring expensive camcorders and 35mm cameras on their fabulous cruise vacations. What better way to preserve holiday memories? With this in mind, consider the following scenarios:

- You are enjoying a fine lunch when your camera topples off a table and falls onto the very hard floor.
- While on a beach at an exotic tropical port of call you go swimming or snorkeling. What to do with your camera or camcorder? Perhaps you will bury it in your beach bag, jump in for a quick dip, and constantly worry about the unprotected equipment.
- While sunbathing on a beautiful tropical beach, a teenager runs by and kicks sand on your blanket, covering your camcorder with the deadly particles.

Believe it or not, such losses often spoil the best of vacations. Happily, Travel Pak covers all the above scenarios. When we suffer such a loss, we feel just as bad as the next person, but only for a fleeting moment. Then we quickly remind ourselves that Travelers will be coming to our rescue.

Why Choose Travel Pak Over Other Policies?

Choose Travel Pak because the following, most desired vacation features are found in Travel Pak:

- *Primary Policy:* Travel Pak is a primary policy, so there is no need to file a claim against your homeowner's policy. This is a great feature, since claims against a homeowner's policy may increase the premiums or even risk cancellation of the policy. With Travel Pak there is no need to be bashful even when it comes to minor losses.

- *Broad coverage:* Coverage for baggage and personal belongings should be broad with few exclusions. Travel Pak covers cameras and jewelry up to $1,000, with $2,000 worth of coverage available for sports equipment. Many other policies severely limit photo equipment and camera coverage to a nominal amount, while other policies exclude such items. Some policies limit a claim to 25 percent of the value of a camera, while others strictly limit losses to $250 per item.

We are always on the lookout for better or cheaper policies. What we have found are many plainly misleading brochures. One policy claims to offer $2,000 worth of coverage for baggage and personal belongings. However, its microscopic print tells refers customers to customer service for further "details." I called the customer service number for this company and learned, to my disdain, that the actual policy has a $250 coverage limit on cameras and jewelry. When checking a policy, get the company's toll-free number. Then call and ask about *all* the company's policy exclusions, including any items that are not covered outright and the loss limits on cameras, camcorders, jewelry, sporting gear, and so forth.

Some policies require customers to purchase a total package that includes medical and accident coverage. Often these duplicate vacationers' other insurance coverage. Purchase only the coverage actually needed. Travel Pak's "à la carte menu" is perfect by our standards, since it permits customized coverage for each vacation.

Trip Cancellation Coverage—How Much Can You Afford to Lose?

Example 1 You have paid thousands of dollars for your dream cruise vacation and the departure date approaches. Suddenly a family member or travel companion becomes ill or has an accident, causing you to cancel the cruise. The very sympathetic tour operator explains that you are not entitled to any refund because you declined to purchase cancellation coverage.

Example 2 The following actually occurred during our Tanzania safari. An elderly member of our small group suddenly had chest pains. He and his wife had to pay thousands of dollars for an emergency flight home. They had no cancellation coverage and therefore saw no recovery of these substantial costs.

Example 3 You and your traveling companion are our neighbors. All of us booked the same fabulous Mediterranean cruise. On this occasion, we are both going first class, paying $10,000 per couple. Your car and my car leave our driveways side by side. We both head down the freeway to the airport to catch the flight to our luxury cruise ship. Both of us purchased $10,000 worth of trip-cancellation insurance coverage. You purchased the top-rated insurance policy recommended by the California State Automobile Association. We purchased our favorite Travel Pak policy. Then it happens: up ahead an overturned tractor trailer is blocking the roadway. Everyone misses their plane and cruise vacation. We each submit our $10,000 claims to our respective insurance companies and are reimbursed the full $10,000 of our loss. Your claim is flat-out denied and you are paid *zero*!

How is this possible? The answer is in the nasty details. Believe it or not, many travel cancellation policies will not honor the above claim, including the policy recommended by the California State Automobile Association. Their policy's fine print states that *no coverage* is provided at all *unless* the delay was caused by the policyholder being *actually involved in a motor vehicle accident* en route to the airport. On the other hand, Travel Pak, with its liberal provisions, may pay such a claim whether or not the policyholder was directly involved in the accident or merely delayed. The delay must be a result of an *unforeseen emergency* and at least one hour in duration.

Trip cancellation insurance is intended to reimburse nonrefundable vacation expenses and also emergency medical transportation back home, whether an illness, injury, or jury duty happens to you, family members, or travel companions.

A Word About Preexisting Illnesses

Travel Pak covers any illness or injury that occurs after the policy is purchased. It also covers any preexisting illness or injury if the condition was "under control" for sixty days before the purchase date. *Under control* means that no treatment has been received or required for the past sixty days. Once you have booked your cruise, if you are in good health, make it a point to purchase Travel Pak trip cancellation coverage quickly. There is no extra charge for buying the insurance early. Then, if an illness, injury, or flare-up occurs anytime after the purchase you are fully covered.

➥ **Steve and Pat's Preexisting Illness Tip:** *When should the purchase of Travel Pak trip cancellation coverage be delayed? Suppose a person had a minor back strain forty-five days ago but is now fully recovered and feels fine. And this person just booked a cruise that departs in two months. Because of the sixty-day rule, the back would* not *be covered for any further problems. All cruise payments would be lost if there is a serious flare-up before departure. Let us assume this person waits fifteen days and then purchases the Travel Pak policy. If, during the fifteen days, there are neither back problems nor treatment, the sixty-day rule is met. Now, any back problem that prevents this person's departure or which occurs during your cruise will be covered. If any reader has ongoing medical problems, we have a great alternative for you!*

Travel Guard: The Ultimate in Preexisting Protection!

Just recently we found a solid travel insurance competitor to Travel Pak. The policy is Travel Guard International. Both policies are excellent and each has strong and weak points. Note that we have never used Travel Guard and cannot vouch for its claims handling. Do you have ongoing health problems? Then Travel Guard is heaven-sent with its 100 percent, preexisting condition medical waiver. If you can, review both companies' flyers, obtain and review their sample policies, and call to ask questions. A brief comparison follows:

- Travel Guard offers a *100 percent waiver of preexisting medical conditions.* However, the policy must be purchased *within seven days* of making a deposit on the vacation.

- Travel Guard is sold as a package that includes personal belongings, medical, and trip cancellation coverage. There are no á la carte options, as with Travel Pak.
- Travel Guard's baggage coverage is weak. The policy includes only $1,000 in maximum coverage. A maximum payment of $500 is payable on the first item claimed, and a $250 per item maximum for items claimed after that, until $1,000 is reached. Travel Pak has a better and higher $1,000 limit per item claimed, and a $2,000 maximum on total coverage.
- Travel Guard requires receipts with every claim. Travel Pak does not require receipts on claims of less than $500. This helps when receipts are lost or difficult to find.
- Both Travel Guard and Travel Pak offer trip cancellation coverage that will pay for a missed vacation that results from "unforeseen circumstances." Most other policies do not.

➥ **Steve and Pat's Tip:** *When is it wise to buy both policies? You may need to buy Travel Guard for the preexisting medical waiver. Then buy additional baggage (personal belongings) coverage from Travel Pak for $5.50 for each $100 of coverage up to the higher Travel Pak $2,000 maximum.*

Contact Travel Guard International to obtain a flyer or ask questions, or even purchase a Travel Guard policy on the phone by calling (800) 826-1300, or fax (800) 955-8785.

Turning in an Insurance Claim

The Travel Pak claim form is simple to complete, since Travelers does not require submission of original receipts. Simply list the place and date of purchase of items lost or damaged and estimated repair or replacement cost. If your loss is less then $500, the claim does not need to be notarized. During the past ten years, our many meticulously prepared claims have always been promptly processed and paid.

Our travel motto is Don't Worry, Be Happy! In this regard,

Travel Pak has kept us smiling through occasionally unpleasant and unpredictable events, the type that occur on even the best of dream vacations.

➥ **Steve and Pat's Tip:** *Can't locate a travel agency that sells Travel Pak policies? Simply contact our good friends at Downtown Travel, our local travel agency in Walnut Creek, California. Send a written request for a Travel Pak application. Then complete the application and mail it to the listed address with the premium check. The policy will be issued and returned by mail. Write to: Downtown Travel, 1609 Locust Street, Walnut Creek, CA 94596, or call (510) 945-8004, or fax (510) 945-8081.*

Effective Date of Coverage

Personal belongings coverage begins the date of departure. Cancellation coverage begins on the date the application is signed and mailed. Always keep a copy of the application. To calculate the number of vacation days for baggage (personal belongings) coverage, first count all the days of the vacation including the departure date and the return date, then deduct one day from the total number of vacation days. That's it!

Medical Care at Sea: Is There a Doctor Onboard?

Usually the last thought crossing a passenger's mind as they book their cruise vacation is the question of emergency medical care. But how smoothly a medical emergency is handled can make or break a vacation. Carnival, Celebrity, Costa, Disney, Holland America Lines, Norwegian Cruise Line, Orient, Premier, Royal Caribbean International, and Royal Olympic Cruises have infirmaries onboard with limited medical facilities staffed by a doctor and nurse and equipped to treat minor nonemergency matters.

A ship's infirmary is generally open regular hours. However, during off hours doctors can be reached by phone, and twenty-four-hour care is available. Maritime doctors even make cabin calls. Remember, only basic services are offered, no specialized expertise or equipment is available. The doctors and medical staff are hired as independent contractors, not employees of the cruise line. Consequently, the cost for medical care is charged at the prevailing rate.

> ➥ **Steve and Pat's Tip:** *Princess Cruises has always been a leader in providing excellent medical care at sea. Princess' medical staff is UK registered and have at least three years' postgraduate medical training including experience in primary care, minor surgery, emergency medical care, and cardiac care and are certified in Advanced Life Support. All physicians are full-time, shipboard doctors with extensive maritime experience, can handle emergencies at sea, and interact with shore facilities around the world. Princess' ships all have full pharmacies onboard stocked with medications approved by the UK Committee on Safety of Medicines.*

All cruise ships advise passengers to bring an adequate supply of prescription medications in their original bottles. Pharmacies are not available onboard except for Princess Cruise Lines. Prescriptions are difficult to fill in port.

> ➥ **Steve and Pat's Tip:** *Norwegian Cruise Lines requires that children under eighteen traveling without a parent or guardian, for example, grandparents, aunts, and uncles, must have a notified parental or guardian consent letter authorizing medical treatment in case of an emergency. This is an excellent tip for nonparental adults traveling with children in similar circumstances on other cruise lines to assure that their charges will always be able to receive the necessary medical care or prescriptions.*

The *Grand Princess*, Princess Cruise Lines' newest ship, sailing in summer of 1998, includes a groundbreaking telemedicine program known as SeaMed. The ship's medical center is linked directly by a two-way video to the emergency department physicians and specialists at Cedars-Sinai Medical Center in Los Angeles to help in the management of complex and emergency situations. Radiographs, ECG, and physiologic signals can be transmitted to the hospital by satellite for interpretation and consultation by a twenty-four-hour medical staff.

Emergency Medical Evacuation While Cruising

If a passenger with a life-threatening medical condition requires transfer to an onshore medical facility, the plan of evacuation depends on the location of the vessel relative to the nearest medical facility. Surprisingly, medical situations requiring that a passenger be evacuated from a cruise ship happen frequently and luckily usually happen in port. The cruise medical staff will make all the arrangements for the patient and accompanying parties to be transported to the local hospital. Medical notes, tests, and observations are sent with the patient. At the hospital, a liaison staff member will take over the necessary translation and instructions to the hospital staff for continued medical care.

Passenger evacuation at sea happens far less frequently than when a ship is in port. In international waters, the only choice is to immediately head to the nearest port with medical facilities. If the ship is near United States coastal waters or near United States islands, like the U.S. Virgin Islands, the captain will divert the ship to the nearest island or port of call with a landing strip. Simultaneously, he will notify the United States Coast Guard that an emergency medivac helicopter is required. Coast Guard helicopter pickups at sea are dangerous and require intense communication and coordination between the ship's captain and the helicopter crew. Today, cruise lines are practicing medivac pickups with the United States Coast Guard to perfect the transportation of patients to shore in an efficient and safe fashion.

Medivac evacuation from a vessel at sea is expensive and costs many thousands and thousands of dollars. Even ambulance charges can run into thousands of dollars depending on local prices, distance traveled and the medical expertise of the ambulance staff.

If you have a medical condition which could possibly require expert care, check with your health insurance carrier before booking a cruise. Then there will be no surprises. You will know if you are covered for catastrophic medical emergency care outside North America including transportation by whatever means to the nearest facility. Of course, if an emergency arises and medical evacuation is needed immediately, even without medical coverage, you have no choice but to go ahead. It would be less stressful to know in advance that these charges would be covered by a medical insurance policy.

➥ **Steve and Pat's Tip:** *Medicare and many private insurance policies do not provide medical coverage while traveling outside North America. Typically their policies will not cover emergency air or ground evacuation to the nearest medical facility.*

If you are not covered and feel that insurance will grant you peace of mind, then check with the cruise line to learn if they offer an insurance policy with medical coverage. Nonemergency, hospital, medical care, and routine doctor visits are generally not covered by these policies. Purchasing a medical insurance plan through the cruise lines may not provide coverage for pre-existing conditions. If you decide to purchase a plan offered by a cruise line, request a description of the policy, and scrutinize the conditions, exemptions and disclaimers, always in tiny print in their brochure, before signing up.

Cruise Lines' Medical Insurance Policies

Celebrity Cruises offers a Cruise Protection Plan that includes TravelGuard Assistance with a twenty-four-hour hotline offering emergency medical assistance and evacuation through a worldwide network of medical and travel professionals to help solve all medical problems. Up to $5,000 is paid for covered medical expenses such as sickness, injury, and emergency dental treatment. If serious illness or injury requires hospitalization, emergency air and ground transportation are covered up to $20,000.

TravelGuard Assistance coordinates all aspects of the transportation to insure the passenger's safe return. The policy ranges in price from $69 to $119 depending on the length of the cruise. Contact the carrier, Insure America, at (800) 826-8210 for Cruise Protection Plan inquiries only.

Premier Cruises offers a Premier Travel Protection policy that includes medical protection. Only emergency medical injury and sickness are covered. Covered medical expenses are reimbursed up to $10,000. Reasonable costs of emergency evacuation by air or ground for covered medical reasons are reimbursed up to $15,000. The policy ranges in price from $39 to $169 depending on the location of the cruise itinerary. Call the plan administrator with questions at (800) 457-7709 for additional information.

Norwegian Cruise Lines offers a Passenger and Baggage Protection Plan that pays up to $10,000 for medical expenses due to accident or sickness and up to $15,000 for emergency evacuation. Twenty-four-hour emergency assistance is available. The cost of the plan ranges from $39 to $79 depending on the length of the cruise. For plan details, including medical condition limitations and what to do in an emergency, contact the plan administrator at (800) 722-5672.

Royal Carribean International has an insurance policy called CruiseCare. The policy provides that if you become sick or injured on a cruise, you will be reimbursed for up to $10,000 for covered medical expenses and up to $25,000 for transportation costs to the nearest facility. Costs of the policy range from $90 to $139 per person depending on the location of the cruise itinerary. Direct your questions to the CruiseCare desk at (800) 453-4022.

PART II

Bargain Cruising: Selection to Bon Voyage

6

Selecting Ideal Cruises: Knowing Vacation Objectives and Destinations

Is this topic necessary? After all, most readers know their vacation objectives and destinations, right? Part of our joy of travel is the "vacation guessing game." A year ago, in mid-July, we were only six weeks away from our Labor Day vacation. We duly marked our work calendars and were ready to go, except we had no idea where we were going. We had yet to make a single concrete vacation plan.

> ➥ **Steve and Pat's Tip:** *Between cruises, readers may just wish to do a South Pacific "wild thing" like our camper-van adventure. If so, contact the super-discount travel consolidator Discover Wholesale Travel at (800) 576-7770 or (714) 833-1136, or fax (714) 833-1176. Their price for our ten-day New Zealand vacation, including round-trip airfare on Air New Zealand, transfers, and the camper-van was $959 per person! In addition, we each received 13,000 frequent-flyer miles, usable on Air New Zealand's partner—United Airlines!*

Our recommended *Los Angeles Times* connection worked like a charm. Within days of spying the ad we booked one of our best vacations ever: a fabulous ten-day New Zealand camper-van adventure. Two highlights were cruising Milford Sound into the Tasman Sea and spending a half day hiking on Franz Joseph Glacier using ropes and pickaxes.

Vacation Objectives

We follow this golden rule: vacation objectives should be mutually agreed upon. Why? Because vacations for most Americans are too few and far apart. Consider the following when formulating all-important vacation objectives:

Shipboard Versus Land-Based Sightseeing Long hours of shore-excursion sightseeing may be arduous, even for members of the younger cruise generation. Disabled passengers, families with small children, and seniors with severe medical conditions may wish to minimize such noble but arduous efforts. Some cruise itineraries schedule many ports of call, like the classic southern Caribbean cruises. Other itineraries offer world-class sightseeing from the ship's decks like the Alaska and Panama Canal routes.

Climate One can select a breathtaking Alaska cruise with its cooler climate, or one may choose to roast at poolsides under the Caribbean's tropical sun. Others may prefer visiting Europe's great cities on a moderate-climate Mediterranean cruise.

Recreation Obtain shore excursion brochures that list available sightseeing and recreation options.

Young Family Considerations Ever more families with young children are taking part in America's favorite pastime. Their objectives may mean considering ships that offer superior child and teen programs. See our section on family cruising at the end of Chapter 1.

Finances Above all else, cruise vacation objectives must be affordable. Our *Cruise Guide* is dedicated to this proposition!

Food Many have special objectives related to shipboard food. Not partial to Italian food? Require kosher meals? Vegetarian entrees at each meal? Want great "healthy" entree selections?

Selecting Ideal Cruises 97

Know your food objectives and keep them in mind when reading our section on dining in chapter 8.

Days at Sea Carnival's one-week Mexican Riviera cruise includes three full days at sea. Princess offers a Mexican Riviera itinerary with two additional ports of call and only one day at sea. We just spoke with a young couple whose objective was rest and relaxation. They were dismayed that their southern Caribbean cruise stopped at five ports of call, giving them only one full day at sea.

Intimacy Among the Hordes On another cruise we witnessed a couple's dismay and outrage when they learned that their requested table for two in the main dining room was not available. Others look forward to romantic alternative dining away from the main dining room that offers gourmet meals. Some may wish for private five-course dinners served in their cabin. Only a handful of cruise lines includes this ultimate option as part of their room service menu. When we say "hordes," could we possibly be referring to grand ships that carry 2,600 passengers? Some prefer smaller, more intimate ships with fewer amenities.

Selecting Destinations

The key to each memorable cruise vacation is selecting the right cruise destination and itinerary. On Alaska cruises, only some itineraries visit Sitka, while others visit Glacier Bay. Want an ultimate shore excursion? A scuba-diving adventure? A Caribbean itinerary that includes Cozumel and the Grand Cayman Islands is a must. One Mexican Riviera cruise offers a one-day visit to Puerto Vallarta, while another adds two full days in Acapulco.

Foreign-registered ships must stop at a foreign port between embarkation and debarkation of passengers in American ports to meet U.S. legal marine requirements. Some Hawaiian Islands cruises (on Norwegian Cruise Line) pick up passengers in Hawaii, visit remote lackluster Christmas Island, and return to Hawaii, where the passengers disembark.

Time itself may be a key factor in selecting destinations. Detailed itineraries show arrival and departure times for each port of call. Imagine arriving at a dream destination only to learn too late that the ship arrives at 5:00 P.M. for a night visit. A port visit may be as short as three hours, from 9:00 A.M. to noon, when the ship departs.

With one's objectives and destination firmly in mind, a bit of homework will ensure a compatible itinerary and a fabulous cruise vacation.

Collecting Brochures and Viewing Videos

The Boy Scout's credo is Be Prepared, and it comes into play here. The first step is to collect helpful, informative cruise brochures on all the major cruise lines. This task is both easy and virtually cost free. Simply turn to our Appendixes at the back of the book. Our complete listing of mass-marketed, bargain cruise lines includes their toll-free numbers. Simply call the cruise lines and request both their main or general brochure and as many specialty brochures as you wish. Many cruise lines offer low-cost videos that convey the sights and sounds of the cruise lines' various ships. Cruise videos cost about $10.

➥ **Steve and Pat's Tip:** *It is a good idea to obtain new brochures each year. This is especially true, since ships' amenities can change quickly.*

Cruise Terminology: A Language All Its Own

With eyes closed, imagine a champagne waterfall. Perhaps your mind is conjuring images of thousands of gallons of bubbly, golden champagne crashing down a mountainside. If so, you have failed our cruise terminology test. A working knowledge of the ins and outs of cruise talk will add to a successful voyage.

Steve and Pat's Special Cruise Glossary

The Bridge The bridge is the ship's upper-deck operations and control center. Each cruise has a bridge tour with the crew explaining the workings of the high-tech instruments. Do not miss it.

Selecting Ideal Cruises

↪ **Steve and Pat's Tip:** *Keep an eye out for local cruise shows or expos put on by local cruise-only travel agencies. Most shows are free. Some deluxe shows include food and charge a moderate $5 to $10 fee. Representatives from five or more major cruise lines will attend such shows, eager to answer questions and provide their latest brochures.*

The Bow No, this is not the final salutation of the stage performers at show's end. This refers to the front area of the ship.

Champagne Waterfall Okay, it is time to break the suspense. This is a time-honored custom on many ships. It is fun, elegant, and a great photo opportunity. First, a pyramid is constructed out of champagne glasses. One lone champagne glass forms its peak. The impressive mountain of champagne glasses stands on a table and reaches a height of five or six feet. Then, one by one, guests step up and pour from a bottle of champagne into the top glass. Onlookers watch in fascination as the champagne cascades down from one level to the next, filling the glasses. When all the champagne is poured, the waiters hand the glasses to the passengers for a toast. What fun!

March of the Flaming Baked Alaska Alaskan passengers are horrified when they hear of this one, but they are quickly reassured that the phrase is *flaming Alaska* not *flaming Alaskans*. This is another time-honored cruise tradition. At the end of dinner, the lights are turned low. The waiters march slowly in single file around the darkened dining room, each carrying a flaming baked Alaska on his tray. Then the waiters serve the delectable dessert to the appreciative passengers.

Shore Excursions These can cost hundreds of dollars but are often worth every penny. Shore excursions refer to exciting sightseeing and recreational activities in each port of call. Most shore excursions are arranged and sold by the cruise line, or, passengers can arrange for private excursions upon arriving in a port of call.

Ports of Call Stops made by the cruise ship where the passengers can disembark and enjoy onshore excursions and activities.

Selecting Early- or Late-Meal Seating We repeat the importance of this decision. Once selected, changing a dining selection may be difficult or impossible. We recommend the late seating and discuss our reasons in Chapter 8.

Captain's Gala This refers to a special formal-dress dinner in honor of the ship's captain. Usually the dinner offers the ship's most exotic menu, such as lobster.

Upper/Lower Berths (Bunk Beds) Imagine a red circle with a diagonal line placed over these words. We do not want this lowest of low-end sleeping accommodations. Newer megaships have done away with bunk bed cabins.

Floor Steward Each deck has a crew of stewards who are responsible for the cabins in their zone. The steward's major duty is to deliver the touted "free" 24-hour room service. Want to snack at 4:00 A.M.? Just ring for the steward!

Ringing Bells and Chimes Not to worry. Passengers are usually resting in their cabin when they first hear the chimes ringing for dinner. Also, the bells or chimes announce special shipboard news items.

Shipboard Credit Think of shipboard credit as a cruise gift certificate. In lieu of a physical certificate, the gift amount is added as a credit to the passenger's account. An example would be a $100 per cabin credit that can cover the cost of bar bills or optional spa charges. Compared with cash-in-your-pocket specials like Pearson Travel's bonus American Express travelers checks, a cabin or shipboard credit is the next best thing. Remember, a shipboard credit is a use-it-or-lose-it item.

Daily Activity Newsletter The crew slips this daily publication under each cabin's door. All the day's scheduled activities and events are listed, including helpful information on business, health, and comfort services. Newsletters are "busy," so read them carefully or risk missing that one-time tour of the ship's bridge or kitchen.

Boat Tenders No, these are not pieces of chicken in the shape of small boats. These are covered motorized lifeboats that hold one hundred or more passengers. Often, ports cannot dock all the cruise ships at the piers simultaneously. When this occurs, the cruise ship anchors offshore and boat tenders are lowered and put into service as water taxis. The boat tenders spend the day ferrying passengers to and from the port of call.

Shipboard Account Most ships follow a "cashless" cruise policy. This means there are no cash transactions during a cruise. Ship credit accounts are set up when passengers leave a credit card imprint at check-in, then there is no need to carry a wallet or purse. Passengers are free to jump into their bathing suits, slip on their sandals, grab their sunglasses, and head for poolside lounge chairs, where they may order all the exotic drinks they wish and sign for them. During the cruise, all optional expenses such as drinks, skeet shooting charges, and shopping arcade purchases are conveniently placed on the shipboard credit accounts.

Port of Embarkation This is the city or town from which the cruise ship sets sail on day one.

Port of Debarkation Now that the dream cruise vacation has ended, the ship arrives at its final destination, called the port of debarkation.

Date of Entry Into Service After a ship is built and a bottle of bubbly is broken over its bow, the ship hits the water and heads out on a shakedown cruise. Then, on its inaugural cruise when it carries its first load of passengers, the ship has entered service.

Date of Refurbishment This usually refers to newly redecorated or upgraded basic amenities such as the ship's cabins, public areas, kitchens, dining rooms, pool areas, spas, fitness centers, i.e., a general makeover. It is always best to learn the age of the ship and the year and extent of its most recent refurbishment.

Cabin Size Bargain-priced cruises include a lower-category inside cabin with two lower beds. Expect a small, intimate cabin and you will not be disappointed. Cabins in this category range in size from 115 square feet to 172 square feet. Some examples follow. The numbers in parentheses refers to square footage. Carnival (170 on all new ships), Celebrity and Grand Princess (171), Costa (160), Royal Caribbean (130), Royal Olympics's *Countess* (125), and Orient's *Marco Polo* (115).

Booking Deposit Check the small print in the back pages of cruise brochures for the deposit requirements. Sample deposit requirements per person are Princess, $250; Carnival, $350; Orient, $500; and Renaissance, $500, nonrefundable.

Cancellation Fees *Know this before you book your cruise!* Here are samples of cancellation fees if the cruise is canceled during the indicated number of days before the cruise departure date. Cancellation penalties (fees) are rated as "average" and "severe":

- Princess Cruises (average): no fee for 60 or more days; 50 percent for fifteen to thirty days
- Carnival Cruise Line (average): no fee for 61 or more days; 50 percent for fifteen to twenty-nine days
- Orient Lines (average): no fee for 120 or more days; 50 percent for fifteen to twenty-nine days
- Renaissance Cruises (severe): $500 fee for 90 or more days; 100 percent for one to eighty-nine days

Too Good to Be True—Cruise "Guarantee"

We are unabashed consumer advocates in our daily lives. We scrutinize advertisements, read travel insurance policies and the fine print on the back of cruise brochures. So, naturally, we are interested in cruise guarantees. Consider the following fruits of our investigative labors.

Carnival's Vacation Guarantee Carnival's "guarantee" applies "if you are not *completely satisfied* with your cruise vacation experience..." If a passenger is dissatisfied with the very early part of the cruise, the passenger must advise the ship's information desk, "... before arrival at the first port of call...." We do not value any guarantee that talks of complete satisfaction with the cruise vacation experience and then self-destructs upon arrival at the very first port of call. This means the guarantee does not apply after arrival at the first port of call. To its credit, Carnival makes no claim that their guarantee covers the total vacation.

Renaissance Cruises' Great Places, Great Times Guarantee This states that their guarantee program "... assures your total vacation satisfaction," and that "no other cruise line offers such a complete satisfaction guarantee." (1998 Renaissance Mediterranean and Greek Islands brochure, pages 3 and 28). Powerful protecting words if they mean what they say. Continuing, this guarantee applies only to passengers who "simply notify the ship's reception desk, before the first port of call, that you wish to disembark." Their Mediterranean and Greek Islands cruise itinerary lists *eight* ports of call. What happens if you are having a horrid time on all the remaining days of the cruise, after reaching the first port of call? What does Renaissance mean when it states that its guarantee "assures your total vacation satisfaction?"

Ask Renaissance. We found no one at Renaissance willing to discuss this with us, and they treated Steve rudely merely for asking. Read all guarantees carefully and understand your rights before leaving on vacation.

Single, Disabled, Food Restricted?

Singles Cruising

Let's face it—if singles wish to participate in and reap the benefits of America's favorite vacation pastime they are at a distinct disadvantage. The pecking order of cruise passengers is the following: seniors and retirees, baby boomers, families, couples, children, and singles. When it comes to traditional cruises, young singles all too often feel like a round peg trying to fit into a square hole. For many singles who are traveling alone, cost becomes the first major hurdle.

Choice of Ship   A general strategy is to choose a larger cruise ship that carries 1,800 to 2,400 passengers. This offers a larger pool of singles on any given cruise.

Cost   If you would like to cause a single vacationer friend instant anguish, simply utter the words *single supplement*. This is the extra or surcharge singles must pay to reserve an entire cabin for themselves. How much does it cost? There is a range of single supplement charges. On the low end, expect to pay 125 percent on Orient, Holland, Celebrity, or Royal Olympic cruise lines. On the high-end, singles must pay a full second fare.

Single Cabins   Several cruise lines offer special cabins designed for single occupancy. They include American Hawaii, Commodore, Costa, Norwegian, Orient, Premier, Princess, and Regal cruise lines. These cabins, as one may imagine, are scarce!

Special Singles Parties All of the mass-market cruise lines offer one or more singles parties during each cruise.

Singles Theme Cruises Check with any travel agent to learn which cruise lines are currently offering singles theme cruises. Commodore Cruise Line offers unique New Orleans departure Caribbean cruises. Not only does Commodore do away with "formal nights," but the cruise line also offers two yearly singles cruises, one in the spring and another in the fall.

Gentlemen Hosts Several cruise lines honor an age-old tradition of providing male hosts for women passengers. Holland America Line provides a cadre of male hosts to provide single ladies with company for dinner, dancing, excursions, or relaxed conversation. Are some male passengers awaiting the arrival of a cadre of women hosts? Better not hold their breaths!

Single-Sharing Programs This may be a make-or-break situation for many singles, men, and women. These programs seek to find a compatible roommate so that single passengers may avoid the hefty single supplement. This is a good time to grab a tape measure and work up a mock cabin, perhaps in the backyard. Then, considering the 115- to 172-square-foot rooms, one may just take a deep breath and decide just how important the savings are, versus sharing this intimate-sized living space with a stranger, compatible or not. Cruise lines that offer such singles sharing programs include Carnival, Celebrity, Holland, Norwegian, Orient, Princess, Regal, and Royal Caribbean.

A best bet may be a Caribbean cruise on the Carnival Cruise Line. This is the cruise line that extols, among its many virtues, the title Fun Ships. Rather than placing its emphasis on food, food, and more food, this cruise line offers more nonstop entertainment and activities than its competitors. It is the best bet for singles and offers more social gatherings (parties) than singles may find elsewhere.

Singles' Activities

While the cruise dining experience dazzles the culinary senses, it is not particularly "singles friendly." The first strategy is to request a singles-only table. Most cruise ships will adapt to their single passengers in this regard. Otherwise, they randomly assign singles to one table or another. In the end, the odds of meeting Mr. or Ms. "Right" at the dining table is slim to remote.

Romantic Dining Alternatives Some cruise lines, like Carnival, have taken up this gauntlet and offer an excellent, romantic alternative. On Carnival's new *Elation,* simply opt for the Tiffany Bar and Grill and enjoy private dining with full gourmet meals. Expect entrees like broiled swordfish, lamb, grilled-to-order New York strip steaks, salads, and pasta dishes. The Seaview Bistro serves steak, prime rib, specialty salads, or grilled breast of duck. And desserts galore!

Target Singles Activities Check the daily newsletter. Carnival's *Destiny* newsletter lists happy hour until 8:15 P.M. at the Onyx Bar, with jazz music.

Sun, Fun, and Water What better place to meet and mingle with fellow passengers than the equivalent of the pool area of a major resort hotel? Check out Carnival's newest luxury "party ship," the *Elation.* Its outdoor entertainment area includes three pools and six whirlpools, including a spiral water slide. Add exotic tropical drinks and live entertainment, and there is every opportunity to meet and mingle.

Cheap Dates A young single passenger at poolside chats with a new "friend." It is 1:00 P.M., time for lunch. Just think of the choices. Without spending a dime he may invite his new friend to join him for lunch at a nearby outdoor buffet lunch of burgers, salads, and snacks, or any of a myriad of choices. And never a check!

No Pain, No Gain Okay, during the day many singles are eager to pay the price for that gourmet dinner. All new megaships and many older refurbished ships offer fantastic nautical spas. There are aerobics and state-of-the-art exercise rooms where the younger crowd congregates. Many ships have outdoor jogging tracks.

Shipboard Recreational Activities Join the fun of outdoor group activities like volleyball and water games.

Dancing This is where the partying on a cruise ship vacation gets downright serious! On Carnival's *Destiny,* one choice is the Romeo and Juliet Lounge, with bar seating and cozy cafe tables.

Nearby is the Jekyll and Hyde Dance Club, with its rocking music from a state-of-the-art speaker system. From midnight till the wee hours, the rocking continues with a spectacular strobe-light system over twin dance floors. On her first day at sea, the *Destiny* had outdoor afternoon music and dancing to the calypso band Bonafide. Happy hour starts at 5:00 P.M. with live music. Try a postgame Super Bowl disco party with dancing till dawn.

So why not be optimistic when it comes to cruise vacations for singles? Singles make up the smallest percentage of passengers on cruise ships. Should singles opt for a cruise vacation? Yes, if they understand its limits. On the plus side, all the amenities of a luxury cruise ship are combined with exciting ports of call and shore excursions. At best, singles will beat the odds with a big splash of romance on the high seas. If they don't anticipate a daily MTV generation hard-rock party at sea, singles have nothing to lose!

Cruising for the Disabled

Disabled passengers come in all sizes, shapes, and ages. On the one hand, we would never catagorize seniors as a group of disabled people. Nevertheless, seniors have a larger percentage of disabled persons than any other category of passengers. At the same time, many middle-aged passengers and some in their twenties and thirties suffer debilitating illnesses. Even youngsters are not immune. My associate Patricia has a seriously disabled thirteen-year-old who suffers from a progressive neurological disease. The daughter is wheelchair bound and needs twenty-four-hour care. Nevertheless, her family recently enjoyed Carnival's fabulous, four-day cruise to the Mexican Baja peninsula, departing from Los Angeles.

The good news is that cruise vacations are more compatible with and accessible to disabled persons than virtually any other type of vacation activity. We say this because of the following:

- One-stop hotel: The cruise ship transports disabled passengers to new, exciting ports of call. No constant packing or unpacking. No arduous land travel.

Selecting Ideal Cruises

- Many cruise ships have specially designed cabins that are slightly larger with wide doors and interior safety rails. Book these special cabins in advance at no extra charge.
- The disabled cabins are generally near the elevators.
- The ships' crew will usually do all they can to help disabled passengers.
- The Carnival chef's efforts to please her disabled thirteen-year-old daughter impressed my associate Patricia. He was ready to prepare special dishes and even puree foods. The words here are *understanding* and *commitment to service* for their passengers. Many other cruise lines will help in similar ways. At least one cruise line ignores the needs of the disabled.
- Many cruises, such as the Panama Canal and Alaska cruises, offer convenient world-class sightseeing from the decks of the ships.
- Disabled passengers who can take mineral baths, Jacuzzis, and deep-body massages will enjoy the nautical spas on the new and refurbished ships.
- All major cruise ships sail with a doctor and medical office for emergencies. The *Grand Princess* has a complete operating room with satellite-TV access to medical experts back home.
- Disabled passengers will often receive special help in getting ashore at ports of call.
- Sightseeing maybe arranged by van or private taxi. A drive through a colorful rain forest is enjoyable to all.
- The disabled passengers can enjoy the luxurious amenities of the cruise ship, including poolside relaxation with cool sea breezes under a tropical sun.

When it comes to disabled persons and cruises, the big picture is both heartening and disheartening. However, things are getting better. On the plus side, the cruise industry as a whole is responding to the special needs of disabled passengers. The industry reports that there are currently 550 disabled cabins available. New and larger ships have more cabins for the disabled, ten to twenty per ship. It is estimated that about 60 percent of all cruise ships currently offer some cabins for the disabled. This percentage is much higher on the newer vessels.

Princess Cruises's newest, biggest, and most expensive ship ever, the *Grand Princess,* has the largest number of cabins for the disabled on a single cruise ship. It carries 2,600 passengers and offers twenty-eight cabins for the disabled. Carnival's new 2,642 passenger ship, the *Destiny* is second, with twenty-five cabins for the disabled. The *Sea Princess, Dawn Princess,* and *Sun Princess* have nineteen cabins each. Older ships and some newer ships have fewer cabins. Celebrity's *Horizon* has only four cabins. Other cruise lines do not try to accommodate the disabled at all.

In a recent letter by Larry Lubin to the editor of the *New York Times,* he describes his interest in a Renaissance cruise on its new ship, the *R1.* He notes his surprise when Renaissance Cruise's personnel "confirmed that there were no [disabled] accessible cabins on the ship and made it clear that I should expect no special handling or attention." He states that he wrote to the vice president of Renaissance Cruises expressing "my disbelief that they designed a 684-passenger ship to discourage disabled travelers. They have not answered my letter." (*New York Times,* March 15, 1998). Mr. Lubin might have asked Renaissance about its brochure promise that the *R1* provides "... all the onboard amenities, facilities, and services discriminating vacationers want." (1998 Mediterranean and Greek Isles brochure, page 2).

Unfortunately, the Americans With Disabilities Act (ADA) is not applicable to foreign-registered cruise ships. This may change for ships using U.S. ports. Meanwhile, Princess Cruises specifically refers to the ADA in formulating the guidelines for its Love Boat Access Program.

Princess's Love Boat Access Program

First launched in 1992, this welcome program is opening the cruise market to the disabled. Their five-page brochure, "Love Boat Access—Making Your Vacation Accessible" is a must for the physically challenged who want to cruise. Here are some highlights of the Princess program that show how fast the industry has changed:

- Princess boasts the highest number of wheelchair accessible staterooms in the industry.
- Special wheelchair gangway mechanisms
- Braille buttons and audible announcements on elevators
- ADA kits that include telephone amplifiers, smoke detectors, door knock sensors, text telephones, etc.
- Princess's ADA staterooms feature wide stateroom and bathroom doors, handrails, steward help packing and unpacking, in-room refrigerators, distress alarms, lower closet bars, and more.
- Wheelchair access to common areas of Princess's ships and to shipboard amenities include the bridge tour, the casino, outside decks, the show theater and cinema, public rest rooms, dining rooms, boutiques, the showroom and the health spa and fitness center.

➥ **Steve and Pat's Tip:** *Carnival is another user-friendly cruise line that not only caters to singles but also to disabled passengers. Carnival has a special desk for disabled bookings. Call Carnival at (800) 327-9501 and request extension 70025. Also, when asking about specific ships, check for elevator wheelchair compatibility, special services, and additional help with shore excursions.*

Food Restrictions and Special Diets

Like chameleons, cruise ships are adapting to modern times. Younger passengers, families, and more singles means change! This translates into more and better options for passengers. Sure, all cruise lines extol the virtues of their gourmet meals and the quantity of food. Today, with advance notice, most cruise ships will prepare special meals, including diabetic, low-salt, and low-fat varieties. Some ships, like Celebrity's, offer kosher meals as well.

More passengers are "body conscious" today and want healthier meal options. On the serious side, "spa cuisine" has become part of cruise nomenclature. Other similar names for healthy meal programs abound. Contact the cruise lines for more detailed information and sample menus. Here is our glimpse of current healthier food at sea programs:

Celebrity Cruises' Lean and Light Menus

Look for the asterisks on the menu. They refer to special items that contain less than 30 percent of total calories from fat. Four-course meals are about eight hundred calories, eight to twelve grams of fat and 1,000 to 1,500 grams of sodium. There is another nutritional breakdown of their healthy meals on the reverse side of the menus.

Sample Celebrity entrees: a four-course meal includes Supreme Chicken Albert (roast chicken) for a total of 807 calories, twelve grams of fat, and about 1,000 to 1,500 grams of sodium. How much does one suffer with "healthy" cruise entrees? Some of Celebrity's other offerings include brochette King Neptune (grilled sea scallops, shrimp, and assorted fish on a skewer), roasted pork loin (stuffed with a mixture of sun-dried tomatoes), rack of veal (oven-roasted with natural juices), and darné of salmon (pan-seared and cooked, placed on a bed of crunchy fennel).

Royal Caribbean International's Ship Shape Menus

RCI carries complete five-course meals on their regular menus. Similar to Celebrity's approach, RCI also puts asterisks next to those regular menu items that they include on their special Ship-Shape Menu.

Samples of Royal's dinner entrees include Caribbean Lobster Tail (broiled with citrus sauce), Entrecote Pizzaiola (sirloin steak cooked in tomato concasse sauce), broiled sea bass fillet, and coq au vin (marinated skinless chicken breast flamed in cognac). They also provide nutritional breakdowns.

Costa Cruises' Health Spa Suggestions

Costa includes a separate Health Spa Menu insert along with its regular dinner menu. One sample of Costa's dinner entrees is grilled swordfish steak Castelana (served with diced tomatoes, garlic, olive oil, and parsley). No nutrition information is provided.

Carnival Cruise Line's Nautical Spa Fare

As part of its regular menu, Carnival includes healthy choice Nautical Spa options. These tagged items are generally lower in fat, calories, sodium, fat, and cholesterol.

Norwegian Cruise Line's Spa Cuisine

Norwegian's healthier fare consists of three-course meals with less than 1,000 calories. Nutritional information is available upon request.

Princess Cruises' Light and Healthy Menus

Princess offers healthier entrees that include broiled fish, chicken, and steak dishes. Most are prepared in lower-fat fashion. Nutritional data is not available.

Kosher Meals

We happily report that most major cruise lines now offer kosher meals and ask that meal requests be made when the cruise is booked. Other cruise lines require requests be submitted up to sixty days prior to the cruise ship's departure date. Always contact your travel agent or the cruise line to confirm kosher meal availability and to determine deadlines for ordering kosher meals.

We must emphasize that not a single major cruise ship offers a kosher dining room and kitchen. This directly affects the options available to orthodox passengers who eat kosher. Those who limit their outside dining to certified kosher restaurants and kitchens must pre-order kosher meals. A specialty kosher catering firm provides ships with oven- or microwave-ready frozen dishes for all daily meals. These items are prepared and served on their own plates and are accompanied by one-time use disposable utensils. Kosher entrees include roast chicken, pot roast, braised veal and Salisbury steak. Other entrees including vegetable dishes are available. Passengers who require further information regarding kosher certification or the specific meal choices should contact the cruise line's customer service department.

Other passengers who eat kosher but do not limit their dining to certified kosher restaurants may enjoy the best of shipboard dining by choosing from the extensive array of regular fresh cooked or prepared gourmet menu items that meet their kosher dietary requirements. Such items most often include dairy, vegetarian, and other delectable meatless dishes.

Just how much of a menu selection is there? Consider the following sample selections from Holland America and Commodore's typical daily menus:

Breakfast: Kippered herring; assorted yogurt desserts; fresh juices; hot and cold cereals; custom omelettes made to order; regular or fruit pancakes; French toast; and an assortment of fresh-baked croissants, muffins, and pastries.

Lunch: Seasonal fruit; mixed green salad; panini Carbonara (pasta with flavored cream sauce and Parmesan cheese); and Salta Di Frutta (fresh pineapple boat filled with tropical fruit chunks served with frozen blueberry yogurt).

➥ **Steve and Pat's Tip:** *Most cruise lines provide paper or plastic plates and utensils upon request. Strictly observant passengers may wish to bring their own supply of such plates and utensils. These may come in handy when ordering items such as whole fresh fruit or boxed cereals and sealed milk containers either in the dining room or via room service.*

Dinner: Smoked salmon with onions, capers and horseradish; heart of lettuce salad with tomatoes and long beans; and sweet-potato soup. Main entrées include choices such as medallions of Alaskan salmon in an egg and Parmesan batter served on Chardonnay tomato sauce; broiled grouper filet with pecan flour; vegetable strudel served with sauteed spinach and shiitake mushrooms; and manicotti alla sorrentina (stuffed with spinach and ricotta cheese topped with light tomato sauce and Parmesan cheese).

Cruise lines that presently offer kosher meals include:

- Celebrity Cruises
- Commodore Cruise Line
- Costa Cruise Lines
- Disney Cruise Line
- Holland America Line
- Norwegian Cruise Line
- Orient Cruises
- Premiere Cruises
- Princess Cruises
- Royal Caribbean International
- Royal Olympic Cruises

Note: Currently, Carnival Cruise Lines does not provide kosher meals.

Vegetarian Meals

Many cruise lines offer vegetarian meals or they will prepare them with prior notice.

In summary, when it comes to special culinary needs, most cruise lines stand ready to help any way they can. Compare this service with the typical land-based vacation, where one may be dining at fifteen to twenty different restaurants during the vacation week! Good luck!

Selecting the Right Cruise Ship

Do we know what cruise ship is best for you? Of course not. Each vacationer must decide what cruise ship suits their needs, desires, and budget.

In this section we do point readers in the direction of the "right" cruise ship. This ambitious task is not an easy one. Consider that there are newer and older cruise ships, ships with narrow decks, and newer vessels that claim their decks are as wide as the Champs-Elysées. There are ships with six decks and newer vessels with fourteen or more decks. There are older refurbished ships. The newest and largest cruise ships offer scores of amenities that may not meet your particular needs. One passenger may want the largest gambling casino on the *Grand Princess*, while others may see an advantage in multiple main dining rooms found on a cruise ship that houses 2,600 passengers.

New vessels preach the virtues of size, grandeur, and sky-high atriums. How, then, do the older and smaller ships compete? They use a strategy that is clear and well reasoned. Whenever cruise lines advertise the smaller and mid-sized vessels, talk turns to old-world charm, expansive use of exotic wood, intimate surroundings, and getting away from the hordes of 2,000 or more passengers. Smaller ships boast that better service and more personal attention is available on a slower-paced cruise vacation. And some of us thought the term *spin* was reserved for Washington types!

Having experienced cruises on smaller and larger ships, we are convinced there is no single, easy answer to the question Which is best? Rather, there are major considerations, and that is what this section is about!

Who Wants a "Previously Owned" Cruise Ship?

Our answer, most of us at one time or another. Select any cruise ship, even today's newest and grandest monarchs of the sea and down the road they will be sold. Over time, cruise ships move from cruise line to cruise line like pawns on a chessboard. Example: In the 1990s, Princess Cruises constructed two super cruise ships, the *Dawn Princess* and the *Sun Princess*. Then, in 1998, it boasted that its newest ship, the *Grand Princess* was the largest, most expensive cruise ship ever built. To accomplish this, in part, Princess sold its older *Fair Princess* and then one of its earlier luxury ships, the *Star Princess*. P and O Cruises, the parent company of Princess Cruise, purchased the *Star Princess* and renamed it the *Arcadia*.

Each ship, old or new, large or small, offers something unique. Always be a good travel consumer and check out the preferred cruise ship, i.e., current amenities besides date and nature of refurbishment before booking the cruise.

Carnival Cruise Line

The emphasis here is on sun, fun, and frolic on the high seas. Expect excellent service from Carnival's Italian officers and international crew. Its goal is to deliver an affordable luxury cruise vacation to the masses at prices they can easily afford. Today, Carnival is the world's most successful and largest cruise line. No doubt Carnival strives to create a resort atmosphere at sea. Or, as Carnival likes to say, "Cruising has evolved into the seagoing resort experience of today." Carnival caters to families, singles, honeymooners, the young, old, and disabled. Did they miss anyone? Add neon and glitz similar to the Las Vegas look and feel, and we are halfway there. Yes, there is plenty of food, though on Carnival the emphasis is on entertainment and good times. Carnival offers one of the best children's programs, known as Club Carnival (for ages two to seventeen). This cruise line is perfect for singles, honeymooners, and the young at heart. Some special Carnival features are:

- Carnival sets itself apart from most by offering a daily second live midnight cabaret show each evening, on all its ships.
- Most twin beds convert to king size.
- A modern nautical spa and exercise room on all ships.
- Excellent quality "alternative" dining.
- Excellent Camp Carnival for kids
- Largest basic cabins, at 170 square feet on all newer ships. The new *Elation* is 50 percent larger in size (77 tons *v.* 50 tons) than most other ships, with three pools and six Jaccuzzis.
- The *Fascination* and *Imagination* have seven-story atriums, three pools, and the largest floating casino.

Celebrity Cruises

Celebrity delivers more luxury cruises at bargain prices than any other cruise line. Its first megaship was the *Century* (1995). Their newest ships, the *Mercury* and *Galaxy* (1997 and 1996) carry 1,870 passengers and offer the finest amenities afloat. With Celebrity, quality, not quantity, reigns supreme. This is one cruise line that has received rave reviews from every quarter of the cruise industry. On average, cabins on its three newest ships are larger and include state-of-the-art amenities. The ships have interactive Sony communications systems that permit passengers to order room service. Passengers may purchase shore excursions and select dinner wine from the comfort of their cabins. Unlike many other ships, all cabins include mini-bar refrigerators, electronic safes, and hair dryers. Then there is Celebrity's excellent cuisine, prepared by Michelin three-star chef Michael Roux. Also, let us not forget the wine, espresso, champagne, and caviar bars. When it comes to a true luxury cruise at a bargain price, we agree that Celebrity is number one!

Commodore Cruise Line

This cruise line succeeds with a single medium-sized, 730-passenger ship, the *Enchanted Isle*, that sails on one-week Caribbean cruises. The ship was built in 1958, refurbished in 1994, and again in late 1997. Commodore offers what *Travel Holiday* magazine called "the best cruise for the money." Passenger testimonials talk in terms of "intimacy," "best of our thirteen cruises," "fun-filled with great food, entertainment, and service," "friendly staff and wonderful ports," "family-type atmosphere," and "charm without neon and glitz."

Commodore leaves from an exciting and unique embarkation port, the city of New Orleans! This gives passengers the opportunity for a second mini-vacation before or after their cruise. The cruise line specializes in bargain-priced, seven-night, round-trip cruises to Mexico and the Caribbean islands. Expect all the usual comforts and amenities without multiple swimming pools. While the ship is low on the glitz scale, it offers a special blend of teak decks, rich wood veneers, and polished brass. Commodore offers excellent cuisine, never in a formal atmosphere, that reflects "Commodore's epicurean New Orleans heritage." Overall, consider a Commodore cruise for an original bargain experience. The cruise line claims a 95 percent "excellent" rating by its passengers, and reports that it was 100 percent sold out last year.

Costa Cruises

Here is an upscale cruise line that offers Italian-style cruising. Costa's fleet consists of mid-sized ships and includes four vessels built in the 1990s. Its newest megaship is the Costa *Victoria* (1996) which holds 1,950 passengers. A Costa cruise means Italian ambience and cuisine. While senior offices are Italian, other crew members are international. The difference with Costa's Mediterranean cruises is the very soul of Costa—its Italian-European essence that draws many European vacationers, including families and a younger crowd of singles, kids, and teens. It offers an extensive array of Italian wines and pleasing meals that are never lacking in quantity. While meals are good to excellent, they are not ultimate gourmet quality. As expected, the newer and larger ships provide the most extensive amenities, like Roman-type nautical spas and multipools. Costa offers solid cruise vacation value with excellent, friendly service.

Holland America Line (HAL)

Holland's is "a tradition of excellence." This cruise line gets consistent high ratings by passengers for its service, food, and cabins. HAL is considered one of the premium cruise lines and offers a relaxed, comfortable, and memorable cruise experience. In 1996, *Ocean and Cruise News* designated HAL as providing the "best cruise value." The cruise line is noted for an older and more mature clientele, though its Caribbean cruises, like those of many other cruise lines, draws a younger crowd.

Expect nothing less than excellent service and constant pampering from HAL's devoted Indonesian and Filipino crew. The cruise line proudly presents a special late-night chocolate buffet and memorable cocktail hours where elegant silver carts serve delectable hôrs d'oeuvres. Its sister ships the *Nieuw Amsterdam* and *Noordam* sport $2 million art collections.

Beginning in 1998, HAL's newest ship, *Statendam*, provides the ultimate in seagoing luxury, with sterling silver and Rosenthal china as part of its dining experience. All decks and the bow are constructed of teak. Its two pools and Jacuzzis are open twenty-four hours. Holland is absolutely tops when it comes to cruise value for cruise dollars. No, HAL is not perfect. It advertises a so-called no-tipping-required policy. We grouse about this, since HAL then goes on to concede that tipping for excellent service is appreciated and accepted by its crew members. What else is new?

Norwegian Cruise Line (NCL)

This is the cruise line that started the cruise revolution in 1980 when it took the big gamble and purchased, for $16 million scrap value, the SS *France*, which was four times larger than the average cruise ships of that day. After spending three years and $60 million to create the first mega-sized cruise ship, renamed the *Norway*, NCL came out the big winner. The rest, as they say, is history, with all major cruise lines following suit, with new ships breaking records for size and passenger capacity. NCL remains one of the industry's most innovative cruise lines, hence NCL's slogan It's Different Out Here. Currently, NCL's fleet consists of six modern ships and the legendary *Norway*, formerly the SS *France*.

NCL has paved the way for true alternative dining (see our section on dining). They provide sports bars with a dozen TVs, another innovation. Unique in the industry, NCL offers full-scale (but not full-length) productions of Broadway shows. It also offers theme cruises, such as "Big Band" and "Comedy." Also, NCL is one of the few cruise lines that permits regular dining room menu items to be ordered from via room service from your cabin. Anyone for a really intimate dinner? Service on NCL is exceptional, and this is the hallmark of a great cruise experience. Believe it or not, their uniformed crew members actually spray passengers with Evian water as they lie overheated on their poolside lounge chairs. Note: Not all their ships have late-night

Selecting Ideal Cruises 119

(after 11:30 P.M.) discos. If this is important to you, be certain to check with your travel agent or NCL directly.

NCL is another major cruise line that delivers memorable luxury cruises at bargain prices.

Premier Cruises

Premicr offers intimate cruising at dirt-cheap prices. Its six ships average only 970 passengers, with its largest ship, the *Star/Ship Oceanic* (Big Red Boat) holding 1,180 passengers. Very good food, service, unique itineraries, and price are hallmarks of Premier. For example, the *Island Breeze* embarks for the southern Caribbean from its home port of Santo Domingo in the Dominican Republic. The *Ocean Breeze* cruises to the Panama Canal, embarking from its home port of Montego Bay in Jamaica. The *Sea Breeze* sails the deep southern Caribbean, embarking from Curaçao. While Premier's ships were refurbished in the early 1990s, its "youngest" ship is thirty-three years old, and the average age of its ships is thirty-eight years. This explains why Premier has only two cabins for the disabled, on the *Seawind Crown*, of the 2,933 cabins in its fleet! This is a sad but historic fact of early cruise construction life.

In 1998, Premier advertised fabulous air-inclusive deals from both the East and West coasts with prices between $900 and $1,100. These air-and-cruise packages are more worthwhile considering the very high cost of airfare to remote embarkation cities in foreign country islands. It is one thing to catch a connecting flight to Miami, Los Angeles, or New Orleans, and quite another to buy a round-trip ticket to Santo Domingo or Curacao. Yet the advantage of embarking from a port in the heart of the Caribbean cannot be overstated—less time wasted on days at sea from the U.S. mainland and more time to visit exotic ports of call like Caracas and Margarita Island. For those who do not mind older ships and enjoy bargain cruising, Premier delivers.

Princess Cruises

We are talking about the "love boats" that sparkle with modern glitz, such as sky-high atriums, multiple pools, expansive decks, less wood, and more brass and glass! Once again, service, from stewards to bartenders, is tops. Food, entertainment, and amenities also get top marks. Princess remains one of the best of the cutting-edge mass-market cruise lines. Their newest ship, the *Grand Princess,* was the largest and most expensive cruise ship ever built at the time this guide went to press. Consequently, it offers more ways to relax, dine, shop, play, swim, sun, and generally indulge oneself. Their "Grand Cruising" experience provides amenities such as true optional dining. Princess extols the virtues of its extensive Alaska experience. It offers many cruise-and-land options and has built interior lodges to be used by its passengers. Its private Midnight Sun Express rail cars offer 360-degree views and large open-air viewing platforms. Princess also excels in the European market, with more ships, destinations, and itineraries than any other major cruise line. Consider the *Grand Princess's* twelve-day Mediterranean cruise. Some special features of the *Grand Princess* follow:

- Nine-hole putting green
- All cabin beds convert to queen size.
- All cabins include refrigerators and hair dryers.
- Eighteen decks
- Jogging track
- Four pools and nine Jacuzzis
- Reef pool with retractable glass dome
- True alternative dining
- Snookers Sports Bar
- Virtual Reality Center with motion simulator
- Three different live shows nightly
- On the *Royal Princess, all* cabins are outside with a window, convertible queen-sized beds, refrigerators, and a bathtub with shower.
- Princess shore excursions are legendary. Princess offers more than 1,000 shore excursions worldwide.

Renaissance Cruises

We consider Renaissance Cruises to be user-unfriendly. We know of no other cruise line that charges a mandatory $500 per person cancellation fee even if the cancellation is made six months or more prior to departure. Or, a fee of 100 percent of all cruise charges for cancellations made less than ninety days prior to departure. To enjoy their bargain early-bird fare, 100 percent payment must be made within *five* days of booking. Their so-called cruise vacation guarantee is discussed earlier in this chapter, as are their handicapped passenger facilities (none on their new *R1* or *R2*). The failure of their executive office to reply to prospective customer inquiries has also been discussed. We have found that other cruise lines treat prospective customers the way they treat their passengers, with courtesy, respect, and customer-friendly policies.

Despite the quality of its final cruise product, Renaissance receives neither our business nor our recommendation. See our section on cruising the Greek islands and Turkey to learn about the money-saving alternative we booked for our land-and-cruise vacation.

Royal Caribbean International (RCI)

Royal Caribbean offers less emphasis on glitz and the Las Vegas look than found on other cruise lines. Its fleet of nine ships and 14,500 berths is impressive, and Royal delivers flawless service from its international crew. It offers a new casual dinner service. Its alternative dining option, the Windjammer Cafe, is open for intimate private dining from 6:30 P.M. to 9:30 P.M. The cruise line is known for constantly high-quality food and service.

RCI provides a more relaxed atmosphere than many other cruise lines. RCI also offers a fine year-round children's program. Consider Royal's twice per year Mexican Riviera cruise, which embarks from San Diego and visits an impressive array of ports of call that include Cabo San Lucas, Mazatlan, Puerto Vallarta, Acapulco, Zihutanejo, and Manzanilla. Its passengers are more mature, cultured, and sophisticated. Hence, its multi-million-dollar art collection, pit orchestra, and champagne bar. Special features on RCI's ships include the following:

- Eighteen-hole miniature golf course on the *Splendor of the Seas* and *Legend of the Seas*
- Full-size movie theater plus pay-per-view TV
- Extensive Ship-Shape programs

- Glass-covered pools and solarium spas on the *Vision of the Seas* and *Rhapsody of the Seas*
- Best room service menu, including regular lunch and dinner items if ordered when the dining room is serving

When it comes to quality, value, and a memorable luxury cruise, RCI delivers in most categories. We are enamored of the eighteen-hole miniature golf course. Now that *is* one up on shuffleboard!

Miscellaneous Considerations

Menus, theme dinners, numbers and sizes of swimming pools, spas, exercise rooms, whirlpools and jacuzzis, or lack thereof, putting greens—the list goes on. When it comes to cruise ships and their amenities, the plain truth is that no two are alike. Take the *Grand Princess,* touted as the "most expensive and largest cruise ship ever built." Clearly, this ship offers much more than the usual array of amenities.

Consider the smorgasbord of today's ship's amenities. Mull them over and check off or circle those that are preferred or considered essential, in order of priority. It may be the option of private alternative dining, twenty-four-hour room service that includes hot dishes off the ship's dining room menus rather than snacks and club sandwiches, a promenade deck under the stars, or Jacuzzis. Without further adieu, dream about the following:

- All inside cabins with two lower beds convert into a queen or double bed and include a refrigerator or mini-bar
- Twenty-four-hour room service that offers the usual snacks, fruit, and sandwiches
- Twenty-four-hour room service that additionally offers hot items off the ship's lunch and dinner menus
- Multiple live evening shows, cabaret acts, and nightclub acts
- Full-scale Broadway productions
- Alternative dining: intimate "private" dining outside the main dining room with a full dinner-type menu
- Under-the-stars outdoor Jacuzzis and all-weather indoor and outdoor pools
- Nine-hole putting greens with professional coaching

Selecting Ideal Cruises 123

- Modern fitness center with the finest electronic equipment
- Full-sized movie theater plus movies on the cabin's TV
- Eighteen-hole miniature golf course
- Daily deck-side lunch and breakfast buffets with hot grill items
- Children's play and day care center with full facilities and amenities
- Tennis, basketball, or handball
- Extensive shopping arcade for duty-free shopping
- Professional aerobic and fitness classes
- Full daily midnight buffets
- Real Kansas City beef and Maine lobster served
- Multiple disco lounges with choice of rock or laid-back tunes
- Daily guest lecturers and/or special events and demonstrations
- Free dance instruction
- Itinerary with sufficient visiting time in the most important ports of call
- Least number of full days at sea and most visits to ports of call
- Cruise ship that caters to special dietary needs
- Cruise ship that offers disabled cabins and facilities
- Wine, caviar, or champagne bars
- Largest casino afloat
- Ship that does away with formal dining nights

➥ **Steve and Pat's Tip:** *Let's assume our advice was followed. Based on vacation objectives, a destination and itinerary were selected. The preferred cruise line was picked and a list of essential amenities was made. Despite this, it is difficult to find the "right" cruise ship. Do not despair. A full-service discount travel agency is ready to help. In the preceding chapter we introduced Pearson Travel. Use this valuable resource to find just the "right" ship. Of course, Pearson wants your booking. Pearson also sells free American Express travelers checks. See chapter 5 and call Pearson at (800) 336-1066.*

7

Be Savvy: Predeparture Essentials

Travel Documents: Don't Leave Home Without Them!

Want to leave your kids, dog, and your stress-filled job behind? In fact, we know husbands and wives who go on vacation without their mates. Regardless, in this chapter we list what must *never* be left behind!

Some years ago we were about to embark on a group scuba-diving vacation with a dozen friends and family members. Our destination was Cozumel, Mexico's largest island and a world-class dive site. At San Francisco International Airport, three of our group were barred from the departing flight to Mexico.

Without notice, the Mexican government changed its policy. The government unexpectedly demanded new forms of identification, such as a current passport or raised-seal birth certificate. Three members of our group had neither one. After some heated discussion, the authorities agreed to accept notarized affidavits. Luckily, with the help of the airport's public address system a notary public was found.

Last spring, an Australian citizen living in California with his American wife was barred from leaving on a flight to Tahiti because he had no Tahitian visa. The husband thought that since his wife did not need a visa, neither did he. Unfortunately for this man, Tahiti requires Australians but not Americans to have an entry visa.

Yes, there is a moral to these stories. Being a savvy traveler is far better than being a travel casualty because of a missing travel document. A list of essential travel documents follows.

Passports Plus Backup Most foreign nations require a valid passport for entry. Exceptions include our closest neighbors, Mexico and Canada, who require that U.S. citizens present only their drivers licenses. Always check with your travel agent and cruise line to learn whether any of the ports of call require a U.S. Passport. Even when not required, it is wise to bring a current passport and a backup I.D. The second piece of I.D. can be an expired passport or a copy of a current passport. Never carry or pack both I.D.s together in one wallet or one carry-on. At the very least, carry a photocopy of a passport when in a foreign port of call.

Entry Visa Many nations require an entry visa in addition to a current passport. Passengers are responsible for bringing the correct travel documents. Check with your travel agent, tour operator, and cruise company to find out what travel documents are required on each cruise. On a Greek island cruise-tour, for instance, Greece requires only a passport, whereas Turkey requires both a passport and an entry visa. Cruise lines often prepare a group visa for its passengers when the itinerary includes ports of call in Turkey.

Obtaining a visa is a hassle, since passports must be sent to the country's embassy, usually in Washington, D.C., and they stamp the visa on a page in the passports. Visa fees range from $25 to $75! Years ago, we sent our passports to the Tanzanian Embassy in Washington, D.C., where they were, horrors upon horrors, lost! It cost us a pretty penny to rectify that sad situation.

Raised-Seal Birth Certificate It is always a good idea to bring such a certificate as an extra piece of acceptable I.D.

Vacation Travel Documents The tour operator or travel agent sends these directly to clients in a tidy packet. The packet may include airline tickets, cruise itinerary, meal seating confirmation, and miscellaneous transfers and car rental vouchers. Keep all documents in your possession and on your person or in a carry-on while in transit to the ship.

AAA Card and Current Drivers License   If rental car plans are part of your itinerary, bring an American Automobile Association (AAA) card. A drivers license is always required to drive in a foreign country.

Travelers Checks   This is the safest form of "cash." Purchase smaller $20 checks that are handy for purchases from street vendors. In California, our AAA Club provides checks without commission, as do many banks. Always leave a copy of the check numbers at home and with a travel companion for safekeeping.

Citibank AAdvantage Card and other Credit Cards   Remember, charge all vacation expenses, including shopping at ports of call, shipboard expenses, and tips. This is a great strategy for banking more miles in your American Airlines free travel accounts. Always take at least one extra credit card. In our case, we each take our own Citibank AAdvantage Visa cards.

Cash   Yes, there comes a time during most vacations when cash works best and other times when only cash will do. Most foreign taxi drivers require cash payment. Then you need cash for that must-have item sold by a small vendor who is ill equipped or unwilling to take credit cards or travelers checks. Often shopkeepers offer super discounts when we pay in U.S. dollars, so then cash is best.

Telephone Calling Card   Carry one with all necessary satellite access numbers for various ports of call.

Health Plan I.D. Card   Even foreign hospitals may ask that infamous question, "Do you have medical coverage?" Most medical cards include necessary phone numbers and other information required by medical providers.

Local Travel Guide and Maps   We include these items because most often we cannot easily replace them if left behind.

Travel Insurance Policy   Should the worst happen, a copy of the policy is a handy reference for determining exact coverage and reporting requirements such as "immediately report loss to a hotel or police."

Be Savvy

Strategy for Cash, Credit Cards, and Travelers Checks

Credit cards   Credit card use is usually safe and convenient. In today's shrinking world, merchants large and small often accept major credit cards. This is true even in most larger stores in China.

Citibank AAdvantage Visa or MasterCard   We are referring to our number-one strategy for future free global travel via the American Airlines AAdvantage program. Charge everything! Today, many merchants in foreign ports take credit cards since cruise passengers often lack local currency.

Travelers checks   Keep a record of the check numbers. These checks are 100 percent secure. Report all loses immediately. If there is a loss, replacement checks may be picked up at the next port of call.

Cash   Cash is the most vulnerable type of fund a vacationer can carry, and is always subject to loss or theft. However, we always take a limited amount, perhaps $300 each, on every vacation for quick purchases and cash-only purchases. Remember. Taxi drivers usually take only cash!

Steve's Beguiling Gypsy Encounter

It was broad daylight in Florence, Italy, when a trusty Coconuts security purse saved my passport, cash, and travelers checks. Patty and I were happily shopping on a busy side street when a young gypsy woman with long black hair and a beguiling smile approached me. With an infant in her arms and a friend waiting nearby, she shoved the baby into my face while begging for money. Imagine my surprise when I next felt her hand in my front trouser pocket! My Coconuts security purse contained cash, travelers checks, and my passport. Being a savvy traveler, it took me only seconds to realize this was no friendly gesture! A brief, canonlike verbal fray followed between the woman, her accomplice, passers-by, an outraged local shopkeeper, and me. She quickly disappeared down the street with her baby and accomplice. I took three deep breaths, calmed down, and all was well in our travel world.

> **Steve and Pat's Tip:** *We highly recommend Coconuts-brand nylon security purses. The manufacturer correctly describes their product as the "world's most versatile, secure, and best-made passport carrier." The purse literally saved our vacation!*

The Coconuts passport carrier is made in California and has two zippered compartments, a belt, and a belt loop. The belt and belt loop contain a steel cable to prevent "cut-and-run" theft. The purse lies flat in a man's front trouser pocket. It may be worn different ways by women. We will not leave home without them. At $15, the Coconut security purse is a bargain. All Coconuts products carry a lifetime warranty. Most travel accessory shops carry Coconuts products, or contact them directly at (510) 532-7449.

The super-security conscious should read Magellan's catalogue. It offers several models of a high-security, leather waist (bunny) pack with a steel-cable-lined belt strap and leather flap covering the front quick-release mechanism. Peace of mind for this one runs high, with $59 (regular) and $69 (large) price tags (items LB431 or LB431L). For an excellent, free travel-accessory catalogue, call Magellan's at (800) 962-4943.

> **Steve and Pat's Tip:** *Do not put all your money in one "basket." Keep cash, credit cards, and travelers checks in separate places. We usually keep some of each in the cabin's safe or in our locked luggage. Do not carry all your money on your person at any one time.*

Who Says You Can't Take It All With You!

Cruise Packing Tips

What a joy it is to be living in a floating luxury hotel that transports us from one exhilarating port of call to the next. On the other hand, when a camera's exotic 6-volt lithium battery runs down you cannot simply leave the ship, jump in the car, and drive to the nearest photo shop. Or that absolutely essential Bullfrog no. 30 may be missing. Where to buy the exact replacement before frying under the tropical sun?

Yes, there are always shopping arcades on cruise ships, including at least one shop that will undoubtedly sell a fair variety of sundry items. However, such shops do not rise to the level of a local K Mart, camera shop, or mega–drug store. Neither are exotic ports of call a guaranteed source for the replacement of personal and electronic items. The next port of call may be a remote, deserted, private island. Therefore, a brief discussion regarding packing is essential.

It is OK to Pack Heavy—If You Must!

There, we have said it! We have put forth the unthinkable, an alternative plan for packing for a cruise. If the vacation package includes transfers between the airport and the cruise ship, why not pack everything that you need for your comfort and convenience? A one-week vacation includes at least four evenings when formal or semiformal dress is required. Dress wardrobes require additional clothes. On Alaska cruises, you need to bring warmer, bulkier sweaters and jackets. On tropical cruises, many bring their own snorkels, masks, and fins.

Most cruise lines suggest one suitcase per passenger. Some admit that there is no actual limit. On U.S. domestic flights, passengers are permitted three checked-in bags per person weighing up to 70 pounds per bag, but do check with the airline for luggage-size and quantity requirements. One large and one medium-sized bag per person are usually sufficient for most packing needs.

The justifying factor for heavier luggage is that air-and-land cruise vacations reduce luggage handling to a minimum. Airline porters and the ship's crew will handle all luggage, crew members deliver the luggage to the cabins. On the final night of the cruise, passengers pack the luggage and place it in the corridor by their cabin's door, where it is magically collected and reclaimed on the dock when passengers depart the ship. It will then be placed on a vehicle for transport to the airport.

Steve and Pat's Tip: With the above in mind, packing light is always the best way to travel. There will always be times when handling luggage is unavoidable and no porter is available. Be savvy and pack all that you need and no more!

Medicines: Absolutely Essential

Despite the hundreds of millions of dollars spent on building today's giant cruise liners, none of them come equipped with a pharmacy. Then, consider that many seasoned vacationers are not savvy travelers. During our second photo safari to Tanzania, we met an older couple from Houston who we will call Joan and David. Joan was a vivacious woman in her early sixties and looked ten years younger. Her husband David was a charming gentleman in his early seventies. The couple had just completed a ten-day tour of Kenya's parks and were joining our one-week Tanzanian safari.

At lunch in Nairobi we were astounded to hear Joan announce that David had run out of his heart medication; he had not brought enough for the entire trip. In a flash, our tour guide whisked the couple from the restaurant to a Nairobi pharmacy, where they purchased the needed medication.

➡ **Steve and Pat's Tip:** Another less-than-savvy couple traveling on our first safari packed their quinine tablets, camera, and film in their luggage. Unfortunately, the airline sent the luggage to the Middle East and it never arrived in Kenya. Again, a local pharmacy came to the rescue. Always keep special medication on your person or in your carry-on luggage; never pack it away in luggage. Better yet, take an extra supply that may be packed in luggage.

However, two days later David developed chest pains. Within hours a Flying Doctors Society plane landed at a military airstrip near our lodge in Serengetti National Park and flew him to a Nairobi hospital, where they stabilized him and sent him home.

While a cruise ship may not be the exact equivalent of a safari van, there are significant parallels. The most popular cruise itinerary, the Caribbean, stops at three to five foreign ports of call, so obtaining prescription drugs is not as easy as it is back home. Passengers may be out at sea for a day or two without their medication. Then, the next full-day stop might just be one of the touted "private" tropical islands with no commercial facilities. Scratch another two or three days without access to a pharmacy.

Packing—Snorkel, Mask, Fins, and Much More!

When it comes to major cruise lines, only one amenity is common to every ship. Each ship has at least one swimming pool, and many new ships have two to five pools in every size and shape. Some ships offer indoor and outdoor pools with retractable glass domes for water fun no matter the weather. Most warm-water cruises offer the following:

- Introduction to snorkeling lectures: Carnival's Caribbean cruises offer a snorkel presentation after their ship embarks.
- Snorkel demonstration in the main pool
- Some ships offer beginner scuba lectures and pool demonstrations, followed by an open-sea, beginner dive.
- Most ships offer certified one-tank dive excursions at many ports of call through local dive shops.
- Major ships rent snorkel gear to passengers. Sometimes underwater cameras are available.
- Organized snorkel excursions and do-it-yourself snorkeling at ports of call

➥ **Steve and Pat's Tip:** *Those who enjoy "power" snorkeling and scuba diving understand why we take our own snorkel gear on a tropical cruise vacation. Doing so avoids potential problems with rental gear. Our "better" fins require rubber booties that protect the feet from nasty coral cuts.*

➥ **Steve and Pat's Packing Tip:** *We hope our eclectic, mini–packing list adds to the pleasure and success of cruise vacations. Gleaned from our years of travel experience, the list covers many basic and not-so-basic items that run the gamut from essential to helpful:*

Travelers checks, cash, credit cards	Large water bottles
Travel and identification documents	All medications, personal items
	Dramamine
Walkman, headset, tapes	Camera and/or camcorder, batteries
Small flashlight, binoculars	
Extra batteries, books on tape	Accessories, charger
	Scissors, Velcro
Lip ice, Noxema, sun screen	All-purpose tool–pocket knife
In-depth travel and itinerary guides	Transformer, adaptor
	Dual-voltage hair dryer
Low-cost telephone calling card	Two large mugs for the room
Extra reading glasses and sunglasses	Mindfold, Noise Busters
Water safe and beach towel	Pocket Pillows, smoke hood
Sturdy walking shoes	Crystal Light–type drink mix powders
Rucksack or picnic bag	
ZipLoc bags, plastic ties	

Cruise Memories: Steve on Cameras and Film

As I write this section, I wish to emphasize that both of us share in our vacation photography efforts, although I am more involved in purchasing and maintaining our equipment. On our African photo safaris to Kenya and Tanzania, I shot the video while Patty shot more than five hundred stills. While shark diving in Moorea, I shot the underwater video and Patty shot stills three to ten feet from forty to sixty *sharks* that encircled us.

Cruises offer some of the best photo opportunities. Because of my many years experience with still, video, and underwater video photography, this is a good time to offer savvy photo advice.

> ➥ **Steve and Pat's Tip:** *A water safe is a small plastic waterproof container worn around the ankle or wrist that holds money, credit cards, and car keys. Vacationers can swim and snorkel in true worry-free fashion. The colorful and inexpensive water safes are available at all sporting goods stores.*

Despite the popularity of home video, 35mm still photography retains its firm grip on the vacationing American public. Forget complicated single lens reflex (SLR) cameras. Today there is a new world of sophisticated point-and-shoot cameras, including the new advanced picture system (APS) cameras. The world of video is more complex than ever, with various formats, not to mention low-versus high-resolution cameras. So, which cameras to consider and choose from in both the still and video photography formats?

Point-and-Shoot 35mm Cameras

Point-and-shoot cameras that use 35mm film offer models in every price range. Most have sophisticated features, are easy to operate, and deliver excellent results. Those planning to purchase a new camera have least two questions in mind: What is the best camera model and what is the lowest available price?

Point-and-shoot camera prices range from $100 for basic models to $450 for advanced-feature models. Camera models can change quickly, however, the best models may be around for several years. So when I describe specific models, generally newer and better models in the future will replace them.

When shopping for a point-and-shoot 35mm camera, consider these essential features:

- Weight: Generally the lighter and smaller the camera, the better. Current models weigh between ten and sixteen ounces.

- Viewfinders: Look for the brightest, largest, and clearest viewfinder image. Do not overlook this most important feature.
- Ease of use: Major controls, including the zoom and shutter buttons, should permit easy one-hand use.
- Zoom lens: Buy a moderately priced 35mm to 160mm zoom lens.
- Autofocus system: All major brands use acceptable autofocus systems.
- Autoflash With red-eye reduction: Do away with red devil-eye photos.
- Macro: Take close-up photos, eighteen to twenty-four inches from the subject.
- Waterproof models: Consider the waterproof Olympus Infinity Zoom 135, with a 35mm to 120mm zoom lens, or my favorite, the Pentax WR-90, with a modest 35mm to 90mm zoom lens.
- Self timer: Press a button and jump into the picture.
- Backlight control: Look for a backlight control, including an exposure lock button. Read the camera's manual and learn to use this important picture-saving feature.
- Panoramic pictures: This features cuts out the top and bottom of the picture and stretches the width to ten inches to include a panorama. Select a model that can change from panoramic mode to mid-role mode. My favorite Pentax IQ models have this ability.

➥ **Steve's Tip:** *I recommend purchasing a point-and-shoot camera with a wide-angle range of either 28mm or 35mm and a telephoto range of 140mm to 160mm, like the Pentax IQ 140 or 160. The price usually ranges between $175 and $350 at local dealers, but the camera can be purchased for far less if you follow my advice.*

Advanced Picture System (APS) Cameras These newer point-and-shoot cameras are a different breed. The camera uses a smaller negative than 35mm film. The camera has a switch that marks the photo so that it may be printed in three sizes, 4" × 6", 4" × 7", and super-panoramic 4" × 10".

I still recommend the Pentax IQ 140 and newer 160 models with panoramic ability rather than the APS models. Although these cameras are "regular" 35mm point-and-shoot models, they allow users to select two sizes of prints, the regular 4" × 6" or panoramic size.

Creating a Cruise Video Masterpiece

Today each of us has the potential to produce a video masterpiece. Some readers may be planning to purchase their first camcorder. The very best buy, for both quality and price, are Hi-Band 8mm camcorders. More reasons why I highly recommend bargain-priced, full-featured Hi-Band 8mm camcorders follow:

- Overall picture quality, including color, brightness, and clarity is 30 to 50 percent better than VHS, VHS-C, and regular 8mm models.
- Unlike VHS tapes, 8mm cassettes are smaller and easier to carry.
- The 8mm tapes run for only two hours; compact videocassettes are available. The tapes are coated with metal particles, so images will last up to fifty years.

➥ **Steve's Video Tip:** *How do you create bright, crystal-clear images that surpass 80 percent of all other camcorders? How do you beat local prices by hundreds of dollars? I recommend the mail order purchase of a high-resolution, Hi-Band 8mm camcorder.*

Today, Hi-Band 8mm camcorders offer the best high-resolution images and hi-fi sound available. In fact, the quality of Hi-Band 8mm rivals video laser discs. I vote for the best picture and sound available at affordable prices. The news gets better. During the past two years, the prices of Hi-Band 8mm models have dropped dramatically. With the additional savings of $200 to $500 by mail order, these camcorders, once priced at $1,400 to $2,000, are available for less than $1,000.

Recommended Hi-Band 8mm Camcorders and Features

My top choices are Sony (TRY-82 or a current replacement model) and Canon's ES-6000 brand Hi-Band 8mm camcorders. I highly recommend the following camcorder features:

- Tilting color viewfinder with optional spare LCD color screen (three to four inches)
- Minimum 10 × (power) optical zoom lens
- Macro-focus for great close-ups
- Built-in digital titles and special effects—the more the better!
- Video stabilization system for steady pictures
- A built-in speaker for easy correction of glitches on playback

The Wonderful World of Mail Order Shopping

Why would anyone buy an expensive camera or camcorder, costing $1,000, by mail order from some seller thousands of miles away? The answer is: big savings. A careful mail order shopper can save hundreds of dollars. For decades I have bought cameras and other major electronic products by mail order and have never lost a dime.

Start by purchasing a current issue of *Popular Photography* magazine. Then flip to the advertisement section in the rear of the magazine and a page titled "Check-Rated Program." Read this page carefully. *Popular Photography*'s program sets forth the magazine's advertising codes, intended to protect readers making mail order purchases. Companies who subscribe to the code have placed a check mark with a small circle that says, "*Popular Photography* Check-Rated Store" in their ad. If something goes wrong with the order, the magazine promises to help resolve the problem. However, I emphasize that I have never used this service during my twenty years of successful mail order shopping.

Shop at your local camera stores and determine their best prices. Return to *Popular Photography*. Avoid "gray-market" items. Many advertisers sell what they call gray-market products and offer an incredible low price. Gray-market equipment does not include the American distributor's "USA warranty." If an ad states, "includes a full warranty" but fails to mention "USA Warranty," these are gray-market items which include either an "international warranty" that is not honored in the United States, or the store may be including their own "in-house" warranty. The microscopic print at the bottom of many ads states that "some products do not come with a USA warranty that may be available at additional cost." I *strongly* recommend that equipment be purchased from stores that offer a full USA manufacturer's warranty. Or, pay extra for a gray-market dealer to include the USA warranty.

> ➥ **Steve's Warranty Tip:** *Gray-market dealers charge $20 to $40 or more for the USA warranty. I do not buy gray-market merchandise because I want the protection of the manufacturer's warranty. I am also a member of Buyers Advantage (800) 553-4948. This wonderful outfit extends U.S. warranties two years from the date of purchase. Makers of expensive camcorders like Sony offer the worst warranty imaginable—only ninety days on labor, the most expensive factor in any repair. Buyers Advantage saves me hundreds of dollars since I have no need to buy expensive extended warranties.*

Study the seller's return policy and the amount of any restocking charge. This is the amount charged for a returned, nondefective item. Keep in mind that mail order sellers make a marginal profit. They expect buyers to know exactly what model they want. If a product is defective, they will accept the return and quickly replace the item. However, dealers are not happy to accept returns of nondefective items. In the latter case, buyers must act quickly, usually within seven to fourteen days and pay shipping charges and restocking fees.

Contact the dealer through its toll-free number. Although

some ads state, "Orders only!" most stores will quote their latest price. Compare prices and decide which check-rated dealer is offering the best deal for a USA warranty and all accessories. Compare return and restocking policies. Is there an additional charge for credit card purchases? Compare shipping and handling charges to figure out the best, final price.

Choose a model, call the dealer, and place the order following the suggestions in the *Popular Photography* program. Follow up on the verbal order with a fax or mailed confirmation. Most dealers ship by United Parcel Service (UPS), and orders will arrive in six to ten days. Of course, express delivery is always available at extra cost. Immediately inspect the item when it arrives. If it appears to function properly, then and only then complete the warranty papers.

➥ **Steve's Camera Kit Tip:** *Some cameras, primarily point-and-shoot models, are sold either "à la carte" or as a kit. The kit version usually includes an expensive lithium battery worth up to $15, a strap, and a case. Check the price quotes carefully. Is it for a kit or just the camera?*

How much are the savings? Greater savings are always made on higher-priced items. Savings range from $75 on items priced at $200 or less and up to $800 on higher-priced equipment. Here are some money-saving examples:

- In 1998, Sony's top Hi-Band, 8mm model TRY-82 sold for $1,189, including sales tax, by my local dealer. Beach Camera sold the same model with a USA warranty, delivered for $879. The net savings was $310.
- Canon's bestselling Hi-Band 8mm camcorder, model ES-6000, sold in the San Francisco Bay Area for $974, including sales tax. Beach Camera sold the same camcorder with a USA warranty, delivered for $779. The net savings was $195.
- Sony's newest digital video (DV) camcorder model TRV9 just arrived at my local dealer. This is the ultimate, state-of-the-art camcorder videophiles dream of owning. My dealer's price is $2,814, including sales tax. Beach Camera is

selling the same camera with a USA warranty, delivered for $1,925. Net savings is $889!
- My favorite point-and-shoot 35mm camera, the Pentax IQ-160 kit, sold at my local dealer for $324, including sales tax. Coast to Coast Camera sold the same model with a USA warranty, delivered, for $255. Net savings was $69.

A short list of dealers that I have successfully dealt with over the past twenty years follows:

- Adorama: (800) 815-1260, (212) 741-0052
- Abe's Camera: (800) 992-2379 (the only check-rated store with a toll-free customer service number)
- Beach Camera: (800) 634-1811; fax: (908) 424-1105 (check-rated store)
- Camera World of Oregon: (800) 222-1557, (503) 227-6008; fax: (800) 729-8929
- Coast to Coast Camera: (800) 788-5555
- Focus Camera: (800) 221-0828; (718) 437-8810; video hot line: (800) 685-9940 (check-rated store)
- Smile Photo and Video: (800) 366-6993; fax: (800) 699-2836 (check-rated store)

Congratulations, you are well on your way to years of huge savings not only on cameras and camcorders but also on sophisticated electronic products of all types and descriptions. Many of these same dealers sell computers, audio and video components, and telecommunications gear.

Better yet, fabulous cruise vacation images will be preserved and kept vibrantly alive with quality stills or on incredible Hi-Band 8mm videotapes.

Comfort, Safety, and Convenience for the Best Cruise Vacation

You have just booked your dream cruise vacation. Soon the stress of daily life will fade. Right? Unfortunately, vacations occasionally breed their own brand of stress or annoyance. Looking for effective and fun means of fighting back? Look no further. We recommend a potpourri of comfort, convenience and safety tips that are surefire winners!

Pocket Pillows We refuse to leave home without our Pocket Pillows! Our interest began when Steve sprained his back one week before our Paris vacation. His back sprain had healed one day before our departure. Nevertheless, there was a ten-hour, nonstop flight ahead and we could only keep our fingers crossed. Steve bought a Pocket Pillow and the ten-hour flight to Paris was easy! He swore that it was like placing an excellent, lumbar support into the plane's seat. Now we both love this super-comfort travel accessory.

Whether sitting, leaning, or sleeping, the pillow provides pure comfort. The 6" × 4" × 1" Pocket Pillow inflates to 15" × 19". It is "magic" because there are two separate air chambers. It works on plane seats, car seats, and cruise chaise longues alike. Pocket Pillows are available at most travel accessory stores or through the Magellan's catalogue (item no. 1F382 at $12.85). Should you have difficulty finding a Pocket Pillow, you may call Dwelly Enterprises at (415) 892-9447, or fax: (415) 897-0927.

Noise Buster Extreme We absolutely adore this amazing product. It weighs only six ounces, comes with a deluxe soft-cushioned stereo headset wired to a tiny box, and uses "white noise" canceling technology. It serves two purposes: first, it acts as a high-quality sound system with a deluxe headset. Simply plug a wire from your portable cassette player to the Noise Buster's miniature control box and enjoy music like never before. Next, it uses state-of-the-art noise-canceling technology. Flick a switch, and—voila—two-thirds or more of all engine noise disappears! In fact, it eliminates up to 75 percent of airline engine noise! During a recent flight, when we handed our units to several British Airways stewards and flight attendants, they tried to buy them! The units work equally well to eliminate ship engine noise! The Noise Buster Extreme price ranges from $49 (on sale) to $69. Contact Brookstone at (800) 351-7222 (item no. 207415). Contact Magellan's at (800) 962-4943 (item no. 1F386E).

Mindfold This is more than a sleep mask, it is a sleep experience. Our hats off to Alex Grey, inventor of this super product. As advertised, the Mindfold delivers "total darkness with your eyes open." The outer shell of this amazing sleep mask is opaque black plastic, while its inner body is soft thick foam. Best are the silver-dollar-sized cutouts in the foam for your eyelashes. Then it happens. No matter if there's surrounding light, you open your eyes and find yourself staring into total, and we mean *total*, darkness. It is eerie, amazing, and awesome! It is like having a personal light switch for the airline cabin, and nothing touches the eyes or eyelashes! It is also recommended for deep relaxation. Mindfold is available from Brookstone (item no.183731) and priced at $17.50. Or, order directly from the manufacturer by calling (888) 705-3805.

Hartman Protech Hair Dryer   Why spend $20 to $30 on a lightweight, dual-voltage hair dryer? We highly recommend the 11.8-ounce American-made Hartman Protech, a 1600-watt dual-speed, dual-voltage hair dryer. Our Hartman dryer has worked for years. Wal-Mart stores sell the Hartman Protech for the amazing low price of $9. For more information, call Hartman Products at (310) 676-7700.

Books on Tape (BOT)   This is the leading company that rents full-length, unabridged books. The company offers over 4,500 titles in a free 460-page catalogue. We have differing votes on this one. Steve's thumb is way up, while Pat's is way down. With that said, here is Steve's pitch.

While driving on my job, Books on Tape are a constant companion. I joyfully listen to wonderful books on planes, under palm trees, and on chaise lounges at poolside. For the same price as local abridged book rentals, BOT rents their books for thirty days. The rental price includes return postage.

Why, you may ask, is Pat's thumb down? She tends to daydream while listening to a book being read on tape and prefers speed reading. I enjoy having it read, especially when the reader adds dramatic touches or other audio effects. Call BOT for a free catalogue: (800) 626-3333; fax (714) 548-6574. Check out their catalogue at: www.booksontape.com, which permits on-line rentals. Ask for their current introductory offer, which can save 50 percent!

The Evac-U8 Smoke Hood   Not that we want to sound dire, but all flight crews carry the same device. Smoke is the real danger in any fire, so savvy travelers always want an edge. This small eleven-ounce packaged hood with a five-year shelf life protects from deadly gases for twenty minutes to permit escape. This item is available from Magellan's, priced at $69 (item no. SP628).

A "cool" hip water bottle carrier The stretchable blue nylon-covered neoprene carrier, with a screw-on push-pull top, holds a standard large water bottle. Available at Magellan's, priced at $14.85 (item no. LB348).

Brookstone This company offers a lifetime 100 percent satisfaction guarantee on their products. After sixty days, Brookstone will give customers an exchange or store credit. Stores are located in major malls in thirty-three states. Stop by and "play," hands-on, with all their fine products. To request a free catalogue call customer service at (800) 846-3000.

Magellan's This company calls itself "America's leading source of travel supplies." Magellan's travel accessory catalogue offers an extensive selection of great travel items. Since their 1989 inception, they have offered a 100 percent customer satisfaction guarantee. This guarantees a full refund anytime after you purchase an item. Their summer 1998 catalogue is sixty-eight pages. To request a free catalogue subscription, call (800) 962-4943.

➥ **Steve and Pat's Tip:** *Keep in mind that neither Brookstone nor Magellan's is a discount seller. They offer unique, quality travel items not found elsewhere. The price is usually retail but backed with lifetime warranties. They occasionally stock major brand items that sell for less in discount stores or discount catalogues.*

When it came time to purchase a second pair of Noise Busters Extreme for Patty, I noticed the same product selling for $49.95 in a discount mail order catalogue from Damark International. Brookstone's regular price for this item was $69.95. I simply presented the Damark advertisement to Brookstone's manager and not only received the discount on our second pair but also a refund of the price differential on the first pair. Although Brookstone's has no formal price-matching policy, the store manager cheerfully "did the right thing" for us, insuring future customer loyalty. Whenever in doubt about price-matching by a reputable store, ask! For a free subscription to Damark's monthly catalogue, which sells items like computers, exercise gear, home furnishings, and electronic language translators, call Damark at (800) 827-6767.

Travisa A funny name, but this company saves vacations. When the Tanzanian Embassy lost our passports several days before we departed for our African safari, Travisa came to our last-minute rescue by "walking" our replacement passports through the embassy, getting the visas stamped in them, and returning them to us by overnight express mail. Travisa's last-minute service is expensive, but all costs are relative when compared with the unacceptable alternative of a canceled vacation. Contact Travisa at (800) 222-2589.

Swaying To and Fro: A Savvy Word About Sea Sickness

One major goal on all cruise vacations is to avoid situations where our faces begin to resemble a St. Patrick's Day shamrock turning a sickly kelly green. In reality, today's modern cruise ships, with their advanced stabilizer systems, offer a rock-solid ride, so sea sickness is not a problem for most passengers.

However, Patty and I will always remember one scene on a Caribbean cruise. There we were, preparing for aerobics in the exercise room. Outside, passengers were enjoying a cloudless sunny day as the ship cruised along on a totally flat, smooth sea. A fellow passenger, a young woman, turned to us and said, "I am really feeling seasick. All this motion is getting to me, how about you two?" We looked at each another and our eyes turned to the rock-solid floor. We were tactful and very perplexed. What in the world was this person doing on a cruise?

We concluded that on occasion seasickness, like beauty and art, is in the eyes and *mind* of the beholder. There are rare occasions where the seas are truly in turmoil and even the hardiest of sailors begin to feel the "queazies." Advanced satellite data also helps avoid bad weather conditions. Prone to seasickness? Take initial precautions. Bring one over-the-counter medication such as Dramamine, pill or patch. Better to be safe than green!

Our general rules for fighting back when it comes to seasickness are as follows:

- *Center of Gravity*: A major cruise line advises booking a cabin close to the dead center of the ship where motion is least felt. How about that inside center cabin?
- When the *"queazies"* strike, go outdoors, stand in a sea breeze, and look at the horizon. Do *not* look at anything that is moving. Do *not* stay inside!
- *BioBand (accupressure wrist band)*: Magellan's describes the "almost-magical" ability of acupressure wrist bands to control the queasiness—without drugs or side effects—that can come with rough seas (item no. IF376, $12.85).
- *Dramamine*: Although this medication works, it does cause drowsiness. A ship's sundry shop or medical office does stock it.
- *NoQweez (drug free):* Magellan's offers a natural ginger complex compound that claims no drowsiness. It costs $9.85 for ten capsules (item no. FV575).

Don't Get Shocked by Shipboard and Foreign Electricity!

Shipboard Considerations Most of today's modern cruise ships' cabins offer outlets for 110 volts for U.S. and 220 volts for European appliances. Check with the travel agent or cruise line to find out if the cabin has a 110-volt outlet that can deliver the 1600 watts needed for hair dryers and other appliances.

> ➡ **Steve and Pat's Tip:** *Every Magellan's catalogue contains four pages devoted to foreign adaptors and transformers, including a worldwide guide listing all countries and required items. Also call the Hybrinetics Company at (800) 247-6900, or fax (707) 585-7313, and request their free "Voltage Valet Foreign Electricity Guide." With this information you will surely never find yourself "shocked" by foreign electricity.*

Foreign Hotels Many cruise itineraries include one or more nights in a foreign hotel as part of their cruise-and-land vacation packages. A typical Greek vacation may include sightseeing for three days in and around Athens, followed by a five-day island cruise with many ports of call. Our Greece and Turkey vacation included seven nights in Greece followed by a seven-night cruise of the Greek islands and Turkey.

Our 1997 Yangtze River cruise included six days of cruising. The following week, we toured China from Xi'an, home of the terra-cotta warriors, to the capital, Beijing, and the Great Wall.

Hotels in foreign countries require adaptors and/or transformers. An adaptor permits one to use a switchable 110/120 volt appliance by permitting it to fit into the hotel room's wall outlet. If an appliance is strictly 110 volts (does not have a switch that changes it to 220 volts) then an additional item, a transformer, reduces the foreign 220 volts to a usable 110 volts.

8

Anchors Aweigh! Finding Your Ship and Cabin

At this very moment, jet planes are flying passengers to their cruise ship's departure city. Upon arrival, there is an additional but brief journey from the airport to the cruise ship's port of embarkation where the passengers are delivered to their luxury cruise ship.

Transfers From Airport to Cruise Ship and Back

Most airports offer shuttle bus service at a reasonable cost. Airport taxicabs are always ready. Want to avoid this additional cost, plus the problem of missed or late connections? A cruise that includes transfers is the answer. If the cruise offers airline connections, then it is responsible for the flight to the cruise ship's departure city, transfers from the airport to the port of embarkation, and luggage handling.

> ➥ **Steve and Pat's Tip:** *On those occasions when the cruise line is not arranging the flight to the cruise ship's departure city there is another great option. Some cruise lines offer à la carte transfers from the local airport to the cruise ship for a small fee.*

Our flight from San Francisco to Anchorage, arranged by Princess Cruises, included transfer by scenic bus from Anchorage Airport to Seward, our port of embarkation. Luckily for us, our bus driver was also a tour guide. As we headed toward Seward, the vehicle came to a sudden stop. There, in a scenic meadow across the road, a family of two adult and four young moose were grazing on the tall grass. The driver encouraged us to exit the bus for a photo opportunity. We were in cruise heaven and had yet to board our ship!

A Cruise Ship's Departure City as a Second Vacation

Often we travel from our home base, the San Francisco Bay Area, to Los Angeles to take a cruise or catch a nonstop flight to Paris or Tahiti. We usually enjoy an extra mini-vacation by arriving a couple of days early.

Los Angeles offers fantastic sightseeing, incredible legitimate and off-Broadway–type theater, and unmatched opportunities for unbridled, frivolous fun. Part of our typical weekend of fun is an obligatory stroll along Venice Beach, where people-watching reigns supreme. Then we may pay a quick visit to Universal City, Universal's City Walk, or one of the city's many world-class museums.

Many other embarkation cities offer similar mini-vacation opportunities. Cruise ships departing for New England, Canada, and Bermuda depart from New York. Premier Cruises ships embark for the Caribbean from New Orleans. Alaska cruises embark from San Francisco, Anchorage, and Vancouver. Some Mexican Riviera cruises embark from San Diego. Each of these cruises offers an excellent opportunity for that second vacation in some of America's and Canada's most exciting cities.

Home Away From Home—Settling in the Cabin

Upon arrival at the port of embarkation, passengers check-in at dockside and finally board their cruise ship. Once onboard, passengers open a shipboard credit account, receive a cabin assignment, and the cabin key. Those passengers paying a bargain price for their cruise may look forward to a small but comfortable cabin. How small? Let us consider Celebrity Cruise Line, one of the highest rated of the mass-market, bargain cruise lines. Their newest ship, the *Mercury*, boasts run-of-the-ship inside and outside cabins that measure 172 square feet. As previously noted, other ships offer inside economy cabins that measure as little as 115 square feet. A typical 12′ × 12′ room in a home or apartment gives a good approximation of the average low-category economy-priced cabins.

Those who have enjoyed overnight or longer sailboat journeys understand that it takes only a slight adjustment to get used to clean, neat, and comfortable downsized sleeping quarters. During our recent adventure in New Zealand, we lived in a Ford Transit camper-van for ten days. The experience was like our one-week sailboat vacation in the Sea of Cortez some years ago. Compared with these venues, even the smallest cabin on a major cruise ship seems luxurious.

Keep in mind that tidiness, only slightly alien to the male species (guess which of us is writing this paragraph), is of paramount importance. On many older and most newer cruise ships, the two lower beds may be moved to form a queen- or king-sized bed. Dressers are built-in and offer ample storage space. Do not expect large hotel room furniture and closets. Unpack quickly, store soft luggage under the bed, and keep the cabin tidy and neat.

All cabins offer a telephone, radio, TV, and a bathroom with a shower. Newer ships offer a mini-bar and/or refrigerators in all cabins, a definite plus. Although theft is rare, *never* leave cash or valuables in open sight. If an in-cabin safe is provided, use it.

Dining on the High Seas—the Heart of Cruising

Food service and selection on cruises are, in a single word, sensational! From flaming desserts like bananas flambé cooked at table-side to lobster and Kansas City beef, cruise lines deliver big-time when it comes to dining on the high seas. There are culinary events such as the famed march of the flaming baked Alaska. As lights dim, the crew marches around the dining room, each member carrying a flaming platter.

Rather than deluge you with copies of out-of-date menus, we provide an overview of the unforgettable culinary experience that cruises deliver. This includes a mention of current trends and some unique food-related amenities now offered by some but not all cruise lines. Our special tips help to optimize the cruise dining experience.

We have a decadent tale for you. It happened on our Caribbean cruise on the *Star Princess*. Our dinner menu was superb. Entrees included mushroom-capped tournedos of beef (filet mignon) and roast Royal Pheasant Flambé with cognac. Such a dilemma! Our eager-to-please waiter was in many respects reminiscent of waiters of bygone days in Catskill Mountains hotels, the type of upstate New York 1950s hotel featured in the movie *Dirty Dancing*. In those early versions of all-inclusive hotels waiters would "kill to please." As déjà vu set in, Steve asked our waiter if we could share another second entree. The waiter eagerly complied. Our tablemates looked on in apparent disdain as both the filet mignon and the royal Pheasant Flambé arrived. Then the metamorphosis took place. The next evening we watched these same tablemates trying to agree on which extra entrees they would be ordering. Soon all were joining in the decadent fray, sampling exotic entrees to their hearts content.

➥ **Pat's Lobster Tip:** *After a sumptuous lobster dinner on a Princess cruise, Patty asked the waiter if they scheduled another lobster dinner during our one-week cruise. Sadly, the answer was no. Still, there was good news. The waiter mentioned that the kitchen had leftovers, and she immediately placed an order for another lobster dinner. Did we mention that Steve does not eat lobster? Poor guy, he does not know what he is missing! The next evening they again served Patty this delectable meal, much to the envy of our tablemates. She was in lobster heaven!*

Although cruise brochures abound with well-deserved self-serving platitudes about the quality and quantity of meals, they rarely suggest the above scenario. Also, Cruise Lines International Association, an organization representing most cruise lines, states that "there is virtually no limit on what or how much (food) you can order." Do we order multiple entrees often? Of course not! This option is reserved for those occasions when we are presented with impossible menu choices.

> ➥ **Steve and Pat's Dessert Tip:** *At another cruise dinner, the menu listed a delicious flaming dessert. After dinner, the desserts, flames and all, were prepared at each table. The next evening we noticed that several tables away, a flaming dessert was being prepared and served only at that table and no others. Being curious, we asked our waiter and he explained that only once during each cruise are flaming desserts served—unless a table makes a special request. We immediately polled our table and obtained a 100 percent vote in favor of a second delectable, flaming culinary event. Everyone at our table applauded, and the next evening the waiter expertly made bananas flambé. You are correct if you see a moral in these two tips. When in doubt, ask!*

Breakfasts Unless a cruise line offers exceptional items, we will refer to regular breakfast dishes listed on the menus. This in no way detracts from the quality of the daily offerings, which include: assorted fruit juices, various hot and cold cereals, eggs and omelettes cooked "your way," pancakes and French toast, seasonal fruits and cheeses, fresh-made pastries, coffee, tea, milk, and hot chocolate.

Lunches Lunch choices are many on all ships. A five-course lunch is served daily in the ship's dining room. The upcoming main culinary event, the famed five-course, gourmet dinner, shapes our daily lunch strategy. We prefer to avoid the temptation of a formal dining room lunch, although salads are available. A better option for us is the festive outdoor lunch buffet with fruit, salads, cold cuts, and countless other choices, including outdoor burger bars offering gourmet made-to-order burgers and grilled chicken sandwiches. Some ships have a potato bar, and every one has a pizzeria and a bistro. Don't forget the dessert buffets and ice cream bars. When it comes to lunch, passengers have unlimited options, so enjoy yourself!

Cruise Lines and Dining

Carnival Cruise Line

Carnival is the "Fun Ships" cruise line with less emphasis on food. Currently, Carnival is upgrading their food service and offering an expanded, twenty-four-hour room service menu. Also, Carnival is committed to developing alternative dining, with its popular Bistro. All Carnival ships offer Bistro dining, starting at 6:30 P.M. The Bistro is a natural extension of Carnival's existing Lido Deck restaurants, which provide an alternative breakfast and lunch. The Lido has been upgraded to include silverware and linens. Morning fare includes an omelette chef for custom orders. Lunch offers a pasta bar, a grilled chicken potato bar, a Caesar salad bar, a Mexican food bar, and a health food bar.

Carnival states that 70 percent of their passengers use the casual, cafelike setting for dinner at least once during their cruise. Bistro meals include such tempting entrees as prime rib, steaks, grilled chicken, specialty salads, and chef's specials like grilled breast of duck, Wiener schnitzel, and swordfish steak.

Breakfast—Main Dining Room Carnival offers an "express" menu with the usual American breakfast, consisting of juice, eggs, bacon, and toast. Unlike the competition, however, breakfast menus offer items like eggs Benedict and lox and bagels.

Lunch—Main Dining Room For those who can take it, a five-course lunch awaits. A typical entree is veal stroganoff. Of course, lighter items are available, such as a tropical fruit plate, omelette, or turkey sandwich.

Dinner—Main Dining Room Look for the usual French, Italian, and American theme dinners, such as American prime rib and roast turkey, French Duck l'Orange or Entrecôte Martinique, and Italian tournedos of beef tenderloin or veal parmigian. Each dinner menu contains special children's choices plus nautical spa fare such as poached fillet of sole, grilled fillet of salmon, and broiled chicken.

Carnival continues its ever-popular twenty-four-hour pizzerias. It has also led the way with one of the first spa cuisine menus, and now additionally offers daily vegetarian items as well.

➥ **Steve and Pat's Tip:** *Those who have the early dinner seating should be aware of the Bistro options when spending a long day in a port of call. When you return to the ship, you may want to relax for a few hours, then grab a late Bistro dinner, perhaps a delectable sirloin steak. This is one of the most popular ways to enjoy Bistro dining.*

Celebrity Cruises

Passengers consistently rate Celebrity as one of the best cruise values. They say that a typical bargain-priced Celebrity cruise should sell for many hundreds of dollars more per person. This likewise applies to Celebrity's attention to shipboard food. Its ships offer regular and alternative dining. Celebrity likes to quote the *New York Post*, which referred to the cruise line's food as "spectacular . . . from sumptuous breakfasts to nightly midnight buffets."

Breakfast—Main Dining Room Celebrity offers the regular menu items plus eggs Benedict, banana pancakes, and fish specialties such as herring, smoked salmon, and broiled Scottish kippers. They serve seven types of omelettes. Express breakfast is always available.

Lunch—Main Dining Room Celebrity offers five full courses. Lunch entrees are exceptional and include such items as beef Bourguignonne, Viennese pork schnitzel, chicken fajitas, Philly cheesesteak sandwich, and rigatoni alla Boscaiola.

Dinner—Main Dining Room Celebrity's fabulous dinner entrees include: Entrecôte l'Echalotes, rack of lamb, Coquilles Saint-Jacques (scallops), baby coho salmon, pork rib roast on Basque onions, filet mignon, rack of veal, shrimp scampi, Duckling l'Orange, ziti alla Gorgonzola, and veal scallopini.

Commodore Cruise Line

Commodore is another cruise line that offers excellent food in abundant quantities. Commodore says its food represents its "Epicurean New Orleans heritage." Passenger testimonials talk about the ship being "fun-filled with great food." Commodore boasts that its twenty-four-hour room service will deliver "most menu requests fulfilled and more!"—and Commodore is referring to its *dining room* menus! This puts Commodore's room service way above most of its competition. Commodore does not have formal dress dinners. Another innovation is the open seating for breakfast, from 7:30 A.M. to 10:30 A.M.

Dinner—Main Dining Room Commodore offers theme dinners that liven up the evening. What to do when the theme dinner is Mexican and some passengers shy away from such spicy foods? Our advice is a great Caribbean song, "Don't worry! Be happy!"

Let's look at Commodore's Mexican Theme Menu. Remember: This example applies to all cruise lines that offer theme dinners. First, the menu offers guacamole dip with sour cream and taco chips as an appetizer. Nevertheless, it also offers a pacific seafood cocktail with crab and shrimp. For soup, there is Consomme Cancun, but also cream of broccoli and a heart of romaine salad. So far so good! Now we come to the all-important dinner entrees. How about trying a spicy Broiled Brochette of Beef Acapulco? As you may have guessed, other entrees include broiled salmon, sugar cured ham, and roast Long Island duck. For a desert, there is caramel flan.

Another example: the Caribbean Menu offers spicy Jamaican Jerk Chicken and Shrimp, but also grilled halibut and rack of lamb. What a wonderful culinary picture! No fear, no pain, no disappointment! Just great gourmet dining choices despite the evening's theme.

Costa Cruises

This Italian line is celebrating its fiftieth year of cruising! Their slogan, Cruising Italian-style, is most appropriate. Costa claims to be Europe's number one cruise line. Its six ships sail the Caribbean, northern Europe, the Mediterranean, and South America. Meal service from Costa's European staff is excellent. Expect attentive waiters ready to meet every request. Their pasta and Italian dishes excel. On European itineraries, steak dishes suffer for lack of the finest U.S. beef. On the other hand, their specialties, like veal roast, are superb.

Breakfasts and lunches, outside the dining room, are served buffet-style and are exceptional. Choices include fresh pasta dishes, burgers to order, salads, grilled chicken breast, beef stroganoff, a carving station serving prime rib, and a fantastic assortment of cheeses and fruits.

Room service is twenty-four-hours and offers the usual snack items, salads, sandwiches, and some hot items. Their menu actually notes that dinner meals cannot be ordered via room service.

Breakfast—Main Dining Room Regular menu items include eggs Benedict, bagels with lox and cream cheese, chopped steak and eggs, fruit pancakes, and waffles with real maple syrup. Costa also provides a daily chef's special, like poached eggs Florentine.

Lunch—Main Dining Room This offers the usual five-course meals "Italian-style." Entrees include beef stroganoff, grilled turkey steak, and sliced roast leg of veal. Then there is pasta, pasta, and more fresh pasta dishes, like ravioli di ricotta ai funghi (in creamy mushroom sauce), lavish fruit salad, a Reuben sandwich, and grilled minute steak (of course it is not *all* Italian!).

Dinner—Main Dining Room Dinner entrees offer a fabulous array of dishes like: marinated roast chicken, broiled fillet of red snapper, prime rib, lots of vegetarian pasta dishes, grilled brochette of shrimp, chateaubriand (note: if U.S. beef is used the menu will refer to American beef), baked mahimahi, roast leg of spring lamb, and roasted marinated pork loin. All meals are served with pasta dishes and offer health spa suggestions like broiled fish, grilled shrimp, and broiled and baked fowl.

Holland America Line (HAL)

HAL's slogan is A Tradition of Excellence! The passengers consistently give the cruise line a high rating for its service and food.

Breakfast—Main Dining Room The menu includes regular breakfast items. There are daily chef's suggestions such as kippered herring smothered in onions with home fries, and Sunshine Parfait (layers of light yogurt, fresh fruit, and granola).

Lunch—Main Dining Room Lunch delivers a five-course meal with entrees such as Vegetable Stuffed Chicken Breast, and bay shrimp and Dungeness crab salad. The sumptuous outdoor Lido Brunch offers an array of delectable salads and omelettes to order. A nearby "food corner" offers burgers. The Veranda Eatery serves Italian pasta and barbecued beef sandwiches. Ice cream bars are available.

Dinner—Main Dining Room HAL offers lavish continental entrees such as strip sirloin, poached halibut, prime rib, center cut roast pork tenderloin, vegetable strudel, and coconut breaded rockfish. Gourmet dishes of beef, fish, fowl, pasta, and vegetarian dishes are always available. Do not forget the daily light-and-healthy entrees like Apple Cider Marinated Chicken Breast, butterfly cornish game hen, and grilled trout. Of course, appetizers, salads, and desserts are of equally high caliber.

HAL serves a famed late-night chocolate buffet.

Norwegian Cruise Line (NCL)

Norwegian was the "inventor" of mass-market cruises several decades ago and is still a major innovator. Its advertising slogan is It's Different out Here. Perhaps most important, NCL has and remains vacationer-friendly. This credo applies directly to dining in several ways.

Most of NCL's ships now have four restaurants. Their commitment to true alternative dining again leads the way as competitors rush to follow in their path. NCL's Bistro restaurants are open from 6:30 P.M. until 11:00 P.M. and provide a private and romantic dining alternative. The ambience, service, and food quality equals that of any fine restaurant back home. A service charge of $5 per person will be added to the bill. While reservations are recommended, they are not required. Note: Formal dress is *never* required at the Bistros. Though passengers are not served main dining room fare, the menu is excellent and include pasta, veal, and steak dishes.

Many ships have sport pubs–snack bars with a dozen TV screens. They offer lunch, breakfast, and light snack buffets.

NCL provides fantastic twenty-four-hour room service that is unique among the giant cruise lines. In the true tradition of excellence, NCL's room service menu first offers regular in-cabin menu items like continental breakfast, ham, roast beef, and turkey sandwiches, Caesar salads, soup, and ice cream. NCL's room service menu then goes the distance and advises passengers that they may order "selections from today's restaurant menu items during main dining room hours," allowing thirty minutes for delivery. This is the ultimate in twenty-four-hour pampered room service that may be a lifesaver if you are ill, tired, or unwilling to dress for that formal dinner. Or, you and your significant other can experience an ultimate romantic private gourmet meal in your cabin. Their ships also offer variations of alternative dining, such as the Lido restaurant on their ship *Rembrandt*.

Breakfast—Main Dining Room   The menu provides regular breakfast items.

Lunch—Main Dining Room   Lunch service includes five courses.

Dinner—Main Dining Room   Dinner menus include customary ethnic theme nights.

Typical dinner entrees follow: American Theme (grilled New York steak, roast turkey, broiled mahimahi); Captain's Welcome Dinner (prime rib, jumbo shrimp with lobster, Veal Piccata); Viking Feast (grilled tournedos, roast rack of lamb, broiled Norwegian salmon); Italian Night (roast rack of lamb, Beef Tenderloin Arrosto, chicken breast parmigiana).

Premier Cruises

The cruise line that offers unique Panama Canal and Caribbean itineraries and special air-and-cruise packages also delivers above average service and food.

Breakfast—Main Dining Room   The menu includes fine quality regular breakfast items.

Lunch—Main Dining Room   The lunch menu includes the usual five-course dining room meal, or alternatives such as a deck-side buffet.

Dinner—Main Dining Room   Theme nights are popular and

held often. Typical dinner entrees include baked Alaska salmon, prime rib, and Sea Scallops Louisiana-style. Premiere also includes a sixth course, a cheese and fruit tray with a selection of international cheeses and seasonal fruits.

Princess Cruises

Would you believe that Princess describes "eleven daily meal and snack opportunities aboard each of Princess Cruises's nine ships? Or that the cruise line's Italian galley staff includes up to sixty chefs working day and night on each ship? The ship's excellent cuisine is continental style, blended with contemporary, and served at popular local restaurants.

Every Princess cruise includes the famed "champagne waterfall" with accompanying flaming crêpes suzette. Princess also offers "breakfast, lunch, light dinners, and snacks in the privacy of their [passengers] cabins." This is another big extra, besides the regular pampered twenty-four-hour room service.

Alternative dining includes a Bistro cafe on many Princess ships. Lunch alternatives include all-day pizzerias and an on-deck buffet featuring pastas, burgers, salads, deli sandwiches, and desserts. The *Grand Princess* offers the Painted Desert alternative restaurant, serving southwestern cuisine. Its Horizon buffet court also offers deluxe dinner meals as an alternative to dinner in the main dining room. Sabatini's serves pizza and pasta dishes.

Room service may be used to order a light evening alternative to the main dining room repast.

Princess offers the well-rounded cruise with more of everything—more activities, shore excursions, and amenities. We rate its attention to cuisine as above most of its competition.

Breakfast—Main Dining Room The menu includes the usual quality items.

Lunch—Main Dining Room Lunch includes five-course meals.

Dinner—Main Dining Room Typical dinners exemplify the fine food offered by Princess Cruises and may include the following: roast duck with orange and Madeira-glazed with apples, tourenados of beef tenderloin in red wine sauce, and baked fillet of salmon with mashed red potatoes. The cruise line provides a special Healthy Choice Dinner Menu offering expertly prepared fish and fowl dishes.

Royal Caribbean International (RCI)

RCI has a reputation for excellent, high-quality food and service. It provides the regular breakfast items plus Royal's famous banana pancakes. Their main dining rooms offer various theme dinners with waiters wearing appropriate colorful dress. Most recently, Royal proudly hailed their new casual dinner service with alternative dining options, like their Windjammer Cafe. The cafe is open for intimate private dining from 6:30 P.M. to 9:30 P.M.

Breakfast—Main Dining Room Besides the regular menu items, shipboard "specialties" are offered, such as eggs Benedict, banana pancakes, and blueberry pancakes all served with Vermont maple syrup. Omelette specialties include lox, eggs, and onions. Lox, bagels, and cream cheese are available.

Lunch—Main Dining Room Five courses with entrees like Wiener schnitzel, sliced Kansas City beef, Sauerbraten Bavarian-style, fettuccini Alfredo, braised lamb shanks, bouillabaisse, and Turkey Breast Piccata con Funghi.

➥ **Steve and Pat's Tip:** *The dining room staff strives to meet a guest's every request. Ask to see the next day's menu so that a special request may be made early. If the request involves special food preparation, the waiter and chef appreciate advance notice.*

Dinner—Main Dining Room Theme dinners include Italian, Alaskan Heritage, Mexican, Russian, Mediterranean, and International. Entrees are sauteed veal loin chops, prime rib, broiled lobster tail, medallions of pork, roast duckling, broiled prime sirloin steak, crabmeat cannelloni, Supreme of Boston Sole Madagascar, poached halibut fillet, sauteed seabass fillet, and broiled Mediterranean lamb shish kabob. All menus offer Ship Shape menu selections.

Dining Alternatives—Fact or Fiction?

There is no better word in our travel vocabulary than *options*. Alternative dining is not a new idea. Some years ago we stayed at a Club Med resort on Turquoise Island in the British West Indies. The club is noted as a dedicated dive center. We were thrilled at the occasion to dive and swim with the island's resident dolphin.

➥ **Steve and Pat's Tip:** *Dining at sea is a highlight of every cruise. Gourmet dinners, from appetizers to flaming desserts, are the pinnacles of the dining experience. We find that cruise-line hype does not reflect the true state of alternate dining. Most ships do not offer alternative dining options that equal the quality and selection of the fare served in the main dinning room. Opting for that intimate trattatoria? Then make certain that you will not be limited to calzone or a slice of pizza!*

The food at this Club Med lived up to its reputation. They served it buffet-style in a large open-air building. This Club Med touted the virtues of its dining alternatives. (Formal seating is not part of the principal Club Med game plan.) There we were at two small bistro-style restaurants. We made reservations for dinner at the intimate Italian restaurant and experienced a quiet, romantic "away from the crowds" dinner. The quality of the food ranged from good to excellent. We both agreed that this was a first-class operation. More than that, this was alternative dining as it is meant to be.

Want more privacy? Have a fear of dinner table "crowds" of ten or more? Alternate main dining room option: How about a private, more romantic table for two in the main dining room guaranteed for your entire cruise! In a recent poll of ten of the most popular major bargain-priced cruise lines, six said two-person seating was readily available and three said only a limited number of two-person tables were available. Only Norwegian Cruise Line stated that it does not provide such seating. Inquiry early if and when you decide that two-person dining is your preference for the entire cruise.

➥ **Steve and Pat's Tip:** *Top choices for full alternative dinners (though not entrees off the main dining room menu) include Carnival's Bistros, Le Bistro on Norwegian Cruise Line's ships, the twenty-four-hour Horizon Court on the* Grand Princess, *Royal Caribbean's room service menu, which includes all main dining room menu items if ordered at mealtime. Alternative dining amenities are changing constantly, and mostly for the better. Since we all look forward to the best gourmet meals served in the main dining room, alternative dining is convenient but not essential.*

Pampered by Twenty-four-Hour Room Service

Want to melt the heart of a seasoned cruiser? Just mention the word *floor steward*. For the uninitiated, let us emphasize (with tongue in cheek) that institution of floor stewards, who bring passengers as close as they will ever get to legal slavery or to having a personal genie, fresh out of the bottle! Several stewards are assigned to each cabin and work various shifts throughout the day and night. Consequently, twenty-four-hour service is available to provide aid, advice, and assistance for your every whim.

Make no mistake about this. The major task of all floor stewards is to deliver on the promise of a twenty-four-hour room service menu. The idea of free twenty-four-hour room service lies exclusively in the cruise ship vacation domain. The rich and famous have little or no problem paying for such service, wherever their travel takes them, by using either hotel staff or their own employees. On the other hand, this is one experience few of "us" will ever savor outside the cruise ship environment.

Room service may vary significantly from cruise line to cruise line. There are two principle types of twenty-four-hour room service:

- Basic twenty-four-hour room service menu. This menu is commonplace and includes cold items such as continental breakfast, snacks, fruit, club sandwiches, and salads.

- Complete twenty-four-hour room service menu. In addition to the regular cold items, these rare menus offer hot entrees identical to the meals served in the main dining room if they are ordered at mealtimes.

Feel too tired for a formal dinner? Under the weather? Want a private, romantic gourmet meal? Very few cruise lines offer this option. Norwegian Cruise Line offers this extra service in writing, while Commodore Cruise Line has "promised" that such in-cabin dinner requests will be honored.

In the Evening: "It's Show Time!"

We have extolled the virtues of evening show times as an integral part of the all-inclusive cruise vacation package, and with good reason. After cruise ship dining, the next most persuasive reason for cruising is probably the included nightly evening shows. Where else does one find such professional entertainment included in the price of a bargain vacation? Nowhere!

Open cruise brochures and there are photographs of glitzy ocean-bound Las Vegas–style shows. Do these photos tell the whole story? Do the cruise lines deliver entertainment the way they deliver gourmet dining? Here is the inside scoop.

Seven-night cruises offer six or seven nights of after-dinner shows, the mainstay of evening entertainment. The shows revolve around a hardworking group of young professional dancers and singers whose primary responsibility is to carry the week with major musical spectacles and occasional solo performances. Very often, one or another of the performers has double duty, working in various capacities during daylight hours. One morning, we found that one of the troupe's best dancers doubled as our aerobics instructor.

At their best, the performers don pastel-colored, sequined costumes with enormous elegant feather plumes. As expected, costumes are not as skimpy as those "almost" worn by Las Vegas showgirls. During a one-week cruise, the performers may present two or three original musical reviews. This is the heart and soul of cruise entertainment. A typical Celebrity cruise show may be called "Broadway," starring the Celebrity Singers and Dancers, with six featured performers and nine additional players for a total cast of fifteen. Two days later another musical review was called, "And the Winner Is . . . !"

On other nights, the shows consist of headline performers whose names are less than household words. Let us take that same week of Celebrity shows. One night saw a variety show headlining the mad-action comedy of Michael James and vocal impressions of Paul Boland. Two nights later international recording artist Mark Preston (formerly of The Lettermen) headlined. Finally, another two days later saw Paul Boland listed not only as impressionist but also as "talented singer." In addition, this triple bill starred the a cappella singers called Grand Slam, and another performance by the ship's players. We would be remiss not to also mention that many cruises headline their shows with evenings of "magic," starring talented prestidigitators. This always makes for a fun evening at sea.

➥ **Steve and Pat's Tip:** *When booking an early or late meal seating, keep in mind that there are two shows nightly. All major cruise ships offer an early show at 8:30 P.M. About 10:30 P.M. the same show is repeated for passengers with a late seating. If the nightly 10:30 P.M. show time is too late for you, then book the early seating for meals so you can attend the earlier 8:30 P.M. shows.*

Who are these cruise ship performers? Most are veterans of years in the "lesser stardom" universe. Many have performed as opening acts for headliners in Las Vegas hotels and other cabarets and dinner theater venues throughout the United States. These talented performers are doing what they love best, although star recognition has eluded them. The youngest may some day see their dreams fulfilled. Meanwhile, we benefit from their multifaceted talents. Unless passengers expect to see Siegfried and Roy, David Copperfield, Whitney Houston, or Wayne Newton, few will be disappointed.

Small Disappointments—the Generation Gap

Let us be honest and up-front on this one. We have never played Tommy Dorsey records. The name "Rosie the Riveter" is alien to us. We were babes in our mother's arms when America's "swing generation" was cutting the last of its "rugs." When we think of golden oldies, it's the Everly Brothers, Elvis, Buddy Holly, the Beatles, the Bee Gees, and so on.

Many segments of cruise shows are geared to the ship's major audience, and that audience is often an "older" crowd. This is evidenced by the numerous shipboard shows that feature popular 1940s tunes or vintage Broadway musical selections that date to the 1920s! Of course, shows occasionally offer some newer Broadway musical numbers from blockbusters like *Phantom of the Opera*. Comedians avoid "toilet humor," which gets our thumbs-up! Veteran singers croon sweet and nostalgic standards and often stretch to do a Beatles number! This is the oldest entertainment game in town, called playing to the audience. Not that there is anything wrong with that!

Entertainment Extras for Those Who Want More!

Again, competition and megaship building give us more options. Today's newest and largest ships offer exciting evening entertainment innovations that may just be near the top of many essential amenities lists. Here is our short list of important evening entertainment extra innovations:

Carnival Cruise Line One professional show per evening not enough? Carnival innovates with an additional "daily bonus" midnight cabaret show, usually starring a veteran comedian or other equally talented performer.

Norwegian Cruise Line While other cruise lines offer a medley of Broadway tunes, Norwegian provides a forty-five-minute to an hour, full-scale production of a Broadway show. Long-standing hits such as *Grease, 42nd Street, George M.,* and *The Pirates of Penzance* are always playing.

Princess Cruises The *Grand Princess*, delivers big time! Three different shows in different locations are offered every night. There is a main-room show, a cabaret show, and a Broadway-style musical revue.

Royal Olympic Cruises Offers more intimate cabaret-style seating during its evening shows. This brings audiences closer to the entertainment action.

Passengers Take Their Turn Stage Center

Have some special hidden talent, one that is ready to come out of the closet and be shared with fellow passengers? If so, show time is close at hand! Every cruise offers a lip synching or talent show that stars the passengers. These amateur crowd-pleasing shows are scheduled for a lazy afternoon while at sea. Videotapes of the grand event make a fun remembrance of the cruise.

Avoiding Costly Option, Onboard Activities!

One taboo topic that is never found in cruise brochures is the fact that all-inclusive vacations have "extra costs." Carnival, to its credit, comes closest by mentioning that "On a Fun Ship cruise, one low price covers *just about* everything." And in extreme cases, these extras can cost passengers more than the price of their cruise!

Most passengers do not wish to spend big bucks, perhaps even hundreds of dollars extra per day, during their cruise. Furthermore, most passengers find it hard to imagine spending such extra cash on an all-inclusive vacation. Consider our admittedly "padded" but quite real examples. All these costs are *per person* and should be doubled for a couple:

- How about ten quick sessions of skeet shooting? Ring up $100 on the cruise cash register.
- Want to visit the beauty salon for a makeover? Ring up another $100.
- How about a visit to the nautical spa for a body massage? Ring up $75.
- Ready for casino gambling or bingo? Remember, the house

always wins. This expensive daily activity can be $20 to $100 or more per day.
- Heard about those elegant new shopping arcades? Many passengers enjoy shopping sprees onboard their very own cruise ship. No spending limit here.
- On mass-market cruise lines, alcoholic and nonalcoholic drinks, other than coffee or tea, are optional extras—like $3 for a Coke! On a long, warm, and supremely relaxing day, ring up a poolside drink tab of $25 per day. Then, add another $25 for dinner wine and evening cocktails.

Here is our complete list of optional spending opportunities on a typical cruise vacation:

> Alcoholic beverages at pools, bars, lounges, and discos
> Nonalcoholic beverages, except coffee and tea
> Beverages ordered from room service except coffee and tea
> Wine at dinners
> Spa and beauty salon services: facials, makeovers, hairstyling, massages, etc.
> Bingo
> Onboard photographs (many photos are great!)
> Skeet shooting
> Golf putting green
> Tennis or golf instruction
> Telephone and computer services
> Shore excursions
> Casino gambling
> Shipboard shopping arcades
> Business expenses and services (better left at home)
> Pay for view in-cabin movies

Even we get momentarily depressed reading the above list. Of course, some of these activities or services are fun and reasonable in moderate quantities. World-class opportunities like a seaplane adventure with a landing on a remote Alaskan lake or the famed Alaska Yukon–White Pass railroad ride were great fun. In the tropics, we enjoy scuba diving in crystal clear waters. Vacation pleasures such as these should be enjoyed, even at extra cost! In this regard, let us reiterate that we have no intent on being cruise party poopers. We would not think of recommending what others should or should not do on their very personal cruise vacation.

What we shall do in lighthearted but serious fashion is demonstrate our own version of a very *free* day at sea on any of today's modern cruise ships.

Steve and Pat's *free* "luxury" cruise day at sea:

- Our day starts with early exercise, perhaps a power walk around the ship or a vigorous outdoor aerobic session.
- Next, a sumptuous but reasonable breakfast at the Lido Deck outdoor cafe.
- We dress for poolside sun and fun. Our poolside gear includes a good book, cassette player with music tapes, and large water bottles in bright neon-colored designer holders. We fill the bottles with Crystal Light tropical fruit punch or lemonade. Since the average one-week tropical cruise has only two days at sea, we savor an opportunity to rest and relax in luxurious surroundings. There we are, stretched out poolside on a comfortable chaise lounge and enjoying balmy tropical breezes!
- When roasted and toasted, we take a refreshing dip in a pool.
- Waiters deliver glasses and buckets of free ice.
- It is high noon, and that means it is time to eat lunch! We opt for an outdoor buffet with endless choices and never a check.
- After lunch, we return to our cabin for a short break from the sun. Then we dress and head out for a stroll.
- This day, free ship activities include a tour of the bridge. Other days, passengers may tour the ship's kitchen. Most passengers find these "insider" tours both entertaining and fascinating.
- Other free daily activities are announced in the ship's newsletter. They include a cooking demonstration, dancing lessons, and guest lectures on topics of general interest.

- Later, we don our bathing suits and return to a poolside lounge chair to do nothing at all.
- Late afternoon, we dress and head for a first-run movie in the large-screen cinema.
- On other days we enjoy free outdoor activities such as shuffleboard and Ping-Pong.
- There is always time for late afternoon window shopping in the ship's arcade. This often provides a price comparison for similar items we will "shop" for in the next ports of call.
- Since we have the late dinner seating, at 8:30 P.M., we head for the pizzeria for a snack. Other varieties of snacks are available from our room service menu.
- At 8:30 P.M. it's dinnertime!
- With only moments to rest after an incredible dinner, we head to the showroom for the Las Vegas–style musical review.
- After the show it is time to work off that dinner. We head to the ship's disco, where we dance until midnight.
- Next, we may take in another cabaret show if available, or . . .
- Believe it or not, it is now time for the famed midnight buffet, or . . .
- We may just jump into our bathing suits and lounge in an outdoor Jacuzzi, where we lay back and stare at a myriad of stars.

➡ **Steve and Pat's Free Picnic Lunch Tip:** *We decided to spend our Puerto Vallarta day at a luxury beachfront resort and came up with a great idea. The prior evening, we placed a room service order for fruit, cheeses, and several super club sandwiches for a picnic lunch. The next morning, when the order arrived, we packed a super picnic lunch using our Ziploc bags. If a cabin has a refrigerator, passengers may raid the midnight buffet for the next day's picnic lunch.*

So goes our exhausting day aboard ship without spending a dime! Our example speaks volumes for saving literally hundreds of dollars or more per couple per week! Do we find ourselves toasting our vacation, poolside, with a very real piña colada or two? Of course!

What if this was not a day at sea? Many ports of call permit independent sightseeing, such as a walking tour of the quaint town of Skagway. The dock is only five minutes from the town, so passengers can easily return to the ship for lunch. In Puerto Vallarta we walked to a nearby lavish beachfront resort. All facilities were free. We unpacked and devoured our tasty and very free cruise-ship take-out picnic lunch.

What about nontropical cruises like Alaska? Even in early summer, we found comfortable temperatures that allowed us to enjoy on-deck lounge chairs on bright sunny days. We do recommend against bikinis and warn against jumping into an empty swimming pool.

➥ **Steve and Pat's Drink Tip:** *We emphasize this one, since it can save $100 or more on drink bills. It can also save thousands of calories. Pack a two-quart Tupperware drink container. Include two, one-quart designer water bottles with shoulder straps and some favorite instant drink powders. We use a variety of diet Crystal Light flavors. Stewards and poolside waiters supply glasses and free ice. This allows for great "free" drinks both in the cabin and while lounging at the pool. If the cabin has a refrigerator, so much the better for having quarts of delicious cold drinks at the ready.*

Looking for Exercise? Look No More!

The late great one-liner comedian Henny Youngman might have said, "take my pounds, please." Let's put this another way. If the words *no pain, no gain* have no place in your cruise vocabulary, we cordially invite you to skip this section.

Let's assure you from the outset that we shall not burst anyone's dream-cruise bubble. We shall offer a helpful, upbeat discussion of a topic that is literally near and dear to many passengers' hearts. The average passenger may pay for a week of bingeing on gourmet cruise meals by gaining three to seven pounds or more. There, we've said it. The genie is out of the bottle. This is many passengers' worst cruise nightmare. So, what options have we? Rest assured, there is hope and quite likely enjoyable salvation ahead.

First, we are offering a sincere admission. We are members of a very large and fashionable club—those midlife baby boomers fighting a constant battle of the bulge. The last thing we need is to gain another three to seven or more pounds. We happily report that in recent years the cruise industry has recognized this problem and has taken giant strides to address it. Today's cruise menus offer a variety of health-conscious choices that include gourmet fish, poultry, and even beef entrees. Vegetarian selections are also available on most cruise menus. Those who are satisfied with these wise selections get our vote of approval and a gold star for willpower given the remainder of the menu's gourmet choices.

For the rest of us, we face a dilemma: How to fend off the extra pounds while enjoying one of the great highlights of all cruises, five-course gourmet meals prepared by master chefs? We are not talking about a fattening cheeseburger. We are referring to incredible, one-of-a-kind entrees followed by mind-boggling world-class desserts such as flaming cherries jubilee prepared by expert chefs at the table. Let's face it. We want both guiltless participation and dancing taste buds—the kind of dance that results from whole lobster dripping in seasoned butter sauce and tourenados of beef cut from the finest corn-fed Kansas City beef.

Enough said about food. Here are our best strategies for, as they say, having our cake and eating it. Let us begin with the good news part of our strategy. First, you may enjoy all of the incredible gourmet dinners, from appetizers to flaming desserts, without any limitation. How is that for a strategy?

Another part of our strategy is a strong recommendation in favor of the late meal seating. This comes into play in a big way. Breakfast is served at 8:30 A.M. for passengers with a late seating. There is ample time to start the day with any number of optional calorie-burning activities. How about power walking around the deck while enjoying an invigorating sea breeze? Today, virtually every cruise ship has well-equipped exercise rooms. During an Alaska cruise we enjoyed early morning thirty-minute sessions on a Life-Cycle while viewing Glacier Bay through picture windows. You can also find the latest treadmills, stair climbers, and other modern electronic equipment as well as free weights for the diehards. Our goal is a minimum of thirty minutes, and hopefully one hour, of exercise.

One or both of us often participate in another great optional exercise activity, aerobics. On another cruise, in the Caribbean, the morning's aerobic instructor had been the star of the previous evening's show. She then beat us into the ground with her high-impact aerobic session. Yet, as we felt the calories burning, we knew this was one trade-off we would take to the dinner table. On another cruise we enjoyed aerobics in the open air on the promenade deck under sunny Caribbean skies. A delightful and invigorating experience.

➥ **Steve and Pat's Tip:** *If the morning aerobic class overlaps with the dining room breakfast hours, do not forget that there is always a totally satisfying buffet breakfast served on the promenade deck. Endless selections include delectable healthy choices such as fresh fruit, Egg Beaters, fruit juices, and an array of cereals. Okay, we also grab one slice of crispy bacon! There is a third option: room service will bring breakfast to the cabin.*

After the early morning exercise, one breakfast option is the regular dining room sit-down meal. Often we would rush from our aerobics class to our cabin for a quick change and then onward to the dining room for the regular breakfast. Here, a combination of guilt and good sense come into play with very excellent results. Cruise ship breakfast menu choices are extraordinary and include every opportunity to either fatten up or enjoy a sumptuous but healthy and nourishing meal! Forget bacon, eggs, sausage, and so on. Remember fresh juices, savory smoked salmon, Egg Beaters, cereals of every kind, and much more.

There are many shipboard activities that double as exercise.

How about swimming, basketball, and tennis? There is also shuffleboard and power Ping-Pong.

Our lunchtime strategy is effective and easy. Our rule at sea is to avoid a major sit-down five-course dining room lunch. Lest you think we are exaggerating the sit-down temptation, consider this typical dining room lunch offered by Royal Caribbean: Start with an appetizer of veal dumpling in a pastry shell. Next, ginger chicken soup followed by a tossed romaine lettuce and cucumber salad. Then a hot entree of Viennese veal goulash followed by blueberry custard pie! Need we say anything further? We opt against temptation and in favor of a guaranteed lighter, more gentle midday meal at the open-air lunch buffet or barbecue on deck. There we can select from salads, fruits, grilled chicken, or even a delicious gourmet burger.

As promised, the real reward comes at day's end with a delectable, no-holds-barred, gourmet dinner. Enjoy everything from soup to nuts, including outrageous flaming desserts. Here is another plus: dinner for the late seating ends at 9:45 P.M., so there is little incentive to attack the famous midnight buffet. Actually, on at least one evening during the cruise, it is fun to "window shop" at the marvelous buffet and have a look at the ice sculpture.

How about yet another option, one that is not only fun and effective but improves relationships and literally brings couples closer together in the best possible way? We are talking about dancing. After dinner and the evening show, why not head to the disco, where fun and calorie-burning meet head-on?

Okay, some passengers are in great shape and have little need for any part of our strategy on calorie control. Regardless, many such passengers are hell bent on keeping up with a daily exercise program. Seniors may also wish to participate in a daily exercise regimen. Today's cruise companies are listening. Most modern ships offer extensive exercise and related activity programs that fit many passengers needs. This may take the form of a senior sit-and-stretch class or water exercises. Be sure to scrutinize the daily activity newsletter for new and innovative exercise ideas.

By following these strategies it is easy, if not totally painless, to keep fit while not overindulging on eight meals a day.

Onboard Port of Call Talks That Help and Hinder

As the phrase implies, cruise directors give talks to passengers regarding each upcoming port of call. In fact, their background and extensive knowledge make them perfectly suited for this well-intended task. At such port talks passengers learn almost everything they need to know about Puerto Vallarta, St. Thomas, Juneau, and all other cruise destinations. There are, however, some caveats.

First, consider ports of call background talks. Cruise ship directors usually schedule ports of call talks on the day before arrival at a new port. The group talk is scheduled in the largest auditorium, either the ship's movie theater or showroom. Today, with modern electronics, cruise ships directly transmit the port talks to the cabins via closed circuit TV. Passengers can view the talks from the comfort of their cabins. However, one cannot ask questions from the cabin.

In our case, we share the best of both worlds. One of us remains lounging in the cabin taking in the discussion on TV while the other, the one who drew the short straw, makes a personal appearance and asks any essential questions.

Take this example: before arrival in Puerto Vallarta the ship's cruise director gave a thirty-minute talk. Literally hundreds of passengers packed the showroom to hear the scoop on this ultimate port of call. I was disappointed to hear the speaker describe every product sold at every shop in town while neglecting the beaches, beachfront hotels, and related activities. How could this be, I pondered, when Puerto Vallarta is a well-known tropical vacation resort? Why others did not ask about where we could go to enjoy ourselves remains a mystery.

As I stood in stunned silence, the meeting came to an abrupt end. It was now or never. I asked the question: Where do we go to enjoy a memorable day of sand, surf, fun, and sun? Without hesitation, the cruise director told me to hang a right as we leave the ship. "Then walk a few blocks until you reach several top-notch hotels. They are happy to allow you to use their premises and facilities if you purchase lunch or a couple of drinks."

The result was spectacular. The advice, as simple as it was, brought us to one of the town's finest oceanfront resorts, Puerto Vallarta's Crystal Hotel. We had a fabulous time.

Our second example faults the cruise line, but only indirectly. During a Caribbean cruise we were headed to the port island of Martinique. The ship's shore excursion brochure listed a half-day van exploration of the island, including the rain forest and famed city of St. Pierre, which was destroyed, Pompeii-style, by the eruptions of a nearby volcano. The cost was $40 per person. We checked our handy Caribbean travel guide and followed some very good advice on how to book a "bargain" private day tour using local taxi drivers.

The prior evening we approached a couple with whom we had gone scuba diving earlier in the week. They quickly agreed to tag along so that we had the necessary foursome when it came time to negotiate with the aggressive taxi drivers. Upon departing the ship, we immediately ran into eager taxi drivers, their shiny Mercedes cabs nearby. The brief negotiation saw the drivers' initial price of $35 per person quickly drop to the bargain price of just $20 each, for a hefty 50 percent savings over the cruise ship price. Besides the savings, we enjoyed the air-conditioned Mercedes Benz sedan versus a crowded van.

Of course, the cruise ships discourage any but their own shore excursions. At the port-of-call talk they warned of unreliable vehicles and drivers, and then presented the ultimate well-intended threat: take a private excursion and you may miss the cruise ship's departure. It is one thing to take an old, broken-down Tijuana taxi and quite another to take a gleaming Mercedes sedan. We noted that the ship's half-day tour lasted four hours and made certain our driver knew the exact time to return to the dock.

Our final port-of-calls talk episode indicates how successful independent shore excursions can be. St. Thomas, one of the finest of our U.S. Virgin Islands, was dead ahead. Our handy Caribbean guide discussed and identified the best snorkeling beach on the northern side of the island. Would our cruise director on this Princess Caribbean cruise do better than his counterpart on our aforementioned Mexican River cruise? We are sorry to report a very large *no*! Not one word was mentioned regarding the island's reefs and beaches. Of course, we did learn the name and address of every diamond and jewelry shop on St. Thomas. We must admit that this information appeared to wet the appetites of hordes of passengers who were eager to spend thousands of dollars at diamond and gold discount jewelry shops.

In short order we hailed a taxi and twenty minutes later found ourselves sacked out on the island's finest beach. A few minutes later we were snorkeling and playing with hundreds of beautiful rainbow-colored reef fish.

Let us discuss another and more helpful aspect of cruise port-of-call talks. During these discussions the cruise directors not only recommend local shops but often discuss the cruise ship's guarantee, which covers all the merchandise passengers purchase at these *recommended* shops. Cruise lines have a business relationship with these vendors.

➥ **Steve and Pat's Tip:** *We have found the Arthur Frommer publications on particular cruise ship destinations, such as the Caribbean, to be an excellent specialty source of intense, valuable, and money-saving information. They cover, in great detail, the three essential areas of sightseeing, recreation, and shopping. We recommend them because we are not competing! As always, our specialty is saving you big dollars in many ways before you book and depart on your dream cruise vacation. We also offer unique ways to save big dollars during the cruise vacation.*

On the plus side, the ship's guarantee permits passengers to closely examine their purchases in the comfort of their cabin knowing that the item may be returned later for a refund to the cruise director or other designated person. Perhaps in the crowded rush to purchase an item a passenger failed to notice the chip on a fine piece of porcelain. This is one solid reason to consider cruise-recommended shops. Then consider that these shops are often upscale and charge more than other smaller stores and street vendors. How do cruise ships deliver on their promised guarantees? Sorry, we have yet to take them up on it.

We suggest you discuss the details with the cruise director, including any limitations on the prices of items covered before making a purchase.

Above all, ask questions! The cruise director and other ship's personnel are there to serve and help all passengers. Make certain they perform that job well!

Tipping on the Seventh Day

After a glorious farewell dinner followed by a final Las Vegas–type musical revue there may be time for a final dance under the stars. Or you can enjoy a final midnight champagne toast while soaking in a Jacuzzi under a star-studded sky. A good moment to recall the sights, sounds, and memories of a glorious cruise vacation.

Upon returning to the cabin, you have to begin packing your bags and placing them in the hallway for late-evening retrieval. This is the appropriate time to show appreciation for the role played by the ship's crew in making your vacation a smashing success. Based on our experience and established cruise customs, a typical tipping guideline follows:

> *Waiter: $3 per night*
> *Cabin steward: $3 per night*
> *Busboy: $1.50 per night*
> *Mâitre'd: $1.50 per night*
> *Luggage porters upon arrival and departure: $1.00 per bag (New York, $1.50 per bag)*

Note: On cashless cruises a 15 percent tip is usually added to all bar bills. Also, each cruise line provides its own recommended tipping schedule. Cruise ships provide tipping envelopes in the staterooms. Drop-off instructions for the tip envelopes suggest you return them to the front desk before leaving the ship.

Do some crew members deserve extra tip money? Of course. If a waiter, busboy, or floor steward has provided exceptional service, this should the reflected in his or her tip.

➥ **Steve and Pat's Tip:** *Nowadays, most cruise ships permit tips to be paid by Visa or MasterCard. Here is yet another opportunity to rack up more free travel program miles on a Citibank Visa or other airline-related charge card. If Visa may not be used for tips, some ship's casinos permit a cash payment on a Visa or MasterCard. The transaction, usually for small amounts of cash up to $150, is done as a credit transaction rather than a cash advance so that no interest is charged.*

Tips "Included" and Other Special Tipping Policies

Tips Included Policy This one is easy. None of the major mass-market bargain cruises lines include tipping in the price of their cruise, and this includes Holland America Line.

Tips Not Required Policy If it looks like a dog, walks like a dog, wags its tail like a dog, and barks like a dog, it's a dog! Enter Holland America Line and their advertising hype. HAL states their policy is "no tipping required," and "while tips are appreciated, they are not solicited." We do not get it. No major cruise line "requires" tipping. We are not aware of any cases where waiters, stewards, or busboys solicit tips. We do know that waiters, stewards, and busboys on every mass-market cruise line, including HAL, appreciate the tips they receive.

PART III

A Smorgasbord of the Best Bargain Cruises

9

Cruising Alaska: America's Last Frontier

The major Alaska cruise activity is sightseeing, and we mean *sightseeing!* Two stupendous, seven-night sightseeing cruise routes are available to discover the last of America's frontiers, the Inside Passage–only cruise and the Inside Passage and Gulf of Alaska.

The Inside Passage–only is a round-trip that starts at and returns to Vancouver. Departing Vancouver, the cruise sails north through the Inside Passage, makes three or four stops at various ports of call, views one or two glaciers, and returns to Vancouver.

The Inside Passage and Gulf of Alaska cruise is a one-way trip that can start at Vancouver and travel north or start at Anchorage and travel south. From Vancouver, the cruise sails north through the Inside Passage, hugs the southeastern Alaskan coast, and ends at Seward on the Kenai Peninsula. Then you can view the Alaskan wildlife while traveling across the peninsula by motor coach to Anchorage, and finally fly home from Anchorage. The alternate route is to first fly to Anchorage, motor coach to Seward, and cruise south along the coast to Vancouver.

While both Alaska cruises sail the thousand miles of the Inside Passage, not all itineraries schedule a full day to view Hubbard Glacier or the towering glaciers of Glacier Bay National Park.

> ➥ **Steve and Pat's Tip:** *Make sure to include an up-close visit to one glacier from the ship's decks. If you are lucky, the ice will break off the face of the glacier, making a loud noise like a canon shot, and crash into the water. It is an experience that is never forgotten.*

All cruise itineraries visit three or four ports of call. These ports are either a part of the round-trip loop or the one-way trip up or down the Alaskan coast.

The Gulf of Alaska cruise has an extra benefit in that instead of returning to Vancouver, it continues at the north end of the Inside Passage. This cruise travels the southeastern Gulf of Alaska to the towering giants of ice, such as the Hubbard Glacier, the largest valley glacier in Alaska, and to Prince William Sound, home of the largest collection of glaciers in North America. Before booking your cruise, decide which Alaska itinerary is right for you and how many glaciers you wish to see.

> ➥ **Steve and Pat's Tip:** *If cost is the most important factor, then book a cruise in the low season—early May or late September. Prices can vary as much as $500 to $700 per person. Often the cruise lines offer special deals to fill its empty staterooms.*

Our Alaska cruise on Princess's *Fair Princess* was for an early sailing in May. This fantastic cruise included round-trip airfare from Anchorage and Vancouver to San Francisco for the astounding low price of $849 per person. We saw the ad and booked it. The weather is quite cool at that time of year; however, a medium jacket is sufficient to view the glaciers from the deck of the ship, and a light jacket for exploring the various quaint towns is adequate.

Once the itinerary is chosen, check with the cruise lines and request their onshore Excursions brochure. Do you want to fish for a day, raft down a glacial river, take a train ride, fly in a bush plane, visit native villages, walk on a glacier, view wildlife, shop for native arts and crafts, or explore frontier towns? All these adventures and more are offered.

Most of the escorted excursions include city, village, historical, and glacier tours on foot or by bus. Prices range between $30 and $75 per person. Plane and helicopter rides are pricey and run from $120 to $250 per person. However, no one will ever forget the thrill of gazing out over the pristine beauty of untouched peaks, glaciers, and misty fjords. Consider your budget and choose activities that will add to your lifetime of wonderful travel memories.

Cruise ships offer various types of prearrival shore-excursion lectures. Some ships play videos describing various ports of call and related shore excursions either on the cabin's televisions or in the ship's movie theater. Often before arrival at a new port of call, the shore excursion manager or cruise director arranges a special shore excursion port-and-tour talk. These fun and informative talks will explain the assortment of available shore activities. Valuable information about the ports of call is presented, pointing the way to the best shopping areas, walking tours, and other local activities and attractions. Ask the cruise director if specific activities interest you.

Booking escorted shore excursions Quickly decide which of the ship's shore excursions are right for you. Then be savvy and book them as early as possible within a day or two after embarkation, popular excursions sell out fast. The purser's desk, the front registration desk, or a special shore excursion desk will book the excursions.

➥ **Steve and Pat's Tip:** *The cost of all shore excursions will be added to your ship account. Eventually, when it comes time to pay, use Citibank AAdvantage Visa, MasterCard or another airline credit card and earn hundreds more program miles for your next trip.*

Later, if you find that you must cancel an excursion, most cruise lines allow refunds that are usually subject to a 10 percent cancellation fee. If a tour is canceled within twenty-four hours of arrival in port, there is usually no refund. Some cruise lines offer packages of assorted tours at a reduced price if booked before departure.

Independent shore excursions The least expensive way to tour ports of call involves independent arrangements made upon arrival at port. Before going ashore, check the daily activity bulletin. It may list information concerning local independent excursions. Usually arrangements are easily made at the dock. Local "entrepreneurs" know that passengers prefer paying 50 percent less than the ship's charge for local sightseeing. Local taxis will line up at the dock waiting for the arrival of each new cruise ship.

➥ **Steve and Pat's Tip:** *Ask dining mates or other passengers you have met to join in and split the cost. Keep in mind that local guides will only accept payment in cash or travelers checks, and negotiation is the name of the game. First, agree on the exact sightseeing itinerary and the entire price for the whole party before jumping into the taxi or other private vehicle.*

It is crucial that your driver knows the time you must return to the ship—the ship's deadline. Make sure you return at least an extra hour before it. Some ships require that passengers return one and a-half hours before sailing. Always check the daily bulletin and signs generally posted by the gangplank to confirm the departure time. Remember the rhyme: "Don't be late! Your ship won't wait!"

The Inside Passage–Only Cruise

The extraordinary, **Inside Passage–only** cruise is generally a round-trip journey starting at and returning to Vancouver, B.C.

Vancouver, B.C.

Vancouver is a picturesque, cosmopolitan city with a population of more than one million. It is Canada's third largest city and its most famous seaport. Better yet, it is one fun town to explore, perfect for a second mini-vacation. If time permits, plan to arrive early or stay an extra day or two at the end of the cruise.

> ➥ **Steve and Pat's Tip:** *Because this cruise starts and ends at Vancouver, generally the airfare to and from Vancouver will be cheaper than airfare to and from two different cities—Anchorage and Vancouver—located in two different countries. However, sometimes the cruise lines will negotiate their own package deals with the airlines, so always check those prices too.*

- Enjoy a city sightseeing tour of the famed gaslight district, known as Gastown, Chinatown, and beautiful Stanley Park, with its famous zoo, aquarium, totems, and playground. ($18)
- Visit the botanical gardens in Queen Elizabeth Park, take a tram sky-ride to the top of Grouse Mountain, lunch at its mountaintop restaurant, and more.
- Want to enjoy some great shopping? Check out the Pacific Center Mall and nearby boutiques.

Inside Passage—Ports of Call and Shore Excursions

Board the cruise ship and sail through misty islands and the sparkling fjords of the Inside Passage. Marvel at the snowcapped peaks that encircle them. Green mountains and waterfalls abound as the ship navigates through protected waters in the company of sea lions and humpback whales. You may occasionally see schools of orcas frolicking and speeding through the waves. Bring your binoculars and watch the swooping bald eagles as they dive for fish or perch on the tall pines at water's edge.

Ketchikan

Ketchikan is the first Alaskan town visitors see when cruising north. Set in an expansive rain forest, Ketchikan is known as the Salmon Capital of the World. It is also the world's foremost site of authentic totems. These two features combine to create fascinating possibilities for excursions. The city is on a large island at the base of Deer Mountain.

Shore excursions:

George Inlet Cannery   Tour the cannery and learn about the nuances of the modern salmon-canning business and its colorful history in this area. ($49)

Saxman Native Totem Village   Tour the Saxman Native Village, home to more than 350 Tlinguit, Tsimpsian, and Haida peoples. This park boasts the largest collection of authentic totems. See authentic tribal dances by a native dance group in native costumes. ($43)

Totem Bight Historical Park   Tour Ketchikan by motor coach and visit the park where local artisans are hard at work practicing their native crafts. ($32)

For the adventurous traveler   Those who wish to experience nature in a pristine environment and explore picturesque waterfalls, backcountry, new flora and fauna, rushing creeks, and timeless shorelines should try the following:

- *Hiking the Tongass National Forest:* Explore Preservation Trail and the lush forest. ($45)
- *Jet-boat* to Loring, a small, quaint waterfront village situated on Neha Bay. ($72)
- *Mountain Lake Canoeing:* Travel by bus to a lake in the Tongass National Forest. ($77)
- *Orca Beach Nature Hike:* Hike through a coastal forest to a secluded beach and take a boat ride on a motorized Zodiac raft. ($69)
- *Whiskey Cove Kayaking:* Explore the waterfront to Pennock Island and up Creek Street. ($75)

Salmon Fishing   For a great challenge to land "the big one," enjoy an excursion on a private sportfishing boat that provides all necessary gear. ($176)

Misty Fjord National Monument   Flight-seeing tours in bush floatplanes visit a 2.2-million-acre wilderness area inhabited by mountain goats, Dall sheep, moose, brown and black bears, and bald eagles. Try a seaplane adventure and land on a remote lake or fjord. Then step out on the floats and enjoy the beauty and quiet serenity of this incredible wilderness. Bring those binoculars! ($159)

Juneau

Towering mountains provide a dramatic backdrop for Juneau, considered by many to be the most beautiful state capital in the United States. Juneau is the third largest city in Alaska. Moreover, Juneau has the unique status of being the only U.S. state capital accessible only by plane or boat. There are no roads to Juneau. Juneau sits in the Tongass National Forest with its incredible scenery and unlimited wildlife. Every cruise ship stops at Juneau and gives its passengers most of the day for stunning onshore activities.

Independent shore excursions:

Juneau Walking Tour   The town was built on top of gold mine tailings. Learn about the Gold Rush days while exploring the narrow streets and historic buildings. View the St. Nicholas Orthodox Church and the governor's mansion. History buffs should visit the Juneau-Douglas City Museum, featuring the area's rich gold-mining memorabilia and tales.

Mount Robert's Observatory   From Juneau, take a tramway ride to the Mount Roberts Observatory and Nature Center and enjoy an incredible view of Alaska's beauty ($18). The Nature Center has a live nature show based on locals' experience with the wild animals. The extensive hiking trail system provides a great excuse for enjoying an excellent day in the outdoors either on one's own or with an escorted tour.

Shore excursions:

Gold Creek Salmon Bake   Experience an outdoor salmon, grilled over an open wood fire with all the trimmings. ($25)

Gold Panning Tours   Get hands-on experience panning for gold. Learn about mining operations in Alaska. ($37)

Hike Through a Rain Forest   Take a stroll through the Tongass National Forest to breathtaking views of Glacier Bay. ($53)

Sea kayaking at Auke Bay   Take in a spectacular view of the Mendenhall Glacier from the ocean. Marine life, birds, and wildlife abound. ($73)

Rafting Down the Mendenhall River Exciting but gentle introduction to white-water rafting on glacial melt. Start on the lake, with a great view of the glacier. Go downriver through moderate stretches of rapids. All gear is provided. ($87)

Sportfishing If time permits and you are inclined, try your hand at salmon or fly-fishing. ($155)

Juneau The city offers many flight-seeing tours to the icefields and glaciers and Taku Wilderness Lodge. Have a lunch of freshly grilled Alaskan king salmon. ($168 for three hours)

Mendenhall Glacier by Helicopter Tour Fly to the Mendenhall Glacier or the 1,500-square-mile Juneau Icefield. ($165 for two-and-a-quarter hours)

Sitka

Sitka is one of Alaska's treasures. Russia explored and ruled Alaska before the United States purchased it in 1867. The stunning architecture with a dramatic backdrop of snowcapped mountains shows Sitka's Russian heritage.

Independent shore excursions:

Sitka Walking Tour This should include a visit to St. Michael's Cathedral, a Russian Orthodox church with an impressive collection of gold and silver icons. Shop for Russian-style souvenirs in the historic downtown.

Sitka Hiking Tour For the athletic, plan a three-mile historical walking tour, including the Russian cemetery, blockhouse, Castle Hill, site of the 1876 land transfer to the United States, James Michener's home, Sitka National Historical Park, the site of the 1804 Battle of Alaska, and the Liberty Prospect Mine. Talk to the local inhabitants about the history of the area. Wander through the verdant forest and then walk along the riverside muskeg and loop back to the ship.

Shore excursions:

Sea Kayaking The hardy can join an escorted tour and two-person sea kayak in the protected bays and inlets that surround Sitka. ($75)

Sportfishing Fish for halibut or salmon. Your catch is cleaned and prepared for shipment home. ($160)

Silver Bay Cruise or Sea Otter and Wildlife Quest Cruise with a naturalist either in the bay ($32 for two hours) or up the narrow passages inaccessible to larger vessels ($95 for three hours) and discover the thrill of Alaskan wildlife—sea otters, sea lions, whales, porpoises, and orcas.

Bald Eagle Raptor Center and Historic Sitka Visit the center and learn rescue and survival techniques to save eagles until they are finally released back into the wild. Drive through Sitka on your return to the ship. ($39)

Flight-seeing Tours by Seaplane or Helicopter Flying over the waters surrounding Sitka affords a wondrous range of views, from active marine life and winding fjords to verdant mountains, high alpine lakes, and ice blue glaciers. ($139)

Glacier Bay National Park

This is shipboard sightseeing at its world-class best! Cruise ships devote an entire leisurely day sailing in Glacier Bay, one of the most beautiful waterways in Alaska. This is a 3.3-million-acre national park. The bay claims to have sixteen glaciers, and twelve of them are active. The cruise ship will sail by the face of majestic glaciers that rise like mountains of ice out of the sea. See giant pinnacles of blue glacier ice break off with earsplitting cracks and crash into the quiet bay. On the way to the glaciers, some ships will pick up a park naturalist who will describe over the public address system the various wildlife and species of birds seen from the decks. Watch the seals and sea lions lazily sun themselves on passing ice floes. Arctic terns and tufted puffins fly in circles over the protected bay.

Hubbard Glacier

A few cruise lines offer a stop at Hubbard Glacier rather than Glacier Bay on the round-trip Inside Passage. Other cruise lines alternate between Glacier Bay and Hubbard on the one-way voyage between Vancouver and Seward. Both glaciers are quite spectacular. Make sure your itinerary includes one, up-close glacier experience. At the head of Yakutat Bay lies the Giant Hubbard Glacier, the largest valley glacier in the world. Also in Yakutat Bay is the Malispina Glacier, which is as big as the state of Rhode Island. The cruise ship will slowly cruise through this awesome wonderland. From the deck, see the six-mile-wide face of the Hubbard while huge chunks of blue glacier ice calve and splash into the quiet waters. See trumpeter swans, geese, ducks, and cranes soar effortlessly over the bay. The Yakutat Forelands offer one of the best bird-watching spots in Alaska—truly a wondrous event. Do not miss it!

Sawyer Glacier

Sail through even more remote icefields to the magnificent Sawyer Glacier and watch the ice crash into the water.

➥ **Steve and Pat's Tip:** *Make sure your round-trip includes sailing close to a mighty glacier in Glacier Bay National Park, Hubbard Glacier in Yakutat Bay, or Sawyer Glacier. You will remember a visit to one of these national treasures long after you return home. Some cruise itineraries skip Glacier Bay or Hubbard Glacier and instead visit the old Russian town of Sitka, so check the itineraries carefully.*

Skagway

Situated at the northernmost tip of the Inside Passage, Skagway dates back to the Gold Rush days of Alaska. This town was the jumping-off point for miners on an overland trek to the Yukon.

Independent shore excursions:

Skagway Walking Tour From the docks, go into this quaint frontier town and take a vintage streetcar tour ($35) or walk through the restored historical district. See the landmark Golden North Hotel, the lookout with its view of the awesome Lynn Canal, the Gold Rush graveyard, and the final resting place of the iron horse steam engines of the White Pass and Yukon Rail-

Cruising Alaska

way. Many different tours are available to the numerous old Gold Rush towns, and gold fields and mines in the area.

Shore excursions:

Klondike Gold Rush Trail Camp This is a restored Gold Rush town with antiques, memorabilia, and frontier clothing left by the miners tucked in the mountains at the foot of the historic White Pass. Take a tour. Gold panning is also available. ($33)

➡ **Steve and Pat's Tip:** *The most spectacular view of the snowcapped, saw-toothed mountains are yours on the White Horse and Yukon Railway. Known as the Scenic Railway of the World, its train travels on a narrow-gauge track up to the summit of White Pass. No trip to Alaska is complete without enjoying this adventure. Leave the docks of Skagway behind and board one of the vintage parlor cars. Travel through glorious Alaskan scenery, pass Bridal Veil Falls, Inspiration Point, and Dead Horse Gulch. See the original Klondike Trail of 1898 worn into the rocks. Remain in the train car as it changes course and returns to Skagway. Enjoy an incredible view of the snowcapped mountains and nearby crystal blue waters. ($79)*

Yukon Territory Scenic Drive Travel by tour bus, following the Skagway River Canyon and winding over the summit of White Pass into the Yukon Territory. Pass the shores of Lake Bennett, old Gold Rush mines, and explore the village of Caribou Crossing with lunch at Spirit Lake Lodge before returning. ($74)

Adventurers will enjoy the following:

Horseback riding high up in the Klondike country on the Dyea Plains ($111)
Mountain biking on the Dyea Plains ($63)
Horseback riding through the Chilkat Mountains ($99)
Sportfishing for salmon in lovely Lynn Canal ($155)
Sea kayaking in beautiful Taiya Inlet ($66)

Glacier Bay by Plane Flight-seeing by helicopter or plane over the glacier country around Skagway is breathtaking. Fly by towering mountain peaks and over lush forests. ($125 for one-and-a-half hours)

Fly and Float Tour   Try a flight to Haines and take a float trip through a bald eagle preserve. ($200 for five hours)

The choices are many but expensive.

Haines

This picturesque Gold Rush town is renowned for the famous Chilkat Bald Eagle Preserve in the Chilkat Valley, and it boasts the world's largest concentration of bald eagles.

Independent shore excursions:

Haines Walking Tour   This will include picturesque Fort Seward, the Alaska Indian Arts Center, and the Sheldon Museum and Cultural Center. Check out the unique galleries in downtown Haines.

Shore excursions:

Bald Eagle Preserve and Chilkat Summit   Drive through the preserve and valley area, noting the many eagles. ($52)

Salmon Bake   Located at historic Fort Seward a few steps from the ship. Enjoy a freshly grilled sockeye salmon and barbecued ribs. ($25)

Chilkat Dancers and Salmon Bake   Same as above, plus a performance by native Indian dancers. ($53)

For the adventurous, try one of the following tours through the Chilkat Eagle Preserve while viewing incredible scenery and wildlife: Do not forget your binoculars.

> *Chilkat Lake Boat Tour: Take a boat ride in an open-air pontoon boat. ($59)*
>
> *Jet-boat Tour: Travel into the remote reaches of the upper Chilkat Valley. ($72)*
>
> *Float Trip Through the Eagle Preserve: Float down the river in a raft. ($78)*
>
> *Canoe Trip: Paddle down the valley through the preserve. ($78)*
>
> *Kayaking and Nature Hike: Hike along the beach and then kayak through the Chilkat Valley. ($105)*

The Inside Passage and Gulf of Alaska Cruise

At the northern end of the Inside Passage, the round-trip cruise will turn around and return to Vancouver. An alternative northern itinerary sails further along the Alaskan coast to the mighty titans of Prince William Sound. See the incredible tidewater glaciers of the sound, home to the largest collection of glaciers on the continent. Here lies College Fjord, with its awesome sixteen glaciers flowing down to the quiet waters of the fjord. View the incredible blue ice of the Columbia Glacier, stretching 260 feet tall and for four miles. Some cruise ships stop at Valdez, the "Switzerland of Alaska," while others continue directly to Seward on the Kenai Peninsula. View the Alaskan wildlife while traveling across the peninsula to Anchorage by motor coach, then fly home from Anchorage. Or fly to Anchorage and cruise south, one-way from Seward to Vancouver.

Inside Passage and Gulf of Alaska—
Ports of Call and Shore Excursions

Wrangell

Norwegian Cruise Line schedules an afternoon stop here instead of Ketchikan on their northbound route. The Wrangell–St. Elias National Park is so vast that all our national parks could fit inside its boundaries.

Independent shore excursions:
Excursions include a visit to Chief Shake's tribal house, Petroglyph Beach, rock carvings, and a private museum.

Shore excursions:
Rain Walker Hike   Enjoy an easy walk through a rain forest, surrounding yourself with ferns and mosses beneath majestic trees of a unique ecosystem.

Stikine River by Jet-boat   Jet-boat through the river system to Shakes Lake and the glacier. Zip around the icebergs in a twelve-passenger, covered boat. See the spectacular array of colors of the ice and the water. ($150 for four hours)

Prince William Sound

Cruise into this 15,000-square-mile wonderland of waterways surrounded by peaks that extend far to the horizon. Many rivers of ice flow down to the water. One of the most awesome and active glaciers is the Columbia Glacier. During the warm summer months, many large chunks of ice break off the face of the glacier. Local ferries and tour boats from Valdez sail close to the face, blast the ship's horn until the ice fractures, and great icebergs crash into the water. Listen for the sound of the horns. The icebergs create dangerous waves when they hit the water. Not to worry—cruise ships stay a safe distance from the glacier's face.

As the ship turns into College Fjord, count the sixteen glaciers that end at the water's edge. The glaciers are named for the colleges that financed the Harriman expedition in the late 1800s. Use binoculars to trace the path of the ice flow. Wildlife abounds. Lazy seals and sea lions sleep on the ice islands and meander through the sound. Pull up a deck chair and enjoy the special sight of the breathtaking mountains of ice. Such a magnificent sight is found nowhere else.

Cordova

Norwegian Cruise Line includes this little-known stop for the bird lovers of the world. Cordova is situated on the shores of beautiful Prince William Sound. To the east lies the Copper River Delta, a wetlands home to migrating waterfowl and varieties of shorebirds, once crossed by the copper trains of the Kennicott. As one of Alaska's oldest communities and only accessible by sea and air, the scenery and wildlife will always remain unspoiled and pristine.

Shore excursions:

Child's Glacier and Copper River Tour Travel over the Copper River Highway to a U.S. Forest Service kiosk. Further along view the Scott, Sheridan, and Sherman glaciers. Visit the Copper River Delta Habitat. ($54)

Raft the Sheridan River Hike along the Sheridan Glacier and raft the river back through the Copper Delta (class two and three rapids). ($75 for four hours)

Sea Kayaking   the Orca Inlet ($50 for four-and-a-half hours)

Orca Bay Sportfishing   A maximum of four fishermen take off for four hours of fishing in the waters of Orca Inlet. All gear is provided. ($129 for four hours)

Glacier by Floatplane   Fly from Lake Eyak over Sheridan Glacier, descend over Child's Glacier, and view Wrangell–St. Elias National Park. Follow the Copper River Delta back. ($154 for one-and-a-quarter hours)

Valdez

Surrounded by towering snowcapped mountains, verdant Valdez is called the Switzerland of Alaska. The many hanging gardens with their marvelous waterfalls plunging to the lush flora below bring back memories of the romantic fairy tale pictures of exotic Kashmir. Unfortunately, the tsunami from the 1964 earthquake destroyed the "Old Town" of Valdez. Valdez is basically an oil town, the tanker terminal of the Trans-Alaskan pipeline.

Shore excursions:

Alyeska Marine Terminal   Take a tour of the tanker berths and watch a tanker take on crude oil while a guide explains the pipeline operation. ($29)

Valdez State Marine Park   Cruise through the park and learn about the cycles of Shoup Glacier with its rich bird population, Cliff Gold Mine, and the Gold Creek and Mineral Creek mining operations. ($49)

Thompson Pass and Worthington Glacier   A tour along the Richardson Highway travels through Keystone Canyon, a narrow break in the Chugach Mountains. View the stunning Horsetail Falls and Bridal Veil Falls, which cascades nine hundred feet to the canyon floor. Pass over the summit and continue to Worthington Glacier State Recreation Site. ($39)

Keystone Canyon Raft Trip   The adventurous can take a thrilling, four-mile river-raft trip back down through Keystone Canyon to the Lowe River Valley. ($69)

Sea Kayaking   Is available through the Valdez Duck Flats, with its variety of bird life, and Mineral Creek Islands, where you can explore for harbor seals, sea otters, and other marine life.

Columbia Glacier by Helicopter Flightseeing by helicopter is incredible. Fly over Prince William Sound, the steep blue face of the Columbia Glacier and Chugach Mountains, and onto Shoup Glacier. ($189 for one-and-a-half hours)

Glaciers by Floatplane Fly a similar route and land in the water next to the Columbia Glacier, offering a close-up view of marine life. ($145 for one-and-a-quarter hours)

Seward

Situated at the tip of the Kenai Peninsula, Seward's deep harbor allows cruise ship passengers to disembark. The motor coach trip to Anchorage along the peninsula offers a wonderful chance to get a look at and photograph Alaskan wildlife.

Shore excursions:

Alaska Sealife Center If time permits, interactive exhibits, habitats designed above and below the waves, and hourly discovery programs provide a unique perspective on the sea. ($12.50)

Kenai Fjords If time permits, take a local cruise through the Kenai Fjord to Resurrection Bay and learn about the history of the bay during World War II. ($59 for three-and-a-half hours)

Portage Glacier Cruise Take a side trip and visit Portage Glacier and then continue to Anchorage. ($26 for one hour)

Anchorage

A bustling town and the largest in Alaska, Anchorage is a melting pot of Indians, Eskimos, and Aluets. Surrounded by the Chugach Mountains and warmed by the Japan Current, Anchorage always has mild temperatures during the summer. On a clear day, you may see all the way to Mt. McKinley. Stretch your vacation if there is time before your flight, or stay an extra day postcruise.

Shore excursions:

Anchorage City Tour If time permits, tour Alaska's largest city. Visit the Anchorage Museum of History and Art, the Alaskan Aviation Heritage Museum, and the Imaginarium. ($23 for three hours)

Chugach Mountains and Matanuska Valley Explore and enjoy the incredible scenery.

Alaskan Cruise Lines and Discount Prices

The Alaskan cruise market has exploded over the past five years. The increased number of even larger ships gives *Cheapskate* vacationers more choices than ever before. More than forty different cruise ships, large and small, will cruise Alaska in 1998 and 1999. Choices abound.

Today's ships offer great food, comfortable staterooms, generous public quarters, and four-star services. Pampering is compulsory on every vessel. Larger ships offer elegant dining rooms, bars, theaters, casinos, swimming pools, and fitness centers.

Our selection of six cruise lines include the largest vessels, and we will provide crucial information to help you pick the right ship for you and your family at the best available price. Basically, we are evaluating seven-night cruises, including the round-trip Inside Passage variety and the one-way north and south Inside Passage and Gulf of Alaska cruise. We will mention special cruises and a few longer cruises as well.

Alaskan Discount Prices

It is a happy fact of cruise travel life that today's discount and sale prices are often matched with similar and even lower prices next month and next year! Our listing of prices and special air-and-cruise deals is a guidepost to the dirt-cheap prices you may expect to pay when you decide to book a dream cruise in the future.

Our listed prices include inside cabins with two lower beds and all port charges. Many prices are "exclusive" from the mentioned cruise-only or "cruise-mostly" agency. Call these agencies for their best current deals.

Sometimes we indicate that prices were advertised directly by cruise lines. These prices can be further reduced by using our strategies for free vacation cash, cash-in-your-pocket deals, and booking with rebate agencies. Before booking your cruise, review all of the strategies in chapters 2 and 4. Other cruise-only agencies, listed in chapter 5, may meet or even beat the following prices. Shop for the best price and you will soon find yourself embarking on a cheapskate-priced dream Alaska cruise!

↪ **Steve and Pat's Tip:** *In this and following chapters, keep in mind that Carnival's lowest category cabins have bunk beds. Add about $100 to upgrade to a two-lower-bed cabin. Celebrity, Princess, Royal Caribbean, and Holland America ships have only two-lower-bed cabins. The Norwegian fleet, with the exception of the* Norwegian Sea, *have two-lower-bed cabins. Costa cruise ships, except for the* Romantica *and* Victoria, *also have only two-lower-bed cabins. On Premier cruises, add $50 for a two-lower-bed cabin.*

Carnival Cruise Line

In 1998, Carnival decided to join the other cruise lines and placed the 1,500-passenger *Jubilee* on the Alaskan route. The Inside Passage and Gulf of Alaska, the north and south one-way route between Vancouver and Seward, is Carnival's only current itinerary. The northbound itinerary and ports of call include Vancouver, cruising the Inside Passage, Ketchikan, Juneau, Skagway, Sitka, Prince William Sound with College Fjord and Columbia Glacier, Seward, and Anchorage. The southbound itinerary and ports of call include Anchorage, Seward, Prince William Sound with College Fiord and Columbia Glacier, Valdez, Hubbard Glacier, Skagway, Juneau, Ketchikan, Inside Passage cruising, and Vancouver. Either itinerary is great, since both visit Prince William Sound. The main choice is between Sitka (northbound) or Hubbard Glacier in Yukatat Bay (southbound). If your motto is the more glaciers the better, then take the southbound route. Carnival scheduled twenty cruises for 1998.

Carnival's *Jubilee* is a Fun Ship that previously sailed the Mexican Riviera and now spends summers in Alaska. The *Jubilee* offers Las Vegas–style shows, disco dancing till 3:00 A.M., a nightclub with live dance music, a casino, and casino bar, and Nautical Spa resort facilities with gym. Late night entertainment that lasts until 1:30 A.M. is diverse and plentiful. With the addition of this cruise route to Carnival's roaster, Carnival is testing the Alaskan market. Generally Alaska cruises attract an older population. Since Carnival typically markets to an under-forty crowd, this ship will have wider appeal than most other cruise lines. If you are under forty, this cruise is definitely for you. However, if you are looking for more formality and ultimate gourmet food you will likely do better on another cruise ship.

The *Jubilee* offers international cuisine plus a midnight buffet. Camp Carnival, with supervised childrens' activities and an electronic game room, keep the kids busy. (See Chapter 1 for more information on cruising with kids.) Note: The ship has Italian officers and a friendly international staff.

Carnival is the giant in the cruise industry, and three out of every ten passengers will be on a Carnival ship. However, this does not necessarily suggest that the cruise price will be the cheapest. In 1998, Carnival only had one ship sailing the Alaska itinerary. In the future, more sailings may be available than the initial twenty in 1998.

Discount prices Travel of America offered May and September departures on the *Jubilee* priced at $849, including port charges, and only $150 extra for an outside cabin. Summer sailings were priced at $1,149. Call Travel of America at (800) 228-8843. Also, review Chapter 4 for additional savings. Check with Pearson Travel and other discount and rebate agencies.

Celebrity Cruises

Celebrity continues to offer some of the best cruise bargains. This is the cruise line that many consider to be hundreds of dollars underpriced for the top-notch luxury cruises it delivers. Two sister ships, the *Mercury* and the *Galaxy*, with 1,870 passengers each, sail seven-night cruises. The *Galaxy* sails the round-trip Inside Passage, starting and ending at Vancouver, and includes either a stop at Glacier Bay or Hubbard Glacier, Skagway, Haines, Juneau, and Ketchikan. *Mercury* primarily travels the one-way, Vancouver-to-Anchorage route—the Inside Passage and Gulf of Alaska cruise. Only a few routes stop at Prince William Sound (College Fjord and Columbia Glacier) and Hubbard Glacier. Other ports are Ketchikan, Juneau, Skagway, and Valdez. See the most spectacular glaciers on this route. The alternate route includes Hubbard Glacier, Juneau, Skagway, Sitka, and Ketchikan, or Hubbard Glacier, Juneau, Skagway, Glacier Bay, and Ketchikan.

Both ships have two indoor pools, one of which is covered by an incredible megadome of glass that slides open and closed. There are three outdoor pools, and AquaSpa with state-of-the-art exercise equipment, casinos, casino bar, gala stage productions, and an outdoor cafe with an omelette chef. The *New York Post* calls Celebrity's food "spectacular ... from sumptuous breakfasts to nightly midnight buffets."

On every ship children have their own Clubhouse, especially designed for their activities. Twenty-four-hour sitting is available on most ships.

Discount prices Time to Travel, a cruise specialty agency, offers May and September sailings on the *Galaxy*'s Inside Passage seven-night cruise, priced at $1,104, including port charges. They also offer May and September seven-night Inside Passage sailings on the new *Mercury*, priced at $1,042, including port charges. Call Time to Travel at (800) 524-3300. On selected sailings, the third and fourth person can sail for just $349 per person. Cruise World, another specialty agency, offers seven-night Inside Passage cruises on the *Galaxy*, priced at $999, including port charges. Call CruiseWorld at (800) 588-7447.

The absolutely best bargain is the *Galaxy*'s last sail of the season repositioning cruise in late September, with the following itinerary: leaves Vancouver, sails the Inside Passage, views Glacier Bay, Juneau, spends a day at sea, stops at Victoria, B.C., spends a day at sea traveling down the Washington and Oregon coast, and disembarks at San Francisco. Space is limited, but the price is a low $799, including port charges. Book through Ethan Allen Travel at (650) 348-5115, or Whole World of Travel at (800) 458-3636.

Cruising Alaska

Holland America Line (HAL)

In 1989, Carnival Cruise Line purchased HAL. However, HAL continues to be run as an independent entity, since its sales are aimed at a different segment of the cruise market. Where Carnival markets Fun Ships, HAL might market its vessels as "Mature Ships." This is our way of emphasizing that HAL's elegant, slower, and more formal pace appeals more to the mature over-fifty crowd. Those looking for a dance-till-dawn party ship had best try the *Jubilee*.

HAL rules the Alaskan cruise market by offering the largest number of sailings on six ships, with a choice of 120 seven-night cruise dates. Although the ships are constantly shuffled between locations, six ships typically sail the Alaskan waters during the summer months. Five of the ships, the two smaller sister ships, the *Nieuw Amsterdam* and *Noordam*, and the three larger sister ships, the *Maasdam*, *Ryndam*, and *Statendam*, carry approximately 1,300 passengers each.

The sixth ship, the *Westerdam*, built in 1986, was purchased by HAL in 1988. It was remodeled and expanded to hold 1,500 passengers and is a ship of *grand* design. The ship has two pools, a retractable dome, spa, casino, and international cuisine.

All ships have British or Dutch officers and a service crew of Filipinos and Indonesians. The sister ships *Nieuw Amsterdam* and *Noordam* have been refurbished. They now match the quality of the larger ships and offer a more intimate cruise environment. Both have pools with a retractable glass dome like the Celebrity ships the *Mercury* and the *Galaxy*. Although HAL's ships were built in the 1980s and '90s, their design, accommodations, and amenities provide one of the best cruise experiences in Alaska.

The one-week, round-trip Inside Passage cruise leaves Vancouver, B.C., sails the Inside Passage, continues to Juneau, Skagway, Glacier Bay, and Ketchikan, and returns to Vancouver. The schedule is very accommodating. HAL has three ships, the *Maasdam*, *Nieuw Amsterdam*, and *Westerdam*, leaving on different days during the week, i.e., Mondays, Thursdays, and Saturdays, respectively, for the duration of the summer sailings.

Discount prices The absolute best deal is the *Nieuw Amsterdam* cruise marketed by Whole World of Travel. In 1998, HAL had four sailings that included airfare from select cities for the low price of $1,079, including port charges. Call (800) 458-3636. CruiseWorld sells Holland America's seven-day Alaska cruises, priced at $950, including port charges. Call (800) 588-7447. Costco Travel sells these cruises priced at $951, including port charges. Call Costco Travel at (800) 800-8505.

HAL's Inside Passage and Gulf of Alaska (Glacier Discovery) Cruise is a seven-day cruise between Vancouver and Anchorage through the Inside Passage. The cruise offers three ports of call: Ketchikan, Juneau, and Sitka. The two itineraries include two glacier viewings: College Fjord and Hubbard Glacier or College Fjord and Glacier Bay. Again, the three ships, *Noordam*, *Ryndam*, and *Statendam*, sail on Fridays, Sundays, and Sundays, respectively, throughout the summer season.

Discount prices The *Noordam*, which has no casino, advertised its seven-night Alaska cruise priced at $898, including port charges. Call Pearson Travel for the latest HAL specials at (800) 336-1066. Costco Travel offers the September sailing on the *Ryndam* priced at $1,001, including port charges. The *Ryndam* offers its last sail of the season, in mid September, priced at $806.

Travelers Advantage offered sailings at $993, including port charges, and a free cabin upgrade. See Chapter 4 for information on joining Travelers Advantage.

Norwegian Cruise Line (NCL)

NCL has two ships cruising Alaska, the *Norwegian Wind* and the *Norwegian Dynasty*. Each is dedicated to one cruise itinerary.

During the summer, the *Norwegian Wind*, sails the round-trip, Inside Passage from Vancouver. NCL recently stretched this medium-sized ship and remodeled it. However, it still holds fewer passengers than most ships her size. Lounges, showrooms, and the casino are grandly scaled, and the decks are extra wide. Staterooms are roomier, and 85 percent are outside cabins with a floor-to-ceiling window for an incredible view. The Inside Passage itinerary embarks from Vancouver, Juneau, Skagway,

Haines, Glacier Bay, Ketchikan, and then returns to Vancouver. Several sailings do change their itinerary and substitute Sawyer Glacier for Glacier Bay.

The *Norwegian Dynasty* sails the Inside Passage and the Gulf of Alaska route from May through September. NCL recently acquired this small, cozy ship in the fall of 1997. It only carries eight hundred passengers. However, all amenities are available, such as TV with CNN, one pleasant main dining room, an alternative dining cafe, a nightclub with live music, a swimming pool, hot tubs, and fitness center. The cruise is one-way, north or south, from Vancouver or Anchorage/Seward, and sails the following route: Inside Passage, Wrangell or Ketchikan, Juneau, Skagway, Hubbard Glacier and Yakutat, Prince William Sound, Cordova, and Anchorage.

Discount prices Travel of America offers these cruises at super-bargain rates. Both cruises are priced at $895, including port charges, for mid-May sailings. The lowest prices for an inside cabin during the low season in early May start at $938, including port charges.

Princess Cruises

Princess Cruises pioneered luxury cruising to Alaska almost thirty years ago. Today, Princess is still leading the way, with "Grand Class" cruises and tours. There are over one hundred cruises from which to choose. Like Holland America, Princess Cruises has designed cruise tours that combine cruising with a land package of three days or more. However, these packages are expensive, so shop well before booking a combo tour.

Princess has five ships that cruise the Alaskan waters with a seven-night itinerary. One ship, the *Island Princess*, offers ten- and eleven-day cruises.

Two ships, the *Dawn Princess* and the *Sun Princess*, are sister ships and members of the Grand Class, carrying 2,000 passengers and weighing seventy-seven tons. Each ship has over four hundred private balconies, five different dining areas, including two intimate dining rooms a twenty-four-hour food court, a fitness center and spa, a sports deck for athletics, and a child's Fun

Zone. Both have one indoor pool, three outdoor pools, and a wraparound promenade deck for great viewing.

The *Crown Princess* and the *Regal Princess* are also sister ships, designed by the French architect Renzo Piano, known for his famed design of the Pompidou Center in Paris. The ships mimic the curvaceous silhouette of a dolphin, carry 1,600 passengers, and weigh seventy tons. Each ship has over 180 staterooms with private balconies, teak decks with two pools, an in-pool bar, an intimate wine and caviar bar, a coffee and pastry cafe, a teen and youth center, and a million-dollar art collection.

The smallest ship, the *Sky Princess*, carries 1,200 passengers and weighs forty-six tons. The ship was previously the *Fairsky*, built in 1984 and refurbished in 1992. Its amenities include two lavish dining rooms, a pizzeria, three pools plus a kid's pool, the Horizon Lounge, with floor to ceiling windows for great viewing, a jogging track, a teen and youth center, a spa and fitness center, and a casino. For a more intimate, uncrowded cruise with elegant appointments, this ship fits the bill.

Only one ship, the *Regal Princess*, offers a seven-day, round-trip cruise from Vancouver through the Inside Passage. The cruise starts at Vancouver, sails the Inside Passage, Juneau, Skagway, Glacier Bay, and Sitka, and then returns to Vancouver.

The primary itinerary for the other four ships is the seven-day, one-way Inside Passage and Gulf of Alaska, north or south, from Vancouver to Anchorage/Seward or the reverse route. The *Dawn Princess*, the *Sun Princess*, and the *Crown Princess* offer the following itinerary: Vancouver, sailing the Inside Passage, Ketchikan, Juneau, Skagway, Glacier Bay, College Fjord, and Anchorage. The *Sky Princess* has an identical itinerary, except that the *Sky* substitutes Hubbard Glacier for Glacier Bay.

If a longer cruise is an option, take the *Island Princess*, the renown "Love Boat" of television fame. This is the smallest of the six ships plying Alaskan waters, with only 640 passengers, built in 1971 and renovated in 1994. The ten- and eleven-day itinerary sails one-way north or south with a cruise route that starts at Vancouver, sails the Inside Passage, continues to Ketchikan, Sitka, Skagway, Juneau, Hubbard Glacier, College Fjord, Seward, Kodiak, Homer, and Anchorage.

Cruising Alaska

Discount Prices   Golden Bear Travel offered a July sailing on the *Crown Princess* at $799. Call (800) 551-1000. Ambassador Tours offered September sailings on the *Sky Princess* ($850) and the Grand Class *Dawn Princess* ($875), including port charges. Princess Cruises advertised June 1998 sailings of the *Crown Princess* and Grand Class *Sun Princess* at $799 and $899, respectively. See chapter 4 for details on this and other cost cutting strategies. Cruise Value Center offers a May *Sky Princess* sailing for $721 and the *Crown Princess* for $821, including port charges. Call for their super-discount prices: (800) 231-7447.

Royal Caribbean International (RCI)

Two ships, the *Legend of the Seas* and the *Rhapsody of the Seas*, offer thirty-five cruises with two different seven-night, round-trip Inside Passage itineraries from Vancouver from May through mid-September.

➥ **Steve and Pat's Tip:**   *In the case of Alaska cruises, airfare can be an expensive add-on. In Chapter 2, we invite readers to enjoy free air travel by using the American AAdvantage program. Just 25,000 miles entitles members to a round-trip ticket from any U.S. city to Vancouver, or two one-way tickets to and from Vancouver and Anchorage. This can cut the cost of an Alaska cruise by $1,000 per couple! The many other strategies set forth in Part I, from using free travel cash to discount and rebate travel agencies, can further reduce the cost of a fabulous Alaska cruise vacation.*

The *Legend of the Seas* is a recent addition to RCI's fleet, with a great design and amenities. Passenger capacity is 1,800. The two-story dining room has floor-to-ceiling windows for spectacular viewing. There is a miniature, eighteen-hole golf course, a retractable glass canopy over the spa and pool area, a fitness center with aerobic classes, a casino, and over 450 staterooms with private balconies. All lower twin beds convert into a queen-sized bed. Here is RCI's itinerary: leave Vancouver, sail the

Inside Passage, Glacier Bay or Hubbard Glacier, Skagway, Haines, Juneau, Ketchikan, Misty Fjord, and end at Vancouver. Cruises depart Sunday.

The *Rhapsody of the Seas* is the flagship of RCI and entered into service in 1997. This is another ship in the Grand Class tradition, carrying 2,000 passengers and of a design similar to the *Legend* but lacking a miniature golf course. The itinerary for the round-trip starts at Vancouver, sails the Inside Passage, Juneau, Skagway, Haines, Hubbard Glacier or Glacier Bay, Ketchikan, and ends at Vancouver.

➡ **Steve and Pat's Best Deal Goal:** *In June 1998, Princess Cruises advertised sailings of the* Crown Princess *and Grand Class* Sun Princess *at $799 and $899, respectively.*

Discount prices Travel of America advertised May, June, and September sailings on both ships starting at $1,179 for double upgraded cabins. Call (800) 228-8843. CruiseOne offers seven-night RCI cruises at $999, plus port charges. Call (888) 703-7245. Time to Travel advertised great deals for the summer sailings of the *Legend*, starting at $1,094, including port charges. *Rhapsody of the Seas* prices start at $1,044. Call (800) 524-3300. Whole World of Travel has advertised prices from $1,044. Call (800) 458-3636.

10

The Caribbean: A Tropical Delight

The allure of a Caribbean cruise is undeniable. The warm sunshine, endless beaches, swaying palm trees, and sparkling waters beckon all. Few other destinations offer such opportunities for relaxation and thrilling recreational activities among a variety of exotic ports of call. The Caribbean stretches from the Bahamas in the north, which lie just off the coast of Florida, to Venezuela, in South America, to the south. From east to west, it reaches from Barbados to Belize. It is made up of more than thirty island nations with a long history of peaceful coexistence. There is a wealth of cultures—African, Ameridinian, British, Chinese, Dutch, East Indian, French, Mexican, Spanish, and many others that blend with the Caribbean's natural beauty. The result is food, drink, colorful art, exciting music and dancing, romantic history, and exciting sports that are distinctively Caribbean.

Hundreds of islands dot the crystal blue, warm waters of this quiet sea. Each island offers its own unique charm. Some islands are natural, untamed, and lush, while others offer sophisticated cities and cuisine. Many of these independent Caribbean islands that were formerly colonial possessions retain their European flavor, language, and culture, making them all the more enticing to visitors.

As you can imagine, there are tough choices to make when deciding where to cruise in the Caribbean.

Three Fantastic Itineraries—Western, Eastern, and Southern Caribbean

Three marvelous, seven-night, cruise itineraries are available to explore the diverse wonders of the Caribbean—the southern, eastern, and western routes. Each offers a unique assortment of islands and ports of call and is packed with fun-filled opportunities to sun, sightsee, and shop to your heart's content. Take a look at any map of the Caribbean and you will quickly see that it is easily divided into three geographical sections.

The Western Caribbean

This area is the easiest to find first, since everyone knows that Cuba is ninety miles south of Miami. The typical western route is a big circle around Cuba. Cruise ships generally embark on a round-trip cruise from Fort Lauderdale or Miami, Florida, sail around Cuba, and make port-of-call stops at Cozumel, Grand Cayman Island, and Ocho Rios or Montego Bay in Jamaica. The cruise ships typically spend three days at sea and three days visiting ports of call.

The Eastern Caribbean

This is a straight finger-shaped route, stretching southeasterly from Florida through the Bahamas and stopping at the U.S. Virgin Islands. Generally the ships embark on round-trip cruises from Fort Lauderdale and Miami, stop at Nassau in the Bahamas, and continue on to the U.S. Virgin Islands—St. Thomas and St. John. Often St. Maarten/St. Martin and San Juan, Puerto Rico are included since they are on the same latitude and make for easy substitute ports of call. Information on St. Maarten/St. Martin are in the "Southern Caribbean" section. The cruise ships typically spend four days at sea and only two days visiting ports of call.

The Southern Caribbean

Our favorite and recommended Caribbean itinerary includes the semicircle of islands laying southeast of San Juan, Puerto Rico, and pointing toward South America. Nearly all ships embark on these round-trip cruises from San Juan. One port of call common to all the cruises is St. Thomas in the U.S. Virgin Islands. Other ports of call vary from cruise to cruise. The most common stops are St. Maarten/St. Martin, Martinique, and Barbados. Antigua, St. Lucia, and Grenada, the farthest point south, are popular alternate choices. The cruise ships typically spend one day at sea and a whopping five days visiting ports of call.

A South American version of the southern route is offered by two cruise lines. Instead of sailing down and back up the semicircle of islands to Puerto Rico, the itinerary becomes a circle. The ships embark round-trip from Aruba, San Juan, Puerto Rico, or Santa Domingo, Dominican Republic. All ships visit the U.S. Virgin Islands and a second area island before sailing south to Venezuela and west to Aruba and Curaçao. The cruise ships typically spend one or two days at sea and five or four days visiting ports of call.

> ↠ **Steve and Pat's Pricing Tip:** *At the conclusion of this chapter, we quote discount prices for many cruise lines and provide contact phone numbers for the latest available deals. However, comparison shopping between rebate and discount companies like Pearson Travel, and others mentioned in Chapter 4 are essential before booking the cruise! Review Chapter 2 for our best advice on obtaining either free travel to any departure city or island, or reducing the cost of air travel by 50 percent using a free companion ticket. Also, whenever a cruise and airfare are purchased, available free travel cash may be used.*

The only drawback to southern cruises is the additional airfare necessary to fly to the more distant ports of embarkation, i.e., San Juan or Santo Domingo. This can range between $100 to

$250 extra per person over the cost of travel from most mainland U.S. departure cities, such as Miami. Always check the cruise lines special low group air fares, which may just save the day. This is especially true when air-and-cruise packages are available.

Spring, Summer, Fall, or Winter—Timing is Everything

Now comes the tricky part. Not all itineraries are available year-round on all cruise lines. Carnival and Royal Caribbean International (RCI) offer the greatest number of year-round cruises in the Caribbean. Carnival has six ships that sail all three itineraries, the *Celebration, Destiny, Fascination, Imagination, Inspiration,* and *Sensation.* RCI has three ships, the *Grandeur of the Seas,* the *Majesty of the Seas,* and the *Monarch of the Seas,* and each is dedicated to one route.

Commodore, Holland America, Norwegian Cruise Line, and Premier each offers one year-round itinerary from ports other than Florida or Puerto Rico. Commodore's *Enchanted Isles* leaves from New Orleans, Louisiana, and sails the eastern route. HAL's *Noordam* sails from Tampa, Florida, and sails the western route. NCL's *Norwegian Star* leaves from Houston, Texas, and sails the eastern, or Texas, route. Premier's *Seawind Crown* leaves from Aruba and sails the southern alternate route. Premier's *Island Breeze* leaves from Santa Domingo, Dominican Republic, and sails the southern route.

High and Low Seasons

Most of the ships spend the fall and winter months, October through April, in the Caribbean. During the summer months, from May through September, many ships leave the Caribbean and travel to the Mediterranean and Europe or through the Panama Canal and up the Mexican Riviera to Alaska or Hawaii. Cruise lines appropriately market their Caribbean cruises as tropical vacation escapes from cold and wet winter climates. Such tropical cruise getaways especially appeal to residents of the northern United States, Great Britain, and Europe.

➥ **Steve and Pat's Tip:** *If cost is the most important factor to consider, then book a cruise in the summer and fall low season rather than the high season that runs from Christmas though the spring. The difference in prices between low and high season can vary as much as $200 to $300 per person. Often the cruise lines offer special deals to fill its empty staterooms and may include low-cost or free airfare. However, not all cruise itineraries are available during the low season on all cruise lines. Some juggling and compromising may be necessary. Is there anything wrong in leaving a hot sweltering Chicago or New York City for a fabulous low-season tropical cruise vacation? No way!*

Shore Excursions

Want to know more about several different itineraries? See our Appendixes for contact phone numbers. Then check with the cruise lines and request their shore excursions brochures. As you review the various brochures, ask the following: Do you want to experience great snorkeling, fantastic drift scuba diving, sail a catamaran, take a helicopter flight over a rain forest, visit world-famous Mayan ruins, shop for local handicrafts, relax on a beautiful beach, view a wildlife sanctuary, shop for jewelry and precious stones, or see a Pompeii-like city that was destroyed by an island volcano? All these adventures and more are available collectively on the various Caribbean itineraries. Reviewing these brochures may just help to tip the scale when making the decision on which itinerary is best for you.

When it comes to the expense of a shore excursion, keep in mind that small Caribbean islands with their quaint towns are easy to explore. They offer great opportunities for low or even no-cost independent walking and shopping tours. On the other hand, ship-escorted excursions include city historical and shopping tours at virtually every port of call. Prices range between $15 and $35 per person. Plane and helicopter rides are the most costly form of "above shore" excursions, and are priced at $70 to $200 per person. The latter refers to an excursion from Cozumel, a thrilling air flight and tour to the Mayan ruins of

Chichen Itza. Review your budget before you book your cruise, then choose affordable activities that will add to your lifetime of wonderful travel memories.

Cruise ships offer various types of prearrival shore excursion lectures. Some ships play videos describing various ports of call and related shore excursions either on the cabin's televisions or in the ship's movie theater. Often before arrival at a new port of call, the shore excursion manager or cruise director arranges a special shore excursion port-and-tour talk. These fun and informative talks explain the assortment of available shore activities. Valuable information about the ports of call is presented, pointing the way to the best shopping areas, walking tours, and other local activities and attractions. If specific activities interest you, ask the cruise director about them.

Booking Escorted Shore Excursions

Quickly decide which of the ship's shore excursions are right for you. Then be savvy and book them as early as possible within a day or two after embarkation, especially the plane ride to Chichen Itza. Popular shore excursions sell out fast. The purser's desk, the front registration desk, or a special shore excursion desk will book the shore excursions.

➥ **Steve and Pat's Tip:** *The cost of all shore excursions will be added to your ship account. Eventually, when it comes time to pay, use Citibank AAdvantage Visa, MasterCard, or another free airline credit card and earn hundreds more program miles for future free air travel.*

Later, if you find that you must cancel an excursion, most cruise lines allow refunds that are usually subject to a 10 percent cancellation fee. If a passenger cancels a tour less than twenty-four hours of arrival in port, there is usually no refund.

Independent Shore Excursions

The least expensive way to tour ports of call involves independent arrangements made upon arrival at port. Before going ashore, check the daily activity bulletin. It may list information concerning local independent excursions. Usually arrangements are easily made at the dock, especially if your goal is a day at an incredible, white powdery beach. Local taxis will line up at the dock waiting for the arrival of each new cruise ship. We recommend the purchase of an in-depth Caribbean vacation guide that devotes hundreds of pages to all the various island ports of call. Be certain the guide discusses those islands of greatest interest to you in sufficient detail. For example, are there good descriptions and maps for free walking tours?

Seven-Day Western Caribbean Cruises

A western Caribbean cruise offers a varied but limited number of ports of call. Typically all cruises leave from Miami, Fort Lauderdale, or Tampa, Florida, or New Orleans, Louisiana. Those living on the East Coast have access to dirt-cheap airfares to Florida departure cities. In general, domestic U.S. airfares to these cities are far less costly than airfares to southern Caribbean departure cities such as San Juan, Puerto Rico. Western Caribbean itineraries usually include three days at sea with three ports of call.

➥ **Steve and Pat's Tip:** *Three days at sea allows plenty of time for shipboard sun, fun, and relaxation. This is the perfect cruise for those wishing to avoid the busy, island-hopping schedule of the southern route. However, if four days at sea sounds even better, read the eastern Caribbean cruise section for the most restful cruises of all.*

The Mayan ruins of Mexico's Yucatán peninsula are the main attraction for the western cruise. Recent archeological explorations date the artifacts of the Mayan religion as far back as 8000 B.C. They combine relaxed days at sea with a choice of three Mayan sites to explore on the peninsula: the walled city of Tulum and Coba on the coast and the incredible, restored city of Chichen Itza in the interior. If you cannot make it to Egypt for a tour of the great Pyramids, a visit to Tulum or Chichen Itza may be the next best thing. The island of Cozumel has one Mayan site in the interior of the island. This Cozumel site is not nearly as intact, extensive, and world-class as Tulum or Chichen Itza.

The second attraction is the fantastic opportunity to enjoy world-class scuba diving and great snorkeling. The western route includes great diving sites such as "the Wall" and Palancar Reef at Cozumel, and the Grand Cayman with its colorful reefs teaming with tropical fish. This cruise is popular with veteran snorkelers and scuba divers who want to try drift diving.

➥ **Steve and Pat's Tip:** *This itinerary emphasizes rest and relaxation. If duty-free shopping for high-ticket items such as jewelry is your goal, then check the eastern and southern routes. Those itineraries spend a full day in the U.S. Virgin Islands at St. Thomas, the capital of Caribbean shopping. American citizens can bring home up to $1,400 worth of purchases, at 40 percent or more off stateside prices, duty free.*

All the ships cruising the western route spend three days at sea with ports-of-call visits in Mexico, Grand Cayman, and Jamaica. Ports of call vary somewhat but always include Grand Cayman Island. Other ports visited are either Mexico's largest island, Cozumel, or Playa del Carmen on Mexico's Yucatán peninsula and Ocho Rios, or Montego Bay. Carnival has the largest number of ships sailing year-round through the Caribbean waters.

Let's use Carnival's seven-day, western Caribbean cruise itinerary as one typical example of a cruise with three days at sea and three ports of call.

➥ **Steve and Pat's Tip:** *In the various itineraries that follow throughout this chapter we note each island's colonial heritage in parentheses. This is important, since the ongoing traditions, "flavor," food, and spirit are often the most enticing reason for tourists to visit.*

The Caribbean

Day one: Depart from Miami in the late evening
Day two: Day at sea
Day three: Visit Playa del Carmen and Cozumel, Mexico, for a full day
Day four: Day at sea
Day five: Visit Grand Cayman Island for a full day
Day six: Day at sea
Day seven: Visit Jamaica (British) for a full day
Day eight: Disembark in Miami

Other common seven-day, western itineraries substitute the third day at sea with a day on a private island (cay) in the Bahamas owned by the cruise line (HAL, NCL, or Princess). This port of call is scheduled either the day after the ship leaves Florida or before it returns. Two cruise lines, Costa Cruises and RCI, substitute Key West, Florida, or Labada, Haiti, for the third day at sea. Then all the ships continue to circle Cuba and return to Florida. Western Caribbean cruise itineraries that offer two days at sea and visits to four ports of call are exemplified by the following Princess Cruises' *Sea Princess* itinerary:

Day one: Depart from Ft. Lauderdale, Florida, in the late evening
Day two: Visit Princess Cays, Bahamas, for a full day
Day three: Day at sea
Day four: Visit Ocho Rios, Jamaica (British), for a full day
Day five: Visit Grand Cayman Island for a full day
Day six: Visit Cozumel, Mexico, for a full day
Day seven: Day at sea
Day eight: Disembark in Ft. Lauderdale, Florida

Western Caribbean—Ports of Call and Shore Excursions

Cozumel, Mexico

Cozumel, Mexico's largest island, lies off the Yucatán peninsula. The island is famous for its pristine coral reefs that invite mind-boggling scuba diving and fantastic snorkeling. Cozumel is considered to be one of the worlds five best scuba-diving sites!

The only major town on the island, San Miguel, is quaint, colorful, and fun. Its slow-paced day changes quickly with the arrival of a cruise ship. Tourism is by far the island's main industry, and cruise ships deliver far more shoppers than scuba divers. Many tiny shops and some larger ones are packed around the downtown square, making San Miguel a shopper's delight. Ceramics, pottery, wood carvings, onyx, brass, reproductions of Mayan artifacts, shells, gold, gems, T-shirts, casual sportswear, perfume, and liquor are abundant at less than reasonable prices. Do not expect a lush tropical island and there will be no disappointment. Cozumel delivers charming, friendly people, a delightful town that welcomes and satisfies shoppers, and some of the world's best reefs for scuba diving and snorkeling.

➥ **Steve and Pat's Tip:** *"Cross-tours" are available to passengers whose ships visit Cozumel versus ships that visit the major mainland port of call, Playa del Carmen. This means that both scuba-diving adventures and explorations of the mainland Mayan ruins are usually available to passengers regardless of whether their ship visits Cozumel or Playa del Carmen. If a scuba-diving adventure is a must and the available itinerary visits Playa del Carmen, make certain that a day scuba-diving excursion to Cozumel is available.*

A word about the areas famed Mayan ruins is in order. The "must-see" ruins are found on the mainland, Mexico's Yucatán peninsula, only a stone's throw away from Cozumel. If time permits, visit the ruins of Chichen Itza by plane. These ancient Mayan ruins are the largest and most famous of the Yucatán ruins, the best example of the ancient monuments of a mysteriously abandoned civilization. In the 1920s, the government began restoration of the Chichen Itza site, which is seven miles square, and today it houses a restaurant, museum, and shop. Although expensively priced at $200, we highly recommend this memorable and exciting excursion, especially the landing at Chichen Itza on the dirt runway. Blow your budget! A great alternative that also saves big dollars is the boat trip to the ruins at Tulum, priced at $79. Do whatever is necessary! These are *not-to-be-missed* excursions!

Independent shore excursions: Why spend hard-earned dollars on ship excursions? In Cozumel, activities are primarily associated with the gorgeous clear water, abundant fish, and dazzling coral reefs. These include world-class snorkeling and scuba diving, sailing parties, shopping in San Miguel, and relaxing on beautiful, white sand beaches. Better yet, pack a box lunch from the ship with your snorkeling gear and grab a taxi at dockside for a couple of bucks and go to Chankanaab Nature Park. Or go to Sol Caribe Hotel, where an upside-down plane lies clearly visible underwater. The plane is found just a bit offshore and is swarming with tropical fish. This is tropical vacation heaven!

Shore excursions:

Following are some typical shore excursions available from Cozumel:

Tulum   Visit the Mayan ruins. This all-day adventure travels by ferry to the mainland. Tulum is the only known architectural example of a walled Mayan city. Tour sixty structures that are remarkably well preserved, perched atop a cliff that overlooks the Caribbean. Note: Mexico charges a $10 tax for use of video camcorders. The visit includes the nearby Xei-Ha lagoon, which offers a fabulous snorkeling opportunity. ($75)

Playacar   Play golf at the Yucatán peninsula's newest course. This is an eight-hour day and the greens fee is steep. ($112)

Remote Beach Party Cruise   Sail in comfort aboard a sixty-five-foot catamaran to a private beach that includes lunch, the use of kayaks, windsurfers, and beach floats. ($36)

Mermaid Sub-Sea Tour   Explore the islands' beautiful underwater reefs. ($33)

Palancar Scuba Dive Reef Tour   For certified divers this is "the big one," which includes the dive boat, equipment, and a two-tank dive to the second largest reef in the world. ($50)

Dzul-Ha Snorkeling Tour   This snorkeling center is designed for easy entry and a day of fun swimming with colorful reef fish. ($30)

Playa del Carmen or Calica, Mexico

Some cruise ships stop at either place on the Yucatán peninsula for the blinding white beaches and easy access to the ancient Mayan ruins of Tulum, Coba, and Chichen Itza. The access to the ruins at Chichen Itza is an eight hour trip by bus rather than by plane. Or travel to the Coba Mayan ruins by motor coach, then hike around the ruins, which are partly hidden by the dense vegetation and are only now being excavated. It was only through infrared photography from an NASA satellite that these structures and canals were discovered. Visit several excavated monuments.

The area's most cosmopolitan city for shopping is nearby Cancun, just north of Playa del Carmen. Of course, Cancun is also home to top-notch five-star resorts. It was off a Cancun beach that we took our first parasailing ride!

Playa del Carmen or Calica shore excursions:

Tulum   Tour of the ruins and snorkel at Xel-Ha. ($79)

Cancun Shopping Tour   The six-hour tour includes a one-hour bus ride to Cancun and three hours for shopping. ($32)

Golf at Playacar   ($104)

Chichen Itza Ruins Tour   Travel is by bus and the tour allows two-and-a-half hours of sightseeing at the ruins. Highlights are the sacrificial wells and climbing the temple, Kulkulcan. ($89)

Jamaica

Jamaica lies ninety miles south of Cuba and is the third largest Caribbean island. Its lively spirit and diverse physical beauty appeal to all visitors. From the heavily forested Blue Mountains to the quiet rivers and dramatic waterfalls, Jamaica is a cool, relaxing retreat for anyone wishing to just get away.

Ocho Rios, Jamaica   Set on the north side of the island, breathtaking countryside surrounds this picturesque town. Since most of the cruise ships stop at this port, it is usually very crowded and busy. Take a short walking tour of the downtown area with its many arts and crafts shops, then escape to lush parks and plantations.

Independent shore excursions: Bring a picnic lunch from the ship and make a day of it! Onshore passengers can arrange for a day at the beach, scuba diving, snorkeling, windsurfing, sailing, or fishing at the many resorts. Just take a dockside taxi cab to any of the nearby upscale hotels. Ask the cruise director for tips on the finest hotels with the most amenities.

Shore excursions:

Shaw Hill Park View-sparking cascades, tropical plants and flowers, and many exotic birds. Bring your binoculars! More than five hundred species of ferns flourish in Fern Gully.

Sundancer Shuttle Cruise to Dunn's River Falls A seventy-five-foot yacht cruises west of Ocho Rios and stops at beautiful Dunn's River Falls. View its waters, which plunge six hundred feet to the river below. ($34)

Jazz Sailing and Beach Tour Enjoy a leisurely catamaran ride, good drinks, and a sail into a secluded cove. Rest, sun, and snorkel to your heart's content, or at least until the "cat" is ready to leave. ($49)

Beach Horseback Riding Start your ride at the Chukka Cove Polo Club, through a trail passing two of the oldest sugar estates to the beach. Ride bare back into the sea and return to the Polo Club. 4 hours. ($79)

Golf Enjoy 18 holes at Runaway Country Club in the Jamaican hills. ($90–100)

Montego Bay, Jamaica Known as "Mo" Bay, it is found on the northwest coast and less of a hassle than Ocho Rios, since fewer ships dock here. Another quaint town, this is the second largest city on the island, and surprisingly, its facilities are better than those at Ocho Rios. However, most shore excursions are not worth your time or money.

Independent shore excursions: The highlight of a town walking tour is Sam Sharpe Square, named for the slave who led the bloody Christmas Rebellion of 1831. Shop for local art at the crafts market and other specialty stores.

Shore excursions: Visit Rose Hall, Great Hall and Plantation, or Croydon Plantation and remember the old plantation days. The best, secluded beach can be found at Rose Hall Beach Club, east of "Mo" Bay. The adventurous should try river rafting, scuba diving, and snorkeling at Montego Bay Marine Park.

Grand Cayman Island

Grand Cayman Island is the largest of the Cayman Islands, a British colony with some of the best diving in the Caribbean. It boasts the famous Seven Mile Beach, an incredible stretch of powdery white sand where sun worshipers can relax and enjoy themselves. It's capital, Georgetown, is a bustling little town of hodgepodge architectural styles.

Grand Cayman is also known as one of the best scuba diving sites in the world. The famed Cayman Wall plunges over a mile down, offering fantastic underwater adventures for certified divers.

Nondivers will enjoy fabulous snorkeling cruises and beach parties.

Shore excursions:

Beginning Scuba Adventure Strictly for those who are not certified divers, this adventure includes all instruction, equipment and a beach dive. ($54)

Certified Scuba-Diving Adventure This two-tank dive to about sixty feet includes a dive on a local shipwreck. ($60)

Stingray Snorkel Tour A boat takes guests to nearby Stingray City, where snorkelers swim amidst the stingrays and marvel as instructors hand-feed them. ($34)

Atlantis Deep-Dive Submarine Want to splurge big time? Here is a golden opportunity. The Atlantis will visit a shipwreck at a depth of eight hundred feet. Not many people experience such a dive. Price tag on this one—a hefty $294!

Atlantis Submarine The shallow ride, to one hundred feet, is priced at $79.

Local Sightseeing Tours the National Museum, the Queen Elizabeth II Botanical Park, and the Majestic Trail, a 2,000-year-old footpath through a two-million-year-old woodland area in the middle of the island, or take locally arranged excursions.

Cayman Turtle Farm This is the island's most popular attraction. View endangered turtles in all stages of development.

The Caribbean

Seven-Day Eastern Caribbean Cruises

Eastern Caribbean cruises follow a straight finger-shaped route, stretching southeasterly from Florida and ending at the U.S. Virgin Islands. Generally the ships leave from Fort Lauderdale and Miami, stop at Nassau or Freeport in the Bahamas or Key West, Florida and continue to the U.S. Virgin Islands--St. Thomas and St. John. Often St. Maarten/St. Martin and San Juan, Puerto Rico, are included, since these islands are at the same latitude as the Virgin Islands. Then the ships return to Florida.

Bahama Islands

Because the Bahamas are so close to the southeastern tip of Florida, many three- or four-day cruises are available from Miami or Port Canaveral. We will mention the Bahamas as a port of call, but not all the different cruises except *Disney Magic* and Premier's *Big Red Boat.* Their seven-day itineraries combine a trip to Disney World or another amusement park and a short three- or four-day cruise to the Bahamas, stopping at Nassau and Port Lucaya or Disney's Castaway Cay. These two packages are a great way to introduce children to the world of cruising, since the cruises are short and on boats especially designed to entertain kids.

Carnival has the largest number of ships sailing year-round in the Caribbean. We will use two of Carnival's seven-day, eastern Caribbean cruise itineraries as a typical example of a cruise with four days at sea and visits to two ports of call. Of course, these cruise ships offer the greatest opportunity for shipboard rest and relaxation. With Carnival you get a Fun Ship, so enjoy its lively daytime activities and evening parties that go on late into the wee morning hours. The next morning you just may want to be pampered by the ship's twenty-four-hour room service with a late breakfast in bed!

Day one: Depart from Miami, Florida, in late evening
Day two: Day at sea
Day three: Half day at sea; arrive at San Juan, Puerto Rico, in afternoon

Day four: Visit St. Croix or St. Thomas, USVI
Day five: Visit St. Thomas or St. Maarten/St. Martin (Dutch/French) for a full day
Day six: Day at sea
Day seven: Day at sea
Day eight: Disembark in Miami, Florida

Another typical itinerary followed by Celebrity Cruises, Costa Cruises, NCL, Premier Cruises, Princess, and RCI spends one day in Nassau, New Providence Island in the Bahamas, or on the private island (cay) owned by each cruise line. Usually it is the first or last day of the cruise, since the Bahamas are so close to Florida. A typical eastern Caribbean cruise itinerary includes three full days at sea and three ports of call in or near the U.S. Virgin Islands. An itinerary of the *Grand Princess* follows:

Day one: Depart from Miami, Florida, in the late evening
Day two: Visit Nassau, Bahamas (British) for a full day
Day three: Day at sea
Day four: Visit St. Thomas, USVI, for a full day
Day five: Visit St. Maarten/St. Martin for a full day
Day six: Day at sea
Day seven: Day at sea
Day eight: Disembark in Miami, Florida

Eastern Caribbean—Ports of Call and Shore Excursions

Bahamas

The archipelago of the islands of the Bahamas is close to the southeastern coast of Florida and stretches more than 650 miles toward Cuba. The Bahamas are known for their perfect year-round climate, combined with spectacular white, sandy beaches with low thick pine forests, mangrove swamps, lagoons, and lakes. New Providence Island and the Grand Bahama Island offer an opportunity for great sightseeing and sun, surf, and fun at local beaches.

Nassau, New Providence Island Nassau has a colorful history as the home base of Blackbeard and commanders of at least twenty pirate ships in the early 1700s. Then the pirates' era ended, and with its balmy breezes and warming sun, Nassau began to develop as a resort. Today it is the capital of the Bahamas and a vibrant commercial center. More than one million cruise passengers visit Nassau every year.

Independent shore excursions: Highlights of a town walking tour are Rawson Square, the Parliament buildings, and the historic octagonal library with its artifacts and historical display about the Lucayan Indians. The famous Queen's Staircase, composed of sixty-six stone steps, is where slaves were bought and sold. Famed Fort Fincastle, located up on the hill, has a commanding view of the city. The Botanical Garden is a recreation of a Lucayan village. Nearby Fort Charlotte has an intriguing mix of connecting corridors between underground dungeons.

Bring a box lunch from the ship. Then take a taxi across the bridge to Paradise Island to the glamorous resort areas of Cable Beach or Cabbage Beach, with its breathtaking two-mile stretch of beach, and savor a day of free sun, surf, and fun.

Shore excursions:

- Take a half-day sail on the catamaran *Yellowbird* around Paradise Island.
- Enjoy a glass-bottom boat tour and view incredible underwater sights.
- Tour the reefs on a moving underwater observatory at the marine park on Athol Island and see waters teeming with tropical fish.
- Take a two-tank scuba dive on one of Nassau's famous reefs.
- Travel to a secluded cay for snorkeling and then relax in the sun on the incredible beaches.
- A once in a lifetime adventure awaits, especially for kids—a dolphin encounter at Blue Lagoon Island, home to "Flipper." Try your hand at petting and feeding a real dolphin in waist-high water.

Freeport and Lucaya, Grand Bahama Island This island is the fourth largest in the chain and the second-most popular destination. It has miles of secluded powder-white beaches and fabulous scuba diving and snorkeling.

Shore excursions: Visit the town of Freeport for a shopping adventure, since the International Bazaar has over eighty shops and goods from all over the world. The center offers more than thirty types of cuisine just in case you miss lunch on the ship. Next door is the Straw Market, where local crafts and other wares can be purchased—watches, jewelry, perfume, crystal and china, cameras, leather goods, and paintings.

The pristine beaches and water sports are the main attraction on this island. Choose sailing, snorkeling, waterskiing, Jet-Skiing, windsurfing, game fishing, parasailing, and more. For solitude, head to Taino Beach or the beach at Williams Town. Both are within easy reach of Freeport. Visit the Lucayan National Park and the Garden of the Groves, two of the island's natural treasures, and discover an exotic world of native flora and fauna.

Half Moon Cay, Bahamas

At beautiful Half Moon Cay, a wide variety of land and water activities are available—snorkeling tours among the coral reefs, hiking though nature trails, shopping for arts and crafts at the Straw Market.

Key West, Florida

Ernest Hemingway found Key West much to his liking, and today it is home to adventurers, artist, and poets. The island's Old Town overflows with colorful bars, restaurants, and unique shopping. Add its pristine reefs, coconut palms, and a laid-back attitude, and it is easy to see why they call it Margaritaville! Key West may be a tiny island, but the ambience and shopping are great fun.

Independent shore excursions: A town exploration begins with a historical walk into Old Town at Mallory Square, where it all began in 1513 with sponging and cigar making. Or take an

Old Town trolley ride while a guide relates the exciting history of this sea town.

Shore excursions:

- Tour Casa Antigua, Hemingway's home, the Hemingway mansion, and Robert Frost's Heritage House.
- View incredible tropical fish and colorful coral reefs while on a glass-bottom boat ride.
- Explore the keys on the famed party boat *Crazy Boat*.
- Enjoy a snorkel and catamaran sail around the island, ending with memorable snorkeling on a colorful reef.

For the more athletic, a two-hour bike tour of the island is available. Also try kayaking (with instructions for beginners), through the many channels around Key West that are teeming with wildlife.

San Juan, Puerto Rico

Although the capital, San Juan, is usually a port of departure for the classic Southern Caribbean cruise, most of the Eastern Caribbean cruises swing by and make a short stop at San Juan on the way to St. Thomas. Consequently, the time in port may be short, so make the most of it.

Puerto Rico has a rich Spanish heritage that fascinates visitors. Steeped in history, San Juan is a great town for sightseeing. The U.S. Congress made the city a National Historic Zone in the 1950s. Of interest are its museums, churches, forts, restored homes, and monuments. Narrow cobblestone streets, tiny alleyways, hidden courtyards, and many public squares are typical of European cities and all part of the charm of Old San Juan.

Shore excursions:

Casa Blanca Visit the family home of Ponce de Leon, the oldest home on the island with gorgeous gardens and fountains, it is authentically furnished with period pieces.

La Fortaleza Tour another elegantly restored home and currently the office of the governor.

Fort El Morro and Forte San Christobal These two forts are fine examples of military architecture and fun to explore, with their panoramic views, massive stone structures, and spooky tunnels.

El Yunque Rain Forest Visit the only rain forest in the U.S. national park system. The 26,000-acre Caribbean National Forest is blanketed with thick green vegetation that extends upward, covering its mountains and peaks and offering an incredible hiking experience.

Great Swimming Beaches These abound on all sides of the island and offer a varied assortment of water activities, such as deep-sea fishing.

Golfers have more than a dozen championship courses from which to choose.

U.S. Virgin Islands (USVI)

Almost fifty islands comprise the USVI. The three principal islands are St. Croix, St. John, and St. Thomas. St. Croix is the largest island. St. John and St. Thomas are next to each other only thirty-five miles away from St. Croix. Holland, France, Britain, Spain, the Knights of Malta, and Denmark once held the islands. The United States purchased the islands from the Dutch after WWI as protection for the Panama Canal, and they became part of the United States in 1917. The islands receive almost two million visitors and 1,000 cruise ship calls per year. This is the number one shopping destination in the Caribbean, and nearly every ship stops here, even cruises that continue to the Panama Canal and South America.

St. Croix, USVI

Christiansted, on the north side of the island, and Frederiksted, on the west side, are the towns to visit. However, only cruise ships with fewer than two hundred passengers can dock at Christiansted, so nearly all cruise ships dock at Frederiksted, a quiet town that offers a quaint heritage walk through streets with 18th and 19th century Dutch architecture adorned with Victorian gingerbread.

Independent shore excursions: In Frederiksted, explore the original 1751 Market square and Fort Frederick with its museum. Other sights include Butler Bay, Ghut Bird Sanctuary, the Estate

Mount Washington Plantation currently being restored and the Whim Great House (a plantation restored to its 1770s splendor), and Christiansted by shuttle.

Shore excursions:

Catamaran Cruise From Frederiksted, the catamaran sails past breathtaking scenery and Sprat Hall, a plantation greathouse built in 1670. Anchor at Sandy Point for swimming and snorkeling. ($39)

Biking Tours Pedal twelve miles through paradise along the coast to Sprat Hall. ($35)

Snorkeling and Sailing Adventures Trips to Buck Island national park are fun. ($45)

Scuba Diving There is outstanding scuba diving beyond the park at Pillar Coral, where tall columns of coral spiral up twenty-five feet, and at the adjacent Cane Bay drop-off, which begins in thirty feet of water and drops to two thousand feet.

Christiansted Tour and Shopping Travel across the island by shuttle to Christiansted. Most of the island's stores are in this town, and they even open on Sunday for the cruise ships. ($12)

A Ferry Ride Take a ride across the bay to the hotel on the Cay, with a lovely beach and great barbecue.

St. John, USVI

St. John is the smallest and least populated of the islands and is three miles east of St. Thomas. The Danish West India Company staked its claim in 1683 and held the island until the United States purchased it in 1917. Cruise ships often stop here on the way to St. Thomas and let passengers off the ship to tour the island. After the excursion, they return to St. Thomas by ferry to link with their cruise ship. From St. Thomas, tours are available to St. John. Again, you would take a ferry from St. Thomas to Cruz Bay and pick up a tour or taxi-guide here.

Two-thirds of the island consists of the Virgin Islands National Park and shares the same lush landscape and dazzling flowers as its neighbors. St. John is world renowned for its idyllic beaches and quiet getaways.

Shore excursions: Since the island is basically a national park, only diehards visit here. Take a tour by safari bus or jeep bus tour, or hire a taxi. Both will stop for photo opportunities of incredible views overlooking the bays and stop at the Annaberg ruins. A beach tour through the park is available and will go to lovely Hawksnest Beach, with a unique snorkel trail offshore or to Trunk Bay Beach, which is lovely. Again, take a taxi to the beach, arrange for a pick-up at a specific time, and enjoy a leisurely day.

St. Thomas, USVI

St. Thomas is the most popular of the Virgin Islands. All cruise ships visit its capital, Charlotte Amalie. This island is without question the shopping capital of the Caribbean, and many travelers say it is the shopping center of the world. Green hills surround the harbor where the postcard city of Charlotte Amalie sits. Not far from the bustle of the downtown area lie great white-sand beaches. Water sport enthusiasts, sun worshipers, and those seeking rest and relaxation need go no farther.

Independent shore excursions: St. Thomas is a fascinating place for sightseeing and shopping because it is steeped in history. Originally, the large warehousers that today are home to duty-free shops were used by pirates in the 1600s to hide their loot. The greatest concentration of shops is on Main Street, on the Waterfront Highway, or in the alleyways that connect them. Just a quick step from the cruise docks and you are in shopper's heaven, where stately buildings were constructed centuries ago and painted in pastel colors. Visit Fort Christian, an imposing brick-red structure, which is the oldest building still in use on St. Thomas. The fort now houses a museum.

Downhill biking is offered, and ends in Magen's Bay Beach with a swim at the beach. The beaches are wonderful and just a quick taxicab ride away from the dock. Water sports are available, and nearly all the beaches have reefs that are perfect for snorkeling. Reefs can be reached from the beach. Head for Stevens Cay or Thatch Cay for a fun day.

Try kayaking at the Kayak Marine Sanctuary and paddle around a cay before returning to the park. Paradise Point Tramway has the most fantastic vistas in the Caribbean.

Shore excursions:

Buck Island One-Tank Scuba Diving Diving to a World War II wreck covered with tropical fish and coral is available after boating to Buck's Island.

Island Sightseeing Tour The tour goes from docksides to the nearby hills. A drive on Skyline Drive offers magnificent views, including Charlotte Amalie below and St. John and the British Virgin Islands in the distance. Visit Mountain Top, the highest point on the island, and the Estate St. Peter Great House. ($31)

St. John Snorkeling The tour goes by ferry to nearby St. John. A short drive away is Trunk Bay an excellent spot for sunbathing, beachcombing, and snorkeling. ($35)

Atlantis Submarine "Odyssey Dive" Take a twenty-minute dive to nearby Buck Island. Underwater excitement peaks at the maximum dive depth of 150 feet! ($82)

Golf at Mahogany Run This famous course is a par 70 and the views are breathtaking from every hole. Transportation, green fees and shared cart provided. ($120)

Seaplane Flight-seeing See the U.S. and British Virgin Islands from "up there!" Flight time is forty- to forty-five minutes. ($99)

Buck Island Snorkeling and Sailing This is our kind of tour. Sail by large yacht to Buck Island then play with the fish while snorkeling in Turtle Cove. All snacks, beer, and soft drinks are provided. ($45)

Seven-Day Southern Caribbean Cruises

Southern Caribbean cruises, often called the Classic Southern Route, offer the widest selection of islands, cultures, and ports of call to explore and experience on a one-week cruise. Because the cruises start in the Caribbean and not in Florida, fewer days are spent cruising at sea. Unlike eastern and western itineraries, these "busy" cruises spend only one day at sea and five days at ports of call. This is the itinerary that delivers the maximum days spent at exotic Caribbean ports. More to see, more to do, and more to buy!

The southern Caribbean includes the semicircle of islands stretching southeast of San Juan, Puerto Rico, toward South

America. Nearly all cruises departing from San Juan stop at St. Thomas in the U.S. Virgin Islands. The other U.S. Virgin Islands ports of call, St. John and St. Croix, offer side trips to St. Thomas for a megashopping adventure. One way or another, this incredible duty-free shopping opportunity will be yours. People come from all over the world to shop for gold and precious gems. Americans can purchase up to $1,400 worth of goods duty free. This is truly a "shop till you drop" cruise adventure.

> ➥ **Steve and Pat's Tip:** *Let's say, again, that cost of the airfare to Puerto Rico and other southern departure ports is higher than the airfare to domestic U.S. cities like Miami. Need free or half-price air travel? This is a good time to review chapter 2!*

The classic southern Caribbean cruise itineraries sail round-trip from San Juan, Puerto Rico, and offer a choice of twenty different ports of call, stretching, like a string of pearls, south from San Juan to Venezuela. In addition to the visit to St. Thomas, the ships continue south to a smorgasbord of tropical islands. The favorites are Barbados (British), Martinique (French), and St. Maarten/Martin. Antigua (British) and St. Lucia are the second most popular ports. The farthest point south is Grenada. Let us compare two popular seven-day classic southern Caribbean cruise itineraries, available year-round, as a basic example of a cruise with one day at sea and five ports of call.

Day one: Depart from San Juan, Puerto Rico in late evening
Day two: Day at sea
Day three: Visit St. Thomas, USVI, for a full day
Day four: Visit Martinique (French) for a full day
Day five: Visit Barbados (British) for a full day
Day six: Visit Antigua (British) *or* St. Kitts (French/British) *or* Dominica (Spanish/British) for a full day
Day seven: Visit St. Maarten/St. Martin (Dutch/French) for a full day
Day eight: Disembark in San Juan, Puerto Rico

A South American version of the southern route is offered by a couple of cruise lines, such as Premier Cruises's *Crown* and *Island Breeze*, Princess's *Dawn Princess*, and RCI's *Rhapsody of the Seas*. They call these the Deep Southern or Exotic Southern Routes.

The port of departure is San Juan in Puerto Rico, Santa Domingo in the Dominican Republic, or the island of Aruba. Again, all ships stop at the U.S. Virgin Islands for incredible shopping opportunities. Then there is another stop in these colorful colonial islands before the ships turn south to Venezuela instead of retracing one's itinerary back to San Juan. After stopping in Venezuela, the ships continue west to Aruba and Curaçao, making a large circle, and then head north to San Juan or Santo Domingo. The cruise ships typically spend one or two days at sea and five or four days in port since they are sailing a longer distance than the Classic Southern Route. A South American Caribbean cruise itinerary will include the following, with typical substitutions:

Day one: Depart from San Juan, Puerto Rico *or* Aruba (Spanish/Dutch) in the late evening
Day two: Day at sea *or* visit Curaçao (Dutch) for a full day
Day three: Visit St. Thomas, USVI, all day *or* a day at sea
Day four: Visit Martinique (French) *or* Curaçao (Dutch) for a full day
Day five: Day at sea or visit Margarita Island, Venezuela, for a full day
Day six: Visit St. Maarten/St. Martin (Dutch/French) *or* Barbados (British) for a full day
Day seven: Visit St. Thomas, USVI, *or* St. Lucia (French/British) for a full day
Day eight: Disembark in San Juan, Puerto Rico

Southern Caribbean—Ports of Call and Typical Shore Excursions

Since southern Caribbean cruises have an extensive list of islands from which to pick for ports of call, we are unable to discuss all thirty possibilities. We picked the most popular islands that we enjoyed from our experiences cruising in the Caribbean.

Barbados

Barbados lies sixty miles east of the chain of Caribbean islands, and because of its geographical location, the island never changed hands during the 350-year period of British colonization. The prevailing winds always blow from the southeast across the island, in the wrong direction for a surprise attack by a man o' war sailing in from the west. While only fourteen miles wide by twenty-one miles long, the easternmost Caribbean island is crisscrossed with more than 975 miles of paved roads, making it easy to explore. The capital, Bridgetown, is one of the most vibrant cities in the eastern Caribbean and dates back to the initial occupation by the British. Its colonial charm blends well with its contemporary commercial buildings. It is a port city, and as the country's economy moves from agriculture (sugar grows in almost every corner of the island) into service industries, its deep harbor is very important.

Independent shore excursions: A walking tour of the capital starts at Trafalgar Square, where an imposing bronze statue of Lord Admiral Horatio Nelson stands next to the Dolphin Fountain. Visit the two coral-stone parliament buildings, built in 1871 and 1874. Inside the House of Assembly building, stained glass windows depict English monarchs from James I to Victoria. Here, visitors can observe Bajan (a contraction of Barbadians) democracy at work.

Bridgetown is considered the duty-free center in the eastern Caribbean. Discover bargain prices on English goods, especially china, crystal, porcelain, and perfume. Broad Street, the main shopping street in the capital, is where upscale the shops and duty-free department stores are located. Excellent shopping can be found in the streets running parallel to Broad Street.

Shore excursions:

Island Tour Visit the major points of interest, such as Tyrol Cot Heritage Village, a living museum, chattel house village, and market. Continue to Gun Hill, a restored signal station, and make a final stop at St. John's Church, rebuilt in 1836 on a cliff edge eight hundred feet above the sea. ($32)

Carlisle Bay Beach   Enjoy the day on one of the island's best beaches and listen to the music from a steel band. All water sports are available, from scuba diving to glass-bottom boat rides. ($33 for four to seven hours)

Harrison's Cave Tour   Pass by Warren's Great House and the unique Moravian Church, dating to the 1700s. Ride a tram through the extensive 150-foot cave with thousands of cave formations. ($36)

Flower Forest Tour   Eight hundred and fifty feet above sea level is the flower forest, located at Richmond, an old sugar plantation dating back to the earliest days of the island. ($32)

A Touch of the Jungle   Travel to Welchman Hall Gully for a three-quarter-mile hike through the jungle. See the incredible variety of plants and maybe the green monkeys, which visit daily on food forays. ($32)

Scuba Diving (Novice or Certified Divers)   Novices will receive instructions and dive over a twenty-five-foot reef. Certified divers will explore a coral reef teeming with fish and many coral formations. All gear supplied. ($70 to $76 for four hours)

Harbor Master Cruise   Sail to a white sand beach for sun, fun, and snorkeling. Snorkel over a coral reef in a marine park. ($19)

Martinique

Gaze upon this island and you will be impressed by the physical beauty of the northern profile, dominated by Mount Pelee, regally crowned by the swirling mist. The island changes from the craggy volcanic shore of the north to the long, white sandy beaches of the south. The center of the island is covered by gentle meadowlands, and everywhere masses of tropical flowers color the landscape. Martinique has all the great attributes of a Caribbean island and a distinctively French atmosphere. The French cuisine, music, and language make the island most unique. A rather long island, Martinique has a great road system for touring outside the main city of Fort-de-France.

Independent shore excursions: Fort-de-France is a bustling commercial center with a verdant park situated in the middle, the Place de la Savane. The green mountains are backdrops for the city, with Fort St.-Louise built for strategic purposes in 1640. It is open to the public on certain days.

Walk through the downtown areas   Filled with shops and quaint apartments complete with wrought-iron French balconies and flower pots of brilliantly colored flowers, it reminds one of Paris.

Shopping   The main shopping is along the side streets, where little boutiques sell fashionable Paris couture and French Riviera sportswear. Larger stores specialize in luxury goods. The biggest bargains are French perfumes, jewelry, and designer fashions.

Saint-Louis Cathedral   This imposing church was rebuilt faithfully according to the original plans created in 1895 by architect Henri Picq. Its impressive spire and metal framework are much admired. See the Schroder Library, built for the Paris Exposition of 1889, dismantled and shipped to the island.

Musée Departemental   Trace the history and culture of the Carib Indians with exhibits relating to developments of European settlements on the island.

Island Tour   For a special tour of the island, take a private tour with the taxis lined up at the dock. For one-half or less the price of a commercial tour, the drivers in their Mercedes Benz taxis will travel to the north shore to Mont Pelee and the town of Saint-Pierre, which was destroyed by a volcanic explosion in 1902 that killed 30,000 inhabitants. Visit the Musée Gauguin and see canvases done by the painter when he lived here in 1887. Return through a gorgeous rain forest, stop at the Sacré-Coeur de Blata, modeled after the famed church in Paris.

Shore excursions:

City and Ruins Tour   Travel by bus on the same tour as described above. ($46)

Beach Snorkel   Board a specially-built snorkel boat, the *P'Ti Punch*, that cruises to a secluded beach. Experienced snorkelers may dive in the famous Black Bat Cave. ($38)

Botanical Gardens   Travel to Sacre-Coeur and onto the Botanical Gardens. ($43)

St. Maarten/St. Martin (Dutch/French)

Truly a unique island, the current boundary is a result of numerous wars between the great European powers of the seventeenth century. Ownership of the island is split between the Dutch and the French, yet no rift exists between the two cultures. It is the smallest island in the world to be divided between two sovereign powers. Erected in 1948, the Border Monument commemorates nearly 350 years of friendly relations between the two nations. The cruise ships dock on the Dutch side of the island, St. Maarten.

St. Maarten belongs to the Netherlands Antilles, along with the islands of Aruba, Bonaire, Curaçao, Saba, and St. Eustatius. However, the Dutch influence is often overshadowed by the Caribbean flavor, so overall the experience is unlike any other. The capital, Philipsburg, is a charming town only four streets wide but lined with quaint shops, colorful hotels, and domestic dwellings. The town is easily explored on foot.

Independent shore excursions:

Walking Tour Start from the main plaza, Wathey Square, bustling with vendors, tourists, and taxi drivers. Little Pier, at the square's southern end, is a departure point for excursions. Stop by the Simarto Museum, which has exhibits of artifacts from the Carib Indians and colonial times.

Fort Amsterdam The first fort built by the Dutch in the Caribbean, on the foundation of an earlier Spanish fortress, is a short drive from the city and dates back to the seventeenth century.

Shore excursions:

Under Two Flags Island Drive Travel by bus from the Dutch capital to the French capital, Marigot, in St. Martin. Tour the countryside and pass through charming French villages on the way to Marigot. Browse through the street with its sidewalk cafes and duty-free boutiques. Then return to the Dutch side and shop in the fine stores in Philipsburg. ($27)

Scuba Diving (Certified) Enjoy a fairly shallow-boat dive through coral reefs inhibited by tropical fish, conch, and lobster. All gear is provided. ($55)

Golden Eagle Catamaran Sail to the pink beaches of the island of Tintamar, perfect for snorkeling and swimming. All equipment is provided. ($69 for four hours)

Explorer's Cruise Travel to the Simpson Bay Yacht Club and board the *Explorer*, a two-decked catamaran, for sightseeing to Marigot. The twenty-minute sail is entertaining, and one hour is spent shopping in Marigot. Then enjoy a short stop at a private island beach on the return trip. ($34 for four hours)

The best strategy is to take a tour through both parts of the island and experience the Dutch and the French atmosphere in language, architecture, and foods. Since most cruises schedule a full day to explore the island, have a grand time.

Caribbean Discount Prices

Given the importance of this chapter, let us reiterate a couple of bargain pricing rules. The following discount and "sale" prices represent cruise deals that proliferated the cruise marketplace at the time of publication. We happily report that six months to one year from now, similar or even lower prices will likely be available. Use our list as a guidepost to the dirt-cheap prices you will be paying.

Our listed prices include inside cabins with two lower beds and all port charges. Many prices are "exclusive" from the mentioned cruise-only or "cruise-mostly" agency. Call these agencies for their best current deals.

At other times we show prices that were advertised directly by cruise lines. These can be further reduced by using our strategies for free vacation cash, cash-in-your-pocket deals, and booking with rebate agencies. Before booking your cruise, review all of these strategies in chapters 2 and 4. Other cruise-only agencies listed in Chapter 5 may meet or even beat these prices.

Travel agencies' phone numbers will be found at the conclusion of this section. Cruise-line phone numbers are found in the Appendixes.

Special Caribbean Cruise Line Notes

Royal Caribbean International All the lowest category cabin beds are two lower beds that convert to queen size!

Celebrity Cruises The *Century* moves from the Caribbean to Europe in 1999.

Premier Cruises The *Island Breeze* leaves the eastern Caribbean in 1999. Premier will sail only its southern South Seas and western itineraries.

Norwegian Cruise Line In 1999, the *Norwegian Sea* will sail only on Texaribbean (Texas and Caribbean) itineraries. Look for the *Norwegian Dream* to take over the southern itineraries, which is good news, since the *Norwegian Dream*, unlike the *Norwegian Sea*, has only lower-bed cabins.

Western Caribbean Discount Prices

Ambassador Tours offered Celebrity's super-luxury liner *Mercury*, an early December 1998 sailing, priced at $802.

Costa Cruises advertised its one-week cruise on the *Costa Romantica* from Ft. Lauderdale at $699. A low-cost upgrade to a two-lower-bed cabin may be necessary. Their air-and-cruise package from San Francisco is $899.

Princess Cruises advertised their *Sea Princess* from Ft. Lauderdale at $677 for the best available inside cabin. Ambassador Tours also offered the new *Sea Princess* from Ft. Lauderdale, a November 1998 sailing, for $749.

Cruises Inc. advertised Royal Caribbean's *Majesty of the Seas* at $709, or an upgrade to category M for $724. Time to Travel offered the same cruise at $699. Or, Cruises Inc. offered the new *Enchantment of the Seas*, embarking from Miami, at $859.

Costco Travel offered Carnival's *Celebration*, sailing from New Orleans, for just $606.

Cruise World advertised Carnival's new smokeless *Paradise* for $749.

Celebrity advertised its new *Mercury* January 1999 sailing for $952.

Premier advertised its *Sea Breeze*, sailing from Ft. Lauderdale, for $648.

Eastern Caribbean Discount Prices

Costa Cruises advertised an incredible air-and-land package for early December 1998 sailings, priced at $808, including port charges and airfare from New York City to Ft. Lauderdale. The ship is the *Victoria*. We happily note that *Victoria*'s lowest-category cabins all have two lower beds. Costa advertised cruise-only sailings on the *Victoria* for $699. Note: Low category 1 on the *Romantica*, used on similar itineraries, have lower and upper berths.

➥ **Steve and Pat's Best Deal Goal:** *Costco Travel offered Carnival's* Celebration *sailing from New Orleans for just $606.*

Costco Travel advertised a super deal on Princess's biggest and most expensive ship ever built, the *Grand Princess*, priced at $889 for a November 1998 sailing from Ft. Lauderdale.

Ambassador Tours offered a cruise on Celebrity's *Century* for December 1998 priced at $702. Time to Travel offered the same cruise at $699.

Cruise World sold cruises on Carnival's spanking-new smokeless *Paradise* priced at $749 for a December 1998 inaugural sailing. The ship embarks from San Juan. Add $100 for a category 4 two-lower-bed cabin.

Costco Travel sells a deluxe Holland America Line cruise on their *Westerdam*, embarking in November 1998 from Ft. Lauderdale, priced at $803.

Holland America Line advertised its *Westerdam*, sailing from Ft. Lauderdale in November 1998, at $653.

Time to Travel offered a Royal Caribbean cruise on the *Grandeur of the Seas* for $749.

Travel in America offered the same deal, Royal Caribbean's cruise on the *Grandeur of the Seas*, for $749. Travel of America advertised Carnival's *Destiny* at $709.

Southern Caribbean Discount Prices

Princess advertised one-week cruises on their new *Dawn Princess* embarking from San Juan priced at $677 for the best inside cabins available at booking. Costco Travel offered this sail-

The Caribbean

ing in high season (January 1999) for $866. Note: Add $100 to Princess cruises for a category 4 two-lower-bed cabin.

Costco Travel offered Royal Caribbean's *Monarch of the Seas* winter 1998 sailings, embarking from San Juan, priced at $717. Time to Travel and Travel of America offered similar sailings priced at $749.

➥ **Steve and Pat's Best Deal Goal:** *Travel of America advertised Carnival's* Destiny, *a Fun Ship, at $709.*

Cruises Inc. advertised Carnival's *Fascination* ($586) and *Inspiration* ($776) cruises from San Juan. Add $100 for a category 4 two-lower-bed cabin.

Ambassador Tours offered Royal Caribbean's *Rhapsody of the Seas* from San Juan for $799. Travel of America offered the same cruise for $749.

Carnival Cruises advertised southern Caribbean cruises for as low as $669 from San Juan. Add $100 for a category 4 two-lower-bed cabin.

Cruise World offered Celebrity's *Galaxy* at $669.

Premier Cruises specializes in air-and-land packages with unique itineraries. Their cruise on the *Sea Wind Crown* with air from New York was priced at $999, and from San Francisco at $1,099. This cruise is round-trip from Aruba. The same cruise without air travel was offered by Costco Travel for just $557. Note: Add $50 for a two-lower-bed cabin. Airfare alone to Aruba ranges from $500 to $600 per person.

Premier's southeast Caribbean cruise, round-trip from Santo Domingo on the *Island Breeze*, including airfare from New York, advertised at $898. Without airfare $799.

Norwegian Cruise Line advertised their one-week cruise on the *Norwegian Sea* from San Juan priced as low as $699. Add $50 for a two-lower-bed cabin.

Texaribbean Cruises Discount Prices Ambassador Tours offered Norwegian's Texaribbean cruise on the *Norwegian Star*. This November 1998 cruise sails round-trip from Houston for a sale price of $611.

> **Steve and Pat's Best Deal Goal:** *Cruises Inc. advertised Carnival's* Fascination *for $586.*

Discount Travel Agency Contacts:

Ambassador Tours: (800) 989-9000
Cruises Inc.: (800) 854-0500
Travel of America: (800) 228-8843
CruiseWorld: (800) 588-7447
Time to Travel: (800) 524-3300
Costco Travel: (800) 800-8505

11

Bermuda: Fun in the Sun

Do not overlook these remarkable islands, where English tradition and hospitality reign supreme just 650 miles east off the Carolina coast. Because of its unique location southeast of New York and northeast of Florida, cruise ships embark for Bermuda from both New York and Florida home ports. Bermuda is an archipelago of more than 180 small islands linked together by causeways and bridges. Only about twenty of the islands are inhabited. Seven of the largest islands are connected by bridges and causeways, making the area easily traveled and unified, close and friendly.

"Le Bermuda" appeared on Spanish maps as early as 1511, and it was known to explorers as the Isle of the Devils. Many a Spanish galleon plying the routes from Cartagena to Cadiz foundered upon the reefs surrounding Bermuda. Survivors brought home tales of horror, shrieking phantasms, and mysterious storms.

The British discovered the islands in 1609 and settled them under the charter of the Virginia Company. Bermuda is now one of Britain's oldest self-governing territories (British Dependent Territory). It has pride in its three-hundred-year-old colonial traditions, like the bell-ringing town crier, afternoon teatime, engaging British accents, and an eagerness to make visitors feel at home.

Since Bermuda is warmed year-round by the gulf stream, the climate is always subtropical, with mild winters and warm summers. American humorist Mark Twain, a frequent visitor, claimed that it was the "right country for a jaded man to loaf in."

> ➥ **Steve and Pat's Tip:** *Since these islands are small and connected by one east-west road, all shore excursions are usually available from any port. Various tour companies offer sightseeing that travels almost anywhere on the islands, from St. George to King's Wharf. So even if a tour that appeals to you is listed as a St. George excursion, ask the cruise tour director if a particular trip is available from another port of call.*

Today, since over half the population is non-British and consisting of descendants of slaves from America and the West Indies, Caribbean music, ranging from calypso to reggae, is heard on street corners and performed at folk dances. Caribbean cuisine, such as lobster, conch fritters, shark hash, turtle steak, fish chowder with black rum, and Portugese red-bean soup, is available at take-out eateries.

> ➥ **Steve and Pat's Independent Excursion Tip:** *A taxi tour is a great way to see the islands. Stop and enjoy the wonderful pink sand beaches, and cross innumerable bridges and causeways. Taxi drivers sporting a blue flag on their hoods are qualified tour guides. Or set out on your own and take an economical tour on the pleasant Pink Buses, with great panoramic windows. The buses travel everywhere in the island. Make your own itinerary and see it all.*

Explore the islands and view the pastel houses with their white roofs and enjoy the endless pink beaches and turquoise surf. More emerald fairways per square mile are in Bermuda than anywhere in the world. The Bermudans intend to keep their spot of paradise unspoiled, so there are no condominiums, developers, or car rentals on the islands. Only five cruise liners are allowed to dock here at one time.

The Great Island of Bermuda is a string of seven islands connected by bridges and causeways. Cruise ships have the choice of three unique ports of call: Hamilton, the capital, located in the center of the island; King's Wharf on Ireland Island North, situated on the far western end; and the old capital of St. George on St. George's Island at the far eastern end.

Hamilton

Hamilton is a small city as capitals go, but its influence is substantial. A magnet for banks and insurance companies because of its stability and tax-free status, it has made Bermuda the second richest island in the world. The town is impeccably clean and picturesque.

Independent shore excursions: Explore its bustling streets and parks, many ancient churches, and English pubs. A quick walk will bring you to the following:

Fort Hamilton Enjoy its lovely moat gardens and panoramic view of Hamilton Harbor. Twenty-four forts on the island are accessible to the public.

Bermuda National Galley View paintings by the Old Masters.

Bermuda Aquarium Over one hundred species of fish range from the cute to the carnivorous.

Natural History Museum and Zoo Both are located in Flatts Village, a short bus ride from Hamilton.

Botanical Gardens A short bus ride will take you to gardens with over 1,000 varieties of plant life, almost all transported to Bermuda by seventeenth- and eighteenth-century seafarers.

Shore excursions:

Catamaran Cruise to the Dockyard An all-day adventure onboard a fifty-foot "cat." Sail round-trip across the Great Sound to King's Wharf and enjoy an hour of shopping at the Dockyard. ($74 for five hours)

Invitation to Tea Visit two of the oldest landmarks, the Tearoom at Gibb's Lighthouse, built in 1844, and the Verdmont

Museum, built in late 1600s, which houses an incredible collection of antiques made of Bermuda cedarwood. Complete the tour with a stop at the Botanical Gardens. ($51)

Glass-Bottom Boat Ride View underwater marine life and see old shipwrecks nestled in thousand-year-old coral formations. ($27)

Snorkel on Devil's Flats One mile offshore, this beautiful inner reef is a garden of hard corals a few feet below the water's surface. ($45)

Wreck Snorkeling The Western Blue Cut, the location for the movie *The Deep*, is only fifteen feet deep and has two different shipwrecks that met the same fate eighty years apart. ($45 for three hours)

Evening shore excursions: Since several cruises arrive in Hamilton at 4:00 P.M. and spend one night in the harbor, there is ample time to enjoy a nightlife tour of the city. If an independent excursion is just what you want, ask the local taxi driver to go to the latest and hottest steel-band club. Otherwise try the following:

Pirate Night at Hawkins Island This is the "best local night" in Bermuda and a short boat trip from downtown. Entertainment includes a steel band playing music from calypso to classical, and local singers and dancers. ($70 for four hours)

Romantic Cruise After dinner, enjoy a special nighttime cruise with Hamilton's city lights in the background. ($37 for two-and-a-quarter hours)

Comedy Cocktail Theater Bermuda's Theatrical Company performs four sensational plays, all of which have been successful, and the reviews have been great. ($25)

King's Wharf on Ireland Island North

Independent shore excursions:

Dockyard Restoration of the Royal Naval Dockyard began in 1809. Today, Dockyard is a restored entertainment and shopping complex at the docks, with restaurants, the Bermuda Arts Center and Crafts Market, Bermuda Maritime Museum, historic Commissioner's House, a cinema, and the Clocktower shopping mall.

Somerset Village Catch a bus or taxi to see lovely old Bermuda homes and English gardens, found there miles from the Dockyard.

Scaur Hill Fort Park Located three miles from the Dockyard. Take a tour or taxi and hike through the park and its lovely gardens to the fort. Enjoy the panoramic view of the Great Sound.

Shore excursions:

Hartley's Undersea Adventure Walk on the floor of the ocean with a special Bermuda peppercorn diving helmet! Descend to the sea floor, feed the fish, and view the exotic life on the coral reef. ($55)

St. George

In 1609, a shipwrecked admiral, Sir George Sommers, built two new ships from the timber on the lush island and made it back to England. Little St. George became the thriving capital of the new British colony of Bermuda. Today it is no longer the capital. Just as well, since further growth would destroy this charming town with the look and feel of Elizabethan England. Stand in the stocks or see where early colonists made their stand against a Spanish fleet with three canon balls.

Independent shore excursions:

Walking Tour Take a leisurely walk on cobblestone streets of old Elizabethan England. Then visit the quaint and colorful King's Square, local art galleries, libraries, private gardens, and churches.

Shore excursions:

Carriage Tour Spend an hour traveling though the city on a lovely horse-drawn carriage. ($21)

Eco Coral Reef and Nature Cruise Board the Coral Sea, the newest glass-bottom boat, and view tropical fish and colorful corals. The history and highlights of St. George will be explained as you travel through town. ($32)

Fort St. Catherine and Museum and St. David's Lighthouse St. Catherine's Fort with its resident ghost is situated on a strategic hill looking north at the far eastern end of the islands. Continue to St. David's Lighthouse and Battery Park. ($35)

Scuba Diving Two-tank reef and wreck dive for certified divers. Over three hundred wrecks surround the island. All equipment is provided. ($70)

Kayak Safari Paddle inside the lagoons and along beaches of the inner coral reef viewing egrets, blue herons, Bermuda longtails, and many others species of birds and fish. All tours are lead by a naturalist guide, and all equipment and instruction is provided. ($54)

Caves and Island Tour to Hamilton (Crystal Caves and Leamington Caves) Bermuda is home to the highest concentration of limestone caves in the world. As early as 1623, Capt. John Smith (of Pocahantas's time) complained that he had encountered "very strange, darke, and cumbersome caves." ($49 for three-and-a-half hours)

Golf in Bermuda: The Ultimate for Every Golfer!

Since its first golf course was designed in 1922, golf has become one of Bermuda's greatest attractions. The incredible lush island setting lends itself to unique courses found nowhere in the world. More than enough time is spent in the islands to allow the most competitive golfer to enjoy a challenging day on the links and with enough time to return to the ship for a gourmet dinner, plus evening entertainment.

➥ **Steve and Pat's Most Excellent Golfer Tip:** *Are you married to or know someone who is a die-hard golfer? Do you need the specifications for the incredible golf courses available on the islands? Call the Bermuda Department of Tourism for a brochure, i.e., "What to Do in Bermuda," which lays out the courses in detail, hole by hole. Write: Bermuda Department of Tourism, Global House, P.O. Box HM 465, Hamilton HM BX, Bermuda, or call (800) 223-6106.*

Norwegian Cruise Line can reserve tee times at any of the following courses. The greens fees and golf cart charges will be added to your shipboard account. Transportation is usually not included, but taxis are readily available at the pier. No refunds on confirmed tee times.

➥ **Steve and Pat's Golfer Dress Code Tip:** *The dress code is strictly enforced. All golfers must wear Bermuda-style shorts or long pants, and shirts must have a collar.*

St. George's Golf Club A short course (4,043 yards, par 62) is found on the eastern tip of the island and north of St. George. Designed by Robert Trent Jones with hillside views of the Atlantic Ocean. ($68)

Port Royal Golf Course Reflects the genius of Robert Trent Jones. The course is situated in some of Bermuda's most lush and beautiful ocean-side terrain. Another long course (6,561 yards, par 71) has free-form greens set against sapphire seas, and graceful fairways skirt coral cliffs. ($95)

Riddell's Bay Golf and County Club Founded in 1922, this short course (5,588 yards, par 70) winds along a narrow peninsula only six hundred yards at its widest. With tight fairways and small narrow greens, it requires considerable accuracy. ($80)

Belmont Golf Club Although a short course (5,769 yards par 70), golfers soon find out the wicked truth: elevated and double-tiered greens, blind second shots, tight fairways, and small, narrow putting surfaces await. ($78)

Castle Harbor Golf Club This challenging course designed by Charles Banks is long (6,440 yards, par 71) and overlooks Castle Harbor's turquoise waters. (cost rumored to be expensive)

Ocean View Golf Course Located in the verdant center of the island known as Devonshire, a couple of miles from Hamilton, Ocean View is owned and maintained by the government. A short, nine-hole course (2,956 yards, par 35) enjoys splendid vistas of the Atlantic from several elevated tees. Its unpredictable terrain and rambling hills are sure to be a challenge. This nine-hole course is just perfect for a short golfing experience for the whole family, and a great way to introduce kids to the world of golf!

Bermuda Cruise Itinerary Options

Although we are not including comparison rates for the shorter weekend cruises, take a look at the activities and those that are appealing to all, regardless of the length of stay on the islands. The four following cruise lines offer one-week Bermuda cruises during most of the year: Celebrity, Norwegian, Royal Caribbean, and Regal. Unlike most other cruise vacations that sail to multiple ports of call, a Bermuda cruise includes several days at sea and, at most, a visit to the three towns of Hamilton, St. George, and King's Wharf.

Bermuda Cruise Lines and Discount Prices

Celebrity Cruises

From April through October, Celebrity has two ships that offer cruises to Bermuda, the *Horizon* and the *Zenith*, from New York or Fort Lauderdale.

In the spring, the *Horizon* sails round-trip from Ft. Lauderdale with four days at sea and three days in port at King's Wharf. When the warm months of June roll around in New York, the cruise ships depart from New York and spend about two-and-a-half days at sea and a little more than three days in port. The following is the *Horizon's* itinerary:

Day one: Depart from New York City in late evening
Day two: Day at sea
Day three: Half day at sea; arrive in King's Wharf at 11:00 A.M.
Day four: Visit King's Wharf for a full day
Day five: Visit King's Wharf for a half day; depart at 2:00 P.M.
Day six: Arrive in Hamilton at 4:00 P.M.
Day seven: Visit Hamilton for most of the day; depart at 3:00 P.M.
Day eight: Disembark in New York City

The *Zenith* sails round-trip from New York during the months of April through October. The itinerary spends two days at sea

Bermuda

and four days in port—two days visiting Hamilton and two days visiting St. George.

Day one: Depart from New York City in the late evening
Day two: Day at sea
Day three: Visit Hamilton for a full day
Day four: Visit Hamilton for a full day
Day five: Visit St. George for a full day
Day six: Visit St. George for most of the day; depart at 3:00 P.M.
Day seven: Day at sea
Day eight: Disembark in New York City

Discount prices Ambassador Tours offers Celebrity cruises on the *Zenith* ($949) and the *Horizon* ($999). Call (800) 989-9000.

Norwegian Cruise Line (NCL)

NCL (*Crown*) sails round-trip from New York City with only two days at sea and two ports of call: one day at St. George and two-and-a-half days at Hamilton. Other NCL itineraries:

- NCL's (*Crown*) round-trip cruise from Port Canaveral, Florida, spends four days at sea and one day each at St. George and Hamilton.
- NCL's (*Majesty*) round-trip cruise from Boston spends only two days at sea and three-and-a-half days at St. George.

Discount prices NCL advertised their *Norwegian Crown* cruise at $1,033, including port charges. The same cruise was advertised by Cruise World at $950, including port charges. Call (800) 588-7447. CruiseOne, another specialty cruise agency, advertised seven-night Norwegian cruises at $799, plus about $130 in port charges, or $930. Call CruiseOne at (888) 703-7245 or (516) 872-1466.

Royal Caribbean International (RCI)

Royal Caribbean is one of the finest of the mass-market cruise companies. Royal delivers quality, luxury, and great prices. RCI also sails round-trip from New York City with two days at sea and two ports of call: one day at St. George and two-and-a-half days at Hamilton.

Discount prices   RCI's discount price for a cruise on the *Song of America* is $752, including port charges. Call Ambassador Tours at (800) 989-9000.

➥ **Steve and Pat's Best Deal Goal:**   *Royal Caribbean International's (RCI)* Song of America *was advertised for $752, including port charges and taxes, by Ambassador Tours.*

12

The Mexican Riviera: South of the Border

Our friends on the East Coast often look to the Caribbean as the most convenient and economical destination for tropical cruise vacations. We on the West Coast turn to Mexico for the best cruise bargains. Caribbean ports of embarkation, including Miami, San Juan, Puerto Rico, Ft. Lauderdale, and New Orleans, are thousands of expensive air miles away for those of us who live in the western states. On the other hand, flights to Los Angeles, the embarkation port for Mexican Riviera and Baja Mexican cruises, are just hundreds of low-cost miles away. In fact, round-trip fares for commuter flights from the Bay Area to Los Angeles range from $70 to $140. Others simply hop into their cars and six hours later arrive in L.A. and save the cost of an airline ticket. Let us not forget the millions of potential cruise customers who live in the Los Angeles metropolitan area.

The two most popular cruise itineraries that embark from Los Angeles and sail down the Mexican coast are the Mexican Riviera seven-day cruise and the popular, lower-priced, three- or four-day Mexican Baja cruises.

> **Steve and Pat's Tip:** *Serious distinctions exist between the Caribbean and Mexican Riviera cruises. Caribbean cruises offer the opportunity to benefit from a higher limit of $1400 for duty-free shopping in the U.S. Virgin Islands and visit four or five islands that were once European colonies. Mexican Riviera cruises do not offer the cultural variety or the shopping opportunities found on the Caribbean cruises.*

Why a Mexican Riviera Cruise?

We love tropical sun, fun, and surf vacations. A Mexican Riviera cruise offers the perfect opportunity to enjoy such activities at incredible bargain prices. While visiting Mexico's ports of call, passengers have access to lavish beachfront hotels with beautifully designed pools and white sand beaches. Shore-based activities include sunning, swimming, snorkeling, and even parasailing high above world-famous tropical resorts. Then there are charming towns that offer fun, if not luxurious, shopping and interesting sightseeing. The success of a Mexican Riviera cruise depends on the enjoyment of sun-and-fun activities, either aboard a luxury cruise ship or at a plush resort hotel at a port of call.

> **Steve and Pat's Shopping Tip:** *Usually the price of many items in Mexico is half the cost of similar items in the states. Most shops, except department stores, close daily for siesta between 2:00 and 4:00 P.M. While larger stores do not bargain over prices, street vendors, flea market sellers, and small shop owners expect to bargain over the best price. Mexico's shopping specialties include the following: silver, leather goods and clothes, ironwood carvings, pure vanilla, pewter crafts, local liquors, and handcrafted items of all kinds and descriptions.*

When we say that shipboard activities play a major role on Mexican Riviera cruises, this is no exaggeration. Consider that most one-week Mexican Riviera cruise itineraries include three full days at sea! This makes a Mexican Riviera cruise the perfect means of "getting away from it all." It is an ideal way to enjoy the best of two worlds, relaxing on a floating luxury hotel for three days at sea and visiting a limited number of Mexican ports of call.

Mexico's Varied, Sun, Surf, and Fun Shopping Ports of Call

Esenada

This small vacation destination is found on the rugged Mexican Baja peninsula. Tourists can partake in any number of available activities. Try an independent shore excursion, such as a walking tour of the town, which should include cocktails and dancing to Mariachi bands on sunny bar terraces. Enjoy Mexican folk art and the many outdoor markets. In the town itself, passengers may visit a historic cantina and wander through scores of shops selling an endless variety of handmade arts and crafts made from ironwood. Other items of shopping interest include leather in all shapes and sizes, from clothing to fine briefcases, vanilla by the quart, fine liquors, and even fabulous Spanish porcelain.

> ➥ **Steve and Pat's Tip:** *During our visit we purchased several hand-carved ironwood statues. One, a sea lion, emerges from a fourteen-inch-high fully round tree trunk. The sea lion itself stands twenty inches.*

Shore excursions:
Baja Bandidos Horseback Trail Ride Ride across the hills of San Miguel, stop at the small Pai Pai Indian village of WI Jasil for a snack and return along trails offering spectacular views of the Gold Coast. ($42)

Blow Hole Tour Tour the town, then travel to the natural wonder, La Bufadora, a natural geyser that sprays its jets of water fifty feet into the air. ($16)

Santo Tomas Bodega and Winery, or the Domecq Winery of Calafia Valley Depending on your ship, take a winery tour and learn about the local customs. Wine tasting? Of course! ($30)

Baja Country Club and Bajamar Oceanfront Golf Resort Check with your cruise director for current greens fees.

Catalina Island

This famed island is only twenty-four miles from Los Angeles and takes passengers back to the 1930s.

Independent shore excursion: Take a cliff-side tour of the picturesque surrounding hills and catch a glimpse of local wildlife, including buffalo. The quaint village of Avalon, once home to the rich and famous, still draws visitors from all walks of life. Enjoy the town's Victorian homes, narrow streets, and slow-paced atmosphere. Consider the island's colorful history and explore its shops and landmarks.

Shore excursions: Shore excursions include helicopter tours of the island, kayaking, and submarine and glass-bottom boat tours:

Lover's Cove Snorkel Tour   Snorkel gear is provided. Enjoy a beach snorkel at Lover's Cove with enough fish food to make the day exciting. ($35)

Avalon Scuba Adventure   At Casino Point, dive at the Avalon Underwater Park, consisting of giant kelp and home to a large variety of marine life. All gear is provided. ($81)

Avalon City and Botanical Tour   Drive along the coast and breathtaking views await. Visit the Botanical Gardens. ($14)

Casino Tour   Visit the Avalon Casino and Ballroom, and the Avalon Theater, with its 1929 murals. Continue to the Catalina Island History Museum. ($9)

Catalina Kayaking   Paddle in the private Descanso Beach Club above the clear water and kelp beds, and spot many of the fish below. ($42)

Land and Sea Adventure   View the island by bus and then board a motorized raft and explore the many sea caves, coves, and secluded beaches. Wildlife abounds. ($58 for four hours)

Puerto Vallarta

The town's popularity soared after John Houston filmed *Night of the Iguana* on nearby Mismaloya Beach and Elizabeth Taylor and Richard Burton built houses there. Today the city of 250,000 is famous as one of Mexico's finest resort areas. Located at the center of one of the world's largest bays, its calm waters offer fine snorkeling and fishing. Did we mention that Puerto Vallarta has 345 days of sunshine each year with average daytime temperatures in the humid high 80s?

Visitors find a wonderful blend of "Old Mexico," with cobblestone streets, red clay tile roofs climbing the mountainsides, and shops galore along the picturesque Malecon. Yet only minutes away are fabulous five-star hotels, a first-rate marina harbor, and luxurious vacation amenities of every kind and description.

Shore excursions:

City Tour, Mismaloya Beach, and Shopping Take a three-and-a-half hour city tour plus Mismaloya Beach, the location for the filming of *Night of the Iguana*. Enjoy the quaint cobblestone streets of Puerto Vallarta and lush tropical foliage. Sightseeing highlights in town include the cathedral, city hall, and the open theater. ($18)

Los Arcos Snorkel Tour Take in the beautiful coastal scenery as the snorkel boat heads for the arched rocky formations called Los Arcos. After a fun snorkeling session, the group heads to nearby Las Animas Beach for sunbathing and swimming. ($39)

Banderos Bay Snorkeling Tour Cruise aboard a fifty-foot catamaran through the spectacular bay to Los Arcos's famous rock formations. All gear is provided. ($29 for three hours)

Beach Party Tour Spend a lovely, three-and-a-half hours at Paradise Village Beach Resort and Spa, one of the most beautiful beaches in the area. The fun never stops on this one! Receive a welcome drink and relax on the white sand beach, swim in the ocean, and enjoy all the hotel's facilities, including its large pool with water slide, a spa, and tennis courts. This is why Puerto Vallarta is known as Mexico's world-famous resort area. ($15)

Backcountry Horseback Riding Travel by bus to the tiny town of La Desembocada, ride along the Mascota River past tropical vegetation and farmland filled with tropical fruit plants. Take a swim in the river before returning. ($37)

Marina Vallarta Club de Golf A golfer's delight. This resort course is unique because it has integrated the area's natural landscape with tropical plants and a thrilling view of the Pacific coastline. Transportation, greens fees and shared golf carts are included. ($108)

➥ **Steve and Pat's Puerto Vallarta Tip:** *When we visited Puerto Vallarta several years ago, our cruise director suggested we walk to the luxury Crystal Hotel, ten minutes from the dock area. To this day, we fondly recall the incredible day we spent at this five-star beachfront resort. The Crystal Hotel is part of a major chain of expensive, high-end properties. The Puerto Vallarta Crystal is part hotel, part time-share, and part condominium, with its own bullfight ring. The ornate lobby gave way to a lovely landscaped garden where mini-villas formed a crescent, with each grouping of four or five villas surrounding its own private pool.*

Steve and Pat's Crystal Hotel experience: Upon arriving at the Crystal Hotel, we made our way to the main pool, settled onto two comfortable lounge chairs, and marveled at this unique property. The pool is elongated and kidney-shaped, with small bridges here and there. It is perhaps four feet deep and made for sun worshipers. In its center is a concrete "flower platform" upon which teenagers stretched out for quality sunbathing and misting from tiny fountains. Soothing light rock music escaped from underground speakers spaced evenly around the area. Water spilled over the pool's edge, giving the illusion of a waterfall emanating from the pool. Just beyond were the beach and ocean. As if all this weren't enough, all around the perimeter of the pool, in the water, were curved concrete lounges. We reclined horizontally, the water only reaching the mid-level of our bodies but keeping us cool and relaxed.

The waiter arrived with giant cored pineapples filled with what tasted like nectar of the gods, a mixture of piña colada and other tropical flavors. We feasted on our Carnival "picnic lunch." At midday we walked to the beach and went parasailing. The hotel was happy to allow us a drop-in visit at no charge whatsoever. Did they expect us to buy lunch or drinks during our visit? Sure. We happily enjoyed several drinks during this fabulous and unforgettable day.

If a port of call is a world-famous tropical resort, why not opt for free day of sun, surf, and fun at a five-star luxury resort? After all, this is why vacationers travel thousands of miles, to visit such famed resorts. Yes, we realize that some others prefer a walk through town with attendant sightseeing and shopping, which justifies the phrase, "each to his (or her) own."

Mazatlan

Mazatlan is another of Mexico's famed seaside resort areas. Recreational and other activities include the following: sunbathing, swimming, snorkeling, scuba diving, parasailing, boating, and fishing. Consider a visit to the local aquarium—one of the largest and best-maintained aquariums in Latin America, with sea lion and bird shows. Other activities include horseback riding, golf, and tennis (check with your cruise director for availability).

Independent shore excursions:

Walking and Sightseeing in Old Town   Visit the 19th-century cathedral, with its carved volcanic façade. Let's not forget shopping in local malls and hundreds of small shops located in the Golden Zone.

Lounge at a Five-Star Hotel   Local hotels welcome ships' passengers for the day, and our tour director gave us the directions to several. We visited an upscale hotel that sported a huge pool with an artificial mountain and waterfall. A live orchestra played at poolside.

Again, we gladly obliged the management and purchased delectable fruity drinks during the hot afternoon. Most Mazatlan hotels are just a short taxicab-ride away. We easily drafted a couple of fellow passengers and cut the taxi fare in half. This time we opted for an inexpensive and delicious poolside buffet lunch. Simply ask the ship's cruise director for the name of the best recommended luxury resort that awaits your arrival as royal guests for the day!

Shore excursions:

The City Tour, Beach, and Shopping Expedition Travel through expensive and exclusive residential neighborhoods en route to the city's downtown area along Olas Atlas and then on to the deluxe hotels on Gaviotas Beach. There is time for shopping and an opportunity to view the memorable Aztec Indian Papantla Show. ($22 for three-and-a-half hours)

Colonial Villages and Papantla Flyers (or the Sierra Madre Tour) Watch how adobe bricks are made at a local brick factory. Then travel to the small village of Malpica and see how concrete tiles are made. See how the locals live in rural villages. Continue to Concordia, founded 1550 and famous for its clay pottery and colonial furniture. Return to Mazatlan to view the Papantla Flyers show. ($35 for four-and-a-half hours)

Sportfishing Tours Enjoy a full-day deep-sea-fishing adventure in search of the great Marlin. Anyone for catching a 750-pound wall hanging? A thirty-five-foot fishing boat provides fun transportation for the day. ($99 for eight hours)

Las Moras Hacienda and Horseback Riding This unique excursion takes passengers to one of Mexico's best-known deluxe hacienda resorts. There is ample time to relax by the pool, stroll in its gardens, and enjoy a one-hour horseback ride in the foothills. A wonderful poolside lunch is served before you return. ($65 for five-and-a-half hours)

Cabo San Lucas

Once a tranquil fishing village, Cabo San Lucas is on the southernmost tip of the Baja peninsula. Famous for its marlin fishing, the town of 25,000 offers a great variety of sun-and-fun activities. Passengers usually have but a half day to visit, and the town's shops offer the full variety of Mexican crafts, silver, ceramics, and wood carvings. A large local flea market is near the docks, offering local arts and crafts and refreshments.

Shore excursions:

Snorkel and Sail Fiesta Tour Swim and play with hundreds of colorful tropical fish and sail a catamaran to Pelican Rock, the snorkel site. On return, the boat passes Lover's Beach and heads toward famous Los Arcos at Land's End, where the crew raises the sails. The "cat" then heads around San Lucas Bay, past the cruise ship, and returns to the dock. ($32 for two-and-a-half hours)

Coastal Highlights Tour Tour along the rugged coastline with its many unusual rock formations, then continue to a glass blowing factory. There are additional stops at the classic hotel Cabo San Lucas, the picturesque town of San Jose del Cabo, a visit to the Mission Church, and a final stop at the Plaza Bonita Mall for browsing and shopping. ($36 for three-and-a-half hours)

Glass-Bottom Boat and Beach Resort Tour View sea lions and pelicans above and colorful tropical fish below on this relaxing excursion. In the background is the dramatic rock formation known as Los Arcos. Then, on to the Hotel Hacienda for optional water sports, or simply relax on its beach. Enjoy a complimentary beverage.

Zihuatanejo and Ixtapa

Found between Acapulco and Puerto Vallarta, these neighboring towns, just four miles apart, represent two vacation worlds. Zihuatanejo remains the sleepy, quaint fishing village that has charmed visitors for years. Here are cobblestone streets, open-air fruit markets, an artists market, and delightful restaurants and shops. All water sports are also available. Eat, Drink, Relax, and Be Happy might be the motto for this place. Consider an early morning walk and see fishermen returning with their catch of the day. This is an ancient regimen that is rarely seen in these modern days.

Independent shore excursions:

Take a walking tour of this delightful village. Passengers may leisurely explore the town's shops, restaurants, and bars along the Avenida del Pescador near the bay. The tourist office is also here. Check out the town's main street, Avenida Cuauhtemoc.

Shopping A fun activity, with shops selling local crafts, such as wood carvings, ceremonial masks, and bright whimsical ceramics. Zihuatanejo's beaches are on a calm bay, so they are perfect for swimming.

Playa Las Gatos (Cat Beach) Take a *ponga* (water taxi) to this beach, with its pristine cove. This spot is ideal for snorkeling.

Playa Principal This is the town's most popular beach, so it may be crowded. Take a short ten-minute walk to nearby Playa Maderas Beach, which has more charm and fewer people.

Ixtapa

Just four miles away is the modern resort town of Ixtapa. Built on twenty-four miles of magnificent beachfront property, Ixtapa is a place of ultimate views in every direction. Luxury hotels and two eighteen-hole golf courses are just the beginning. Marina Ixtapa is the home for 662 yachts. The principal resort beach is two-mile-long Playa del Palmar. A better beach near Club Mediterranean is Playa Quieta. These beaches afford wonderful opportunities for sunbathing, swimming, and snorkeling. Others opt for fishing, scuba diving, golf, and tennis.

Tourists can shop for traditionally crafted items, clothes, and leather goods, and then visit great restaurants and, at the end of the day, frequent dance-til-dawn discos.

Shore excursions:

Ixtapa Island Consider the boat ride to this nearby island, a nature preserve. Boats leave from Playa Quieta. Of the four beaches on the island, Coral Beach is best for snorkeling.

➥ **Steve and Pat's Tip:** *Ixtapa-Zihuantanejo is not a port of call on Carnival's Mexican Riviera cruises. Consider the longer eleven-day RCI cruise which includes not only Ixtapa-Zihuantanejo, but also two days on Acapulco. Read on for details.*

Acapulco

Acapulco is the famous glamour capital of Mexico. This incredible seaside resort is famous for its magnificent sand beaches, captivating nearby mountains, and dazzling crescent-shaped bay. Luxury resorts with an endless list of amenities abound. In Acapulco the action never ends; this is Mexico's twenty-four-hour-a-day glitz city. When it comes to recreation, the word is *everything!* This means golf, tennis, all water sports, sightseeing, and shop-til-you-drop opportunities. Add 360 days a year of sunny weather, and Acapulco is a perfect port of call.

Shore excursions:

City Tour With Cliff Divers   Drive to scenic overlook that offers a marvelous view of the city. The tour continues to either the Acapulco Princess Hotel, which resembles an Aztec pyramid, or the Vidasel hotel with its mile-long swimming pool. Finally, visit the Hotel El Miradon to watch the daring cliff divers of Quebrada plunge gracefully into the sea below. ($27 for four hours)

Other shore excursions include snorkeling, fishing, and boating. There are many opportunities to play golf and tennis on world-class courses and courts.

Manzanilla

This is not one of the usual Mexican Riviera ports of call. It is found on Royal Caribbean International's innovative eleven-day itinerary. Manzanilla, located on a narrow peninsula that is separated by two bays, is one of Mexico's lesser-known resort areas. The town's narrow winding streets are teeming with shops and boutiques selling all types of Mexican crafts. Just beyond the town are jungles and fruit plantations. The immediate area of Manzanilla is known for its uncrowded fine beaches. Expect to see some of Mexico's finest scenery.

Shore excursions: Outdoor recreations options include some of the best deep-sea fishing in the world, scuba diving, and all the usual water sports, as well as golf and tennis. Check with RCI for Shore Excursions.

Mexican Riviera Seven-Night Cruise Itinerary

This is the itinerary used by Carnival and most other cruise lines:

Day one: Depart from Los Angeles
Day two: Day at sea
Day three: Day at sea

Day four: Visit Puerto Vallarta for a full day
Day five: Visit Mazatlan for a full day
Day six: Day at sea
Day seven: Disembark in Los Angeles

Baja Mexico Four-Day Cruise Itineraries

Here is the typical four-day Baja Mexico Cruise itinerary:

Day one: Depart from Los Angeles in the late evening
Day two: Visit Avalon, Catalina Island, California for a full day
Day three: Visit Ensenada, Mexico for a full day
Day four: Day at sea
Day five: Disembark in Los Angeles

Note: The typical three-day Mexico Baja itinerary is identical to the above four-day itinerary, except that it omits the port of call Catalina Island.

Mexican Riviera Cruise Lines and Discount Prices

Carnival Cruise Line

Carnival offers more one-week Mexican Riviera and three- and four-day Baja Mexico cruises than all other cruise lines put together. Recently, Carnival proudly announced that its cruise ship *Elation* is "the newest and largest ship ever to sail to the Mexican Riviera!" We happily report that Carnival's 1998 to mid-1999 sailing schedule shows at least sixty-four, one-week Mexican Riviera cruises on the *Elation*. Here are some of the ship's special features:

Holds 2,040 passengers
Six-story atrium lobby
Large outdoor entertainment area
Marble floors and art collection
State-of-the-art fitness center
Duty-free Galleria Shopping Mall

South of the Border

Full Camp Carnival facilities for kids
Casual dining in Tiffany's twenty-four-hour Bar and Grill
The largest casino at sea
Dance into the wee hours in the Jekyll and Hyde Dance Club.
The Mikado two-level showroom

Discount Prices Costco Travel offers a seven-night Mexican Riviera cruise on Carnival's new *Elation* for just $813, including port charges. Call Costco at (800) 800-8505.

➥ **Steve and Pat's Tip:** *Since its inaugural sailing in April 1998, Carnival's new* Elation *has been carrying sun-and-fun-loving passengers to the Mexican Riviera. Given the three full days spent at sea, we highly recommend the* Elation. *Why not enjoy those days on a spanking new luxury cruise ship that offers three pools, six whirlpools, a spiral water slide, and miles of deck for sunning and strolling!*

Carnival's ship, the *Holiday,* used on three- and four-day Mexican cruises, hold 1,452 passengers and has eight decks. It offers typical ship's amenities, including two pools, plus a children's pool.

Royal Caribbean International (RCI)

Royal Caribbean is one of the finest of the mass-market cruise companies. Royal delivers quality, luxury, and great prices. RCI's Mexican Riviera cruise on the *Song of America* embarks from Los Angeles and visits Puerto Vallarta, Mazatlan, and Cabo San Lucas. *Song of America* is an older midsized ship that was built in 1982 and carries 1,402 passengers. Amenities include two pools and movie theater.

You deserve an ultimate eleven-day Mexican Riviera cruise that visits more and better ports of call! RCI's eleven-day cruise uses the *Legend of the Seas*. This is one of RCI's two ships that have eighteen-hole miniature golf courses as well as an endless array of other luxuries. This cruise sails round-trip from San

Diego and visits Mazatlan, Cabo San Lucas, Puerto Vallarta, Acapulco (for two days) and Manzanilla. For surf, sun, and fun lovers, this cruise offers three days in Mexico's top tropical resorts, one day in Puerto Vallarta, and two days in Acapulco.

➥ **Steve and Pat's Tip:** *First the good news: Whole World of Travel offers round-trip airfare and transfers to the ship for $99 from Northern California. They can also arrange great air-and-cruise packages from other cities. The not so bad news: a reminder that Whole World is a volume agency that prefers to hear from customers who have done their homework, selected their dream cruise, and plan to depart within six months.*

Discount prices The words here are "lower cost option." Where Carnival's new megaship *Elation* is priced at $813, Whole World of Travel offers winter 1998 sailings on RCI's *Song of America* for just $577, including taxes and port charges.

Whole World sells RCI's eleven-day cruise on the *Legend of the Seas* for just $910, including taxes and port charges. Call Whole World at (800) 458-3636.

➥ **Steve and Pat's Best Deal Goal:** *Royal Caribbean International's* Song of America *was advertised for $577, including port charges and taxes, by Whole World of Travel.*

13

The Greek Isles, Turkey, and the Mediterranean: A Shimmering Necklace of Pearls

The Greek Isles, land of romance, mystery, and antiquity. These words conjure pictures of the most exciting vacation ever imaginable! All of us have dreamed of traveling to the fantastic Greek Isles as a wonderful adventure. Few vacations offer such a fantastic opportunity to combine a restful and relaxing vacation with a trip back in time to the beginning of western civilization. We lived our dream cruise-and-land vacation in the summer of 1998.

Greece is bordered on the west by the Ionian Sea and on the east by the Aegean Sea. The Greek Isles stretch around Greece like a shimmering necklace made of a double strand of pearls with a precious gem, the island of Crete, connecting both strands.

The first strand of pearls is the group of Ionian Isles found a few miles off the western shore of Greece, which include Corfu, Paxos, Lefkada, Cephalonia, Ithaca, and Zante. Because these islands are in the Ionian Sea between Italy and Greece, they escaped occupation by the Turkish Empire and were instead conquered by the Venetians, French, British, and Russians. Consequently, the culture of these islands is unique, western, and quite different from the islands in the Aegean Sea to the east.

The second strand of pearls lays off the eastern shore between Greece and Turkey in the Aegean Sea. Four main island groups contain ports of call visited by the cruise lines. The northeastern Aegean Islands stretch down the Turkish coast and to a few miles offshore, and include Chios, Lesbos, and Samos. Continuing south down the Turkish coast is the Dodecanes Islands that include Patmos, Kos, and Rhodes. Switching across the sea to the northern Greek coast is the Sporades Islands of Skiathos, Skopelos, and Skyros, favorites of the European communities for their mixed Greek, Roman, Venetian, and Turkish culture.

By far the largest and most popular eastern group of islands is the Cyclades located in the middle of the Aegean Sea just north of Crete. Several of these islands are well known. A violent volcanic explosion of ancient times destroyed most of Santorini, which is rumored to be the location of the lost city of Atlantis. Mykonos is the "party island" and is a favorite of the younger vacation crowd. Delos is the most sacred of the Greek Isles and the birthplace of the twin Greek gods Apollo and Artemis.

Further south, below Greece and this group of islands, lies the large island of Crete with its distinct Minoan culture, history, and ruins. Crete dangles like a large precious stone in the southern Aegean Sea and connects both the west and east strands of the "pearl necklace."

➡ **Steve and Pat's Tip:** *When beginning to plan your trip to the Greek Isles, several decisions must be made immediately. First, determine the maximum amount of money available for your vacation. Second, figure out how many days you have available for a trip, (seven, ten, or fourteen). Third, do you want to explore mainland Greece as well as travel through the islands?*

Some cruise lines offer additional ports of call at other middle eastern countries located in the eastern Mediterranean Sea. Such countries and ports of call include the following: The Turkish ports of Kusadasi (Ephesus), Canakkale (Troy), and Istanbul, Israeli ports of Ashdod and Haifa, Egyptian ports of call at Alexandria and Port Said and a planned excursion to Cairo, and the split Greek-Turkish island of Cyprus.

The western and eastern islands and Crete make up most Greek Isles' itineraries, cruising between the past and present Greek worlds. Because of the many combinations of ports of call available, picking a cruise itinerary can be challenging and may require tough choices.

Discovering Greece by Land and by Sea

We read all the brochures and then decided that a combination land-and-cruise package appealed to us.

Because most cruises either begin or end at the port of Piraeus, Greece, located south of Athens, a major opportunity presents itself to explore the historic city. Extra days at a hotel can easily be arranged. A stay of two or three days provides time to discover the charm and friendship of the Greek people and life in the capital, to visit the archeological sites at your leisure, or to wander through the many museums containing Greek artifacts and sculptures, such as the National Archeological Museum.

➥ **Steve and Pat's Tip:** *Land-and-cruise packages may be booked directly through the cruise lines or specialty tour operators. Our cheapskate choice is specialty-tour operator Homeric Tours. Other specialty cruise operators include Tourlite International and Gate One. These operators offer the best selection and bargain prices. Their packages offer a range of hotel prices that can reduce the overall cost significantly. Most of these companies offer more combination packages than the cruise lines.*

Combine a two- to three-day stay in Athens with a three- or four-day land tour of Greece on the Peloponnese peninsula that will include visits to various exciting archeological sites and overnight stays at Naupelion, Olympia, and Delphi. You can then board your cruise ship to visit the Greek Isles.

Land tours are also offered by Royal Olympic Cruise Lines and Orient Cruise Lines. However, cruise line arrangements tend to be more expensive than a specialty tour company.

➥ **Steve and Pat's Tip:** *Airfare from New York to and from Athens, Greece, or Istanbul, Turkey, is usually included in land-and-cruise packages offered by the cruise lines and specialty tour operators. Departure is usually from a major east coast gateway city such as New York. It's a veritable bargain. Olympic Airways is the most frequently used air line especially by Royal Olympic Cruises. Both of our nonstop, Olympic Airways flights were on time and offered the usual amenities including free drinks, hot meals and free movies. Orient Cruise Line also uses Lufthansa Air Lines.*

The Greek Isles—Fascinating Itineraries and Ports of Call

Cruises though the Isles involve day stops with visits to Greek, Minoan, Roman, Byzantine, Venetian, and Turkish ruins and present-day museums preserving the antiquities. Greek Isles vacationers can appreciate the Greek influence on the arts, architecture, culture, foods, history, and philosophy of Western Civilization.

Three cruise lines offer a variety of intensive Greek Isles cruise-only itineraries and cruise-and-land itineraries. The cruise lines are Royal Olympic Cruise Lines (ROC) with eight ships; Orient Line with its one ship, the *Marco Polo*; and Renaissance Cruises with two ships, the *R1* and *R2*. Other major lines such as Princess Cruise Lines' *Grand Princess* may offer a couple of ports of call in the Greek Isles on their Mediterranean cruise that includes Spain, Italy, or Russia (Black Sea). These itineraries usually require fourteen days since the ship must cover more miles at sea than is needed for a compact Greek Isle cruise.

Typical three-, four-, or seven-night cruises visit one to two islands each day, traveling between islands at night. In the morning or afternoon, passengers disembark and explore new surroundings and ancient ruins, relax lazily on the beach, wander the well-worn cobblestone streets of picturesque towns or prowl through innumerable shops until it is time to board the ship. The days at sea are few, so consider how many days you require for relaxing versus exploring ports of call; factor that requirement into the decision-making process.

Royal Olympic Cruises Itinerary

Royal Olympic Cruises offers a varied array of cruise itineraries since their fleet of eight ships sails the Greek Isles from March through November. All ROC's cruises begin and end at Piraeus, Greece. ROC's two ships, the *Olympic* and the *Odysseus*, sail the three- and four-day cruises.

The three-day cruises are called the "Aegean Hellenic" or "Aegean Discovery" and offer the following itinerary:

Day one: Depart from Piraeus, Greece, at 11:00 A.M.; visit Mykonos, Greece, from 6:00 P.M. to 10:00 P.M.
Day two: Visit Rhodes, Greece, for a full day
Day three: Visit Kusadasi, Turkey (Ephesus), for the morning; visit Patmos, Greece, in the afternoon, *or* Patmos, Greece, in the morning and Kusadasi, Turkey (Ephesus), in the afternoon
Day four: Disembark in Piraeus, Greece at 7:00 A.M.

If a four-day cruise is your cup of tea, then try the "Aegean Classic" or the "Aegean Venture." The four-day itinerary adds one day to the three-day Aegean cruises listed above. The additional cruising day takes you to Crete in the morning and then on to Santorini in the afternoon.

ROC's three seven-day cruises are designed to cover everyone's fantasy islands. Two cruises, the "Golden Fleece" on the new *Olympic Countess* and the "Mediterranean Odyssey" on the *Stella Solaris* offer a nearly identical cruise itinerary. The "Mediterranean Odyssey" cruise offers one more port of call at Canakkale, Turkey, for an excursion to Troy instead of an additional afternoon in Istanbul, Turkey. Royal Olympic's brochure invites you to "Sail back through time to the Minoan Palace of Knossos on Crete and to the medieval city of the crusaders on Rhodes. Climb to the clifftop village of Thera on Santorini or sip an ouzo at sunset in a seaside cafe on Mykonos. Sample the delights of Istanbul by night." We chose the "Golden Fleece" cruise and enjoyed the variety of ports of call. The "Golden Fleece" and "Mediterranean Odyssey" itinerary is as follows:

Day one: Depart from Piraeus, Greece in the evening
Day two: Visit Santorini, Greece, from 7:00 A.M. to 12:00 P.M.; Heraklion, Crete, from 2:00 P.M. to 7:00 P.M.
Day three: Visit Rhodes, Greece, for a full day
Day four: Visit Patmos, Greece, in the morning; visit Kusadasi, Turkey (Ephesus), in the afternoon
Day five: Half day at sea; visit the Dardanelles in the morning; and Canakkale, Turkey (Troy), *or* Istanbul, Turkey in the afternoon
Day six: Depart from Istanbul, Turkey, at 6:00 P.M.
Day seven: Visit Mykonos, Greece, in the afternoon, with an excursion to Delos, Greece.
Day eight: Disembark in Piraeus, Greece, at 7:00 A.M.

The third seven-day itinerary is the "Classical Aegean and Ionian Voyage." This cruise combines the stunning Ionian Isles of Corfu, Ithaca, and Zante off the western shores of Greece with the scenic and charming Aegean Isles of Santorini, Mykonos, and Crete. This cruise truly completes a string of pearls around Greece.

Day one: Depart from Piraeus, Greece in the evening; ship should go through the Corinth Canal at midnight
Day two: Visit Itea (Delphi) in the morning; Ithaca in the evening until midnight
Day three: Visit Parga in the morning; Corfu in the afternoon through evening
Day four: Visit Zante in the morning; Katakolon (Olympia) in the afternoon through evening
Day five: Visit Rethymnon, Crete in the afternoon to midnight

Day six: Visit Santorini in the morning; Mykonos, in the evening until 10:00 P.M.
Day seven: Visit Nauplia (Mycenae) for a full day
Day eight: Disembark in Piraeus, at 7:00 A.M.

Orient Line Itinerary

Orient Cruises offers a twelve- and a thirteen-day vacation package that includes a basic five-day cruise on the *Marco Polo* traveling through the Greek Isles and Turkey. The ports of call are Athens, Delos, Mykonos, Santorini, Crete, Rhodes, and Kusadasi and Istanbul, Turkey. Of the five cruising days, none are exclusively spent at sea. Each day finds the ship visiting one or two ports of call. However, even though there are no cruising days set aside just for rest and relaxation, this short cruise should not be taxing even if you do an excursion every day.

Orient Lines cleverly adds a pre- and post-cruise hotel stay to the cruise itinerary. Thus, Orient's "Aegean Odyssey" becomes a twelve- or thirteen-day trip consisting of the basic five-day cruise and pre- and post-cruise hotel stays, for example, one stay in Athens (two days) and the other stay Istanbul (three days). The typical itinerary for the "Aegean Odyssey" on the *Marco Polo* follows:

Pre-Cruise Hotel Stay

Day one: Depart from the United States
Day two: Arrive in Athens, Greece in the morning
Day three: Tour Athens for a full day
Day four: Tour Athens in the morning

Cruise Itinerary

Day four: Embark in Piraeus, Greece in the evening
Day five: Visit Delos in the morning; Mykonos from 1:00 P.M. until 10:00 P.M.
Day six: visit Santorini in the morning; Heraklion, Crete, from 4:00 P.M. until 10:00 P.M.
Day seven: Visit Rhodes for a full day

Day eight: Visit Kusadasi, Turkey (Ephesus), in the morning
Day nine: Disembark in Istanbul, Turkey, at 8:00 A.M.

Post-Cruise Hotel Stay

Day nine: Tour Istanbul, Turkey for a full day
Day ten: Tour Istanbul, Turkey for a full day
Day eleven: Tour Istanbul, Turkey for a full day
Day twelve: Depart from Istanbul for the United States

The second itinerary is the combination "Classical Aegean" tour that becomes a thirteen-day trip. The tour includes the basic five-day cruise with the two pre- and post-cruise hotel stays in Athens (two days) and Istanbul (two days) and a two-day, "Classical Greece" tour exploring mainland Greece by motor coach, staying overnight at Nauplia and Delphi.

Because the *Marco Polo* cruises the Mediterranean extensively from May through October, not all Greek Isle cruises are available at all times. The Greek Isles cruises are usually offered in two-week blocks starting the first two weeks in May, the first two weeks in June, the last two weeks in July, the last two weeks in August, the last two weeks in September, and all of the month of October. The low season for Orient Cruises included the first two sailings in May and the last two sailings in October. If the timing fits your schedule and the weather cooperates, several hundred dollars can be saved by booking during this time, for example, $500 per person. However, October's weather can turn stormy and dampen your vacation in Greece.

Renaissance Cruises

Renaissance Cruises offers a one-way, ten-day cruise between Athens, Greece, and Istanbul, Turkey as well as one going the opposite way. Pre- and post-hotel cruise stays in Athens and Istanbul are added to the package, creating a fourteen-day trip. We found that Renaissance's low end–priced cabins on this cruise were unavailable for ten months. The gauntlet was dropped! Could we beat the Renaissance itinerary and low-price challenge? We will let you decide.

➥ **Steve and Pat's Tip:** *Orient Lines and Renaissance require a pre- and a post-cruise overnight stay at a hotel, usually in Athens and Istanbul. This means checking into a hotel, (unpacking and packing for one day) before or after the cruise. We relished one unique aspect of our Homeric "Grecian Voyager" itinerary through Royal Olympic Cruises: Upon concluding our cruise, we simply left the ship in Piraeus, and headed straight for the Athens Airport and our flight home.*

Specialty Greek Tour Operators

Homeric Tours, Tourlite, and Gate One offer various combinations of Royal Olympic Cruises' three-, four-, and seven-day cruises plus land tours on mainland Greece and extended hotel stays in Athens, Istanbul, or Mykonos.

➥ **Steve and Pat's Recommendation:** *After our Greek Isle vacation we are pleased to report that Homeric delivered as promised throughout our sixteen-day trip. We enjoyed a high level of comfort, convenience, and enjoyment. Top amenities and facilities were provided. At journey's end Homeric was again waiting dockside to transfer us to the Athens Airport. Our hats are off to Homeric Tours, which receives our top Cheapskate recommendation. Call Homeric Tours for information and brochures at (800) 223-5570.*

We booked Homeric Tour's "Grecian Voyager," a sixteen-day land-and-cruise package. This is really two one-week vacations rolled into one super package! First, the Grecian Voyager's land vacation includes two full days at a hotel in Athens followed by a four-day Classical tour of Greece by motor coach, staying overnight at Nauplion, Olympia, and Delphi in Amalia Hotels.

Our Homeric Tours "Grecian Voyager" vacation with its much longer sixteen-day itinerary in the summer of 1998 was priced at $2,650 per person. This includes hotels, breakfasts and dinners while on the road outside Athens, a seven-night "Golden Fleece" cruise on Royal Olympics' *Olympic Countess*, port charges, and round-trip airfare from New York. Because the Homeric package is fourteen nights, we saved an additional $500 using Jonny Cat Litter free travel cash so that our net price was $2,400 each.

➥ **Steve and Pat's Tip:** *Our best breakfasts on the mainland were at the Esperia Palace Hotel. Our standard is a breakfast that serves hot and cold items. Many hotels only serve the minimum required continental repast. Check this out before booking. Esperia served great daily breakfasts including three types of eggs (hard boiled, scrambled, and sunny-side up), cold cuts, cheeses, fruit, and cereals.*

Our cruise ship, the *Olympic Countess*, is a smaller and older refurbished vessel that was formerly the *Cunard Countess*. Homeric offers a choice of hotels to suit any pocketbook. The above price reflects our choice of first-class rather than the higher priced deluxe hotels.

➥ **Steve and Pat's Outdoor Movie Tip:** *Seen the Acropolis? Want to mingle with locals and enjoy a unique movie experience? Check the English daily tourist newspaper provided by all hotels. The movie section will list nearby outdoor movie theaters that are set up on rooftops. Price is about $5 and the experience was joyful. Arrive a half-hour early and take a seat behind a table for the best view.*

Jump Back in Time—Explore Greece with a Land Tour

The following sampling is taken from our cruise and land vacation, Homeric's "Grecian Voyager" and other favorite ports of call. Most or all of these dream destinations are a major part of the scores of Greece vacations available in the travel marketplace:

Greece Mainland Highlights:

Athens, Greece The capital of Greece and the birthplace of western civilization retains the old and new side by side. Visit the Parthenon and National Archeological Museum. We stayed at the Esperia Palace Hotel on Stadiou Street. This is a first-class hotel with spacious rooms and a very good location; it is within walking distance to major sights, museums, the plaka, the Acropolis, and much more. However, the air conditioning is barely adequate. Request a quiet room off the main street.

➥ **Steve and Pat's Acropolis View Tip:** *Go to the Dionysos Zonar's Cafe on Rovertou Galli Street beneath the Acropolis. Leave the restaurant and walk through the park up the hill to the Monument of Filopappou. Arrive before dark and enjoy a spectacular sunset over the acropolis.*

Greek food is the most reasonably priced in Europe. We enjoyed the Neon Restaurant located in Syntagmatos Square with its glitzy self-service counters. Food stations for salads, ice cream, pasta, and omelettes offered entrees made to order and a grill area for meat dishes. Entrees were less than five dollars apiece. The plaka offers a wide selection of reasonably priced restaurants tucked away in pleasant parks and plazas.

➥ **Steve and Pat's Taxi Tip:** *The taxis are great and cheap. But be alert: Make certain the meter is on and reads #one for day rates or #two after midnight. Day rates start at two hundred drachmas (about 75 cents). Tip to the next even 100 drachmas. We took about ten taxis in the city: Average prices are about $1.75 to $3 tops including a tip.*

Athens Side Trip to Vouliagmeni Lake

This is a fresh-water lake sheltered in a quarrylike lake site. The entrance fee is inexpensive. The changing booths and showers, chairs, and sun beds are free. The resort is well-kept and cool. Food service is quick and the salads are great. A taxi ride cost 2,000 drachmas (about $7) one way.

Four-Day Tour of Classical Greece

The tour company used the Amalia chain of hotels, which were the best available. They were not up to the four-star standard of major Athens hotels. Our bus coach was super deluxe with reclining seats, individual air ducts, and panoramic windows.

> ➥ **Steve and Pat's Tip:** *Take a seat in the rear of the bus. The front of the buses have limited overhead space. The rear has more effective air conditioning.*

New Greek highways made travel a joy. Numerous and convenient rest stops were scheduled during each leg of our travels. We always felt that we had sufficient time to explore all major ruins at each city visited. Irene, our tour guide, has a master's degree in art history and was very knowledgeable. Her tales, explanations, and exuberance made her a first-class tour guide.

> ➥ **Steve and Pat's Tip:** *Meals in Greece include a tip but the custom is to add another five to ten percent for good service. There is usually a cover charge for the table cloth and silverware and also a bread charge for a grand total of about sixty-five cents per person.*

The daily breakfasts served at the Amalia hotels were certainly adequate. Lunches were not included. On two occasions we checked into the hotel and then went to their dining room for lunch. Each hotel has the same menu and prices are reasonable. Amalia's in-hotel restaurants offer a bland atmosphere compared to the fun ambiance of the colorful outdoor cafes. On the third day we enjoyed an outdoor lunch at a beachfront roadside restaurant on the Ionian sea.

Our Trip Itinerary

Day One Drive along the Saronic Gulf via the Corinth Canal to Mycenae, the site of the oldest culture on Greece with the famed Lion Gate and the tomb of the murdered Agamemnon. Continue to the famous theater of Epidarus, the finest example of an amphitheater in design and acoustics. Then to the quaint tourist town of Nauplion, the first capital of Greece from 1829–1834. Enjoy wandering through the cobblestoned streets and shopping in numerous boutiques.

➦ **Steve and Pat's Lounge Chair Tip:** *Rush to the hotel pool and snag a chaise lounge for the one or two precious hours before dinner. Better yet, bring one of your own colorful beach towels so that you may speedily reserve a lounge. This is the daily custom, although lounges should only be reserved when they are intended to be used.*

Day Two Travel through the middle of the Peloponnese Peninsula to Olympia in western Greece, the birthplace of the Olympic games. Visit the inspiring Olympic Stadium, Temples of Zeus and Hera and the museum.

Day Three Travel up the western Peloponnese coast through the towns of Illia, Achaia, and Patras to Rion and take the car-ferry to Antirion. We stopped at a lovely seaside restaurant for lunch and continued to Delphi. We arrived in Delphi in the afternoon and visit the Museum.

Day Four Delphi sits on a steep slope and overlooks a ravine. Visit the temple of Apollo, the Athenian Treasury, and the Delphi Theater and Stadium. Return to Athens via Levedia and Thebes.

Royal Olympic Cruises' Golden Fleece Seven-Day Cruise

On arrival, you'll experience an easy check-in and boarding and you'll be pampered dockside with glasses of juice. Our inside cabin made maximum use of its 125 square feet through the designer's excellent choice of lighting. It had plenty of closet and dresser space. Mirrored walls created the illusion of spaciousness. There was a telephone and stereo, but no TV. In-room ice buckets are filled in the morning and afternoon. There was no refrigerator in the room.

The mealtimes were as follows: Breakfast is served until 9 A.M.; lunches are between 12 noon and 1:30 P.M. The early seating for dinner starts at 7:30 P.M. and the late seating is at 9:00 P.M., or as late as 9:30 P.M., depending on the day's port of call. Afternoon tea and cookies are served, as well as a midnight snack buffet.

The food was very good. We experienced all of the usual dining-room amenities, including the march of the flaming baked Alaska, except that there was no lobster. There was no formal room-service menu, except for the Continental breakfast, which was very convenient on the days we departed for port as early as 7:00 A.M. Otherwise, ham-and-cheese sandwiches and cheese and crackers are available between meals. Best of all, you can order room-service food from the dining room menu during mealtimes. They served a good selection of beef, fish, and veal dishes, Pacific rim (oriental) items, and spa cuisine.

➥ **Steve and Pat's Tip on Tipping:** *All shipboard charges including excursions and end of cruise tips can be paid by major credit cards. The recommended end-of-cruise tips are as follows: $9 per person, or $126 per couple per week. Don't forget to use your Citibank AAdvantage card to rack up those airline program miles!*

There was also a daily outdoor buffet on deck. Shaded dining areas are available on the Brazilian deck, and the upper mezzanine offers scores of tables with large blue shade umbrellas, which were super for dining and relaxing under during sunny days. The terrific buffet offered salads, cold cuts, four hot dishes (including vegetarian pasta, ravioli, and moussaka), steak, pork chops, and a meat carver serving turkey, ham, or roast beef. There was also a fruit table, replete with bananas, apples, pears, plums, nectarines, peaches, grapes, and apricots. The buffet always serves regular dining-room entrees such as sweet-and-sour chicken or grilled chicken breasts.

Glasses of ice are available anytime on any deck and at any bar. There is a small movie theater with laser disc projection.

Please note that on a Mediterranean cruise, women may sunbathe topless, and about 5 to 10 percent do so.

Wonderful Ports of Call and Delightful Shore Excursions

On the *Olympic Countess*, all questions concerning independent shore excursions must be directed to the staff at the tour desk. The person giving the shore excursion talk in the theater would not take any questions after she finished her presentation. She referred us to the tour desk.

➥ **Steve's and Pat's Independent Excursion Tip:** *Always leave at the earliest time you can so you can go with the majority of people going ashore to better snag partners for sharing taxicabs. Better yet, line up excursion partners in advance. In Crete and Kusadasi, Turkish cabs lined up and waited for passengers and offered a fixed fee of $75 per cab. The price was the same whether two or four persons were in the cab.*

Santorini, Greece

This is the most picturesque of the Greek Isles. It was simply beautiful! Take a cable car or mule ride to the clifftop town of Thera, which costs about $2.50 each way. Explore the town of Thera with its whitewashed houses and narrow winding streets and many outdoor cafes and boutiques. The early morning hours are quiet and peaceful so it is the next-best time to arrive, other than sunset. Stores open by 9:00 A.M. By 10:00 A.M. the town is mobbed with tourists.

Shore Excursions: Was this island the site of the lost city of Atlantis? Take a short trip by motor coach to the ancient Minoan excavations and ruins at Akrotiri and view an archeological dig that dates back to the second millennium B.C. Many two- and three-story house complete with wall paintings, staircases, and a variety of rooms were frozen in time by Santorini's volcanic eruption 3,500 years ago. Return to Thera for a quick trip through the town before returning to the ship. ($47)

Heraklion, Crete

From Heraklion, visit the incredible prehistoric ruins of the Palace of Knossos, once thought to be the original Labyrinth which housed the mythological Minotaur. The palace was the seat of the ancient Minoan culture. The ruins were unearthed and restored in 1899 by Sir Arthur Evans.

Independent shore excursions: Upon leaving our ship with another couple, we hired George, a taxi driver, for $75 for a three and one-half hour tour. He took us to Knossos, which cut the cost of our excursion, including the price of admission, to less than half of the cruise line's price of $48 per person. Purchase a guide to the ruins from the stalls outside the Place for $3–$4, which makes a great souvenir. The guide describes the ruins in detail. Follow the guide's map and explore the ruins at your leisure. Also, our private tour guide gave us a city tour; a visit to the hilltop tomb of Kazantzakis, author of Zorba the Greek; a stop at the Archeological Museum; and gave us time to shop at the city's only shopping area open on Saturday. We shared our tour with Greg and Kim from Phoenix.

Shore excursion: A guided tour of Knossos is available by motorcoach. Or, for the same price, enjoy a panoramic drive through the countryside of eastern Crete to the quiet town of Agios Nikolaos. Visit ruins, a monastery, and a beach on the way. ($47)

Rhodes, Greece

Sail into the beautiful harbor with its detailed architecture, designed by the architect Hippodamos, that made Rhodes one of the most beautiful ancient cities. The famed Colossus of Rhodes, a hundred-foot-tall bronze statue of Helios, once stood here beside the harbor. In 237 B.C., the statue was allegedly destroyed by an earthquake, and was sold and melted down into weapons of war.

Independent shore excursions: Visit Old Town, a medieval walled city built by the Knights of St. John in the fourteenth century, surrounded by an amazing stone fortress. The town is packed with cobblestoned streets, churches, and palaces. The best place to begin is Symi Square with its temple of Aphrodite, close to the harbor. Continue on into town to the Palace of Armeria, which is now the Archeological Institute; it resembles a medieval fortress. Continue to the Museum of Decorative Arts in the byzantine church of Saint Mary. The former hospital of the knights is now an archeological museum which contains antiquities. The athletic, can take a walk to the top of the hill and pass through the second archway that leads to Kleovoulou Square. To the right is the Palace of the Knights of Saint John, the pride of the city with three hundred rooms, drawbridges, moats, and heavy walls. Walk along the city walls for an incredible photo opportunity.

Lindos, Rhodes is a picturesque ancient town of whitewashed houses decorated colorful vines and cobblestone streets. It is located high on the hillside and a must-see in Rhodes.

➥ **Steve and Pat's Tip:** *Luckily, we brought our own picnic lunch compliments of the Olympic Countess. Earlier I raided the morning buffet, made great turkey sandwiches, and selected oodles of fresh fruit. We also took our large bottle of cold lemonade.*

The most fun way to visit Lindos was on an incredible boat trip, instead of an excursion by bus.

➥ **Steve and Pat's Donkey Ride Tip:** *For the same price, the ride goes either two-thirds of the way up the hill to the Lindos town center or further up to the medieval ruins perched far above. The same is true on the ride down. Make certain you will be taken first to the ruins and visit the ancient acropolis dedicated to the goddess Athena, and then decide whether, on the return ride, you with to return to the starting point near the beach for a swim or to the town center for sightseeing and shopping.*

Upon departing ship at 8:30 A.M., we took a cab to the excursion boats in Mandraki Harbor, a quick fifteen-minute walk from the ship. These boats leave around 9:00 or 9:30 A.M., trace the beaches from Rhodes to Lindos, and return in the late afternoon. We picked the *Love Boat*, with great lounge chairs, lots of shade, a bar, mini shop, pop music, and well-designed, clean washrooms.

➥ **Steve and Pat's Tip:** *On Rhodes we saved $58 per person by taking the boat ride for $7 as compared to the ship's $65 price plus a walking tour of the Old City. Our independent boat trip did not offer a walking tour of the Old City, but did include a nine-hour excursion versus Royal Olympic's four and a half hour bus excursion. Plus we took an extra dip in the Aegean on the return trip!*

The trip took two and a half hours each way and the boat made several stops. The boat waits in Lindos for two and a half hours. In the summer Lindus is very hot and humid. Take a donkey ride up to the Old Town for $2.50 one way.

➥ **Steve and Pat's Tip:** *Whenever doing independent shore excursions always be aware of the boarding time and the "buffer period" permitted for late returns. At some ports, the return time was 6:30 P.M. and the posted departure time was 7:00 P.M., a buffer period of up to thirty minutes. Other times the buffer period between return time and departure time was only fifteen minutes. There is no way to know just how long the ship will wait for errant nonreturning passengers beyond these stated times.* Always *assume your ship will leave at the posted departure hour! We assure you that on occasion ships* do *leave errant passengers behind.*

The total boat cost for a nine-hour, all-day cruise was an astounding $7 round-trip. It is best to arrive earlier, at 8:30 A.M., then buy your tickets and tour the dock area until sailing.

Patmos, Greece

An early-morning arrival in the port of Scala is simply wonderful; just two steps off the ship and you are in the downtown square. The tiny, quiet town of whitewashed houses slowly wakes up and is so restful and picturesque with the vibrantly-colored flowers of the bougainvillea climbing over balconies and porches. We passed on the shore excursion and instead elected to explore the cobblestone streets, visited the many boutiques that opened around 8:30 A.M., and watched the town and harbor come to life.

Shore excursion: Patmos offers a shore excursion to the Monastery of the Apocalypse and the hilltop Monastery of St. John. ($32)

Kusadasi, Turkey (Ephesus)

Visit the incredible ruins of Ephesus that date back to early Greek times. Walk through the restored, two-story Library of Celsius, the temple of Diana, the great amphitheater where St. Paul was arrested, and the two-mile, colonnaded Roman road that lead to the harbor thousands of years ago.

Independent shore excursion: We shared a private cab with four people to Ephesus for $80. The ship tour cost $47 so we cut our cost by 50 percent, since we only paid $20 per person, even with a four-dollar admission charge. The driver waited for us at the exit at the end of our downhill walk through the town. There were no crowds and we explored everything at our own pace. Wonderful.

When we returned to Kusadasi, the streets were lined with a bazaar, like a shopping mall. It was very nicely laid out with benches in center. Shop vendors sit waiting to "attack" shoppers.

Istanbul, Turkey

What an incredible and magnificent mix of eastern and western cultures. The Golden Horn and adjacent harbor is outstanding as you arrive in the early evening. The harbor is filled with large, rapidly moving ferry boats taking commuters across the water. This is the great ancient city of Constantinople, captured by the Turks, lost again, captured again, over the ages.

Night shore excursion: A bus is available to take passengers for traditional Turkish cuisine and belly dancing in a fine nightclub. ($65)

Independent night shore excursion: Walk across the Galata Bridge or take a cab and continue along the banks towards Agia Sophia until reaching the lit sign for the Gulhane Park Festival that happens only in the three months of summer. For a $1 admission charge, you get to explore a half-mile of shops; enjoy the tavernas serving grilled chicken and other meats; visit the dessert stands and the many ice cream stands; listen to live outdoor music on two concert stages; and meet lots of friendly Turks anxious to help tourists and practice speaking English. Half a chicken only cost $2. Our dinner plus many Turkish coffees totaled $16 for two including three entrees of kebabs and rice, tip, fruit, and more.

➥ **Steve and Pat's Tip:** *Cabs are everywhere. Cabs meters run on a day rate of 120,000 Turkish lira (fifty cents). Cabs are cheap, but do make sure the setting is correct while getting into the cab. At night the rate is higher and you'll usually decide on the price of a destination before getting in the cab.*

On our second day in Istanbul, many excursions were offered. The ship's tours of Istanbul are seven or eight hours long. This is simply too long to be stuck in a bus when the city is quite easy to explore on your own. At $80 per person, the tour is expensive.

Independent shore excursion: A quick trip by taxi from the port ($4 for the cab) will allow you to start your tour at the Grand Mosque, revered by Muslims and decorated with 21,000 blue Iznik tiles. Then, move on across the formal garden to Aghia Sophia, the church of divine wisdom and once the largest church of Christendom. Nearby is the Topkapi Museum, previously the official residence of the Sultans of the Ottoman Empire, and now a wonderful museum filled with incredible treasures. After lunch, continue to the covered Grand Bazaar with its four thousand vendors and shop until you drop. Then after a quick trip by cab over the Galata Bridge, pull up a lounge chair and a cold drink and wait on the front decks to enjoy the changing view of the awesome skyline of Istanbul. The ship will sail out of the harbor around 6:00 P.M. This is truly a sight not to be missed.

➡ **Steve and Pat's Tip:** *The street area around the port offers little or no quality shopping. Go across the Galata Bridge and use the underground walkways to cross the main boulevard. There are blocks of fine shops and eateries as well as banks and money-changing booths.*

We interrupted our touring with a cool and restful three-hour boat ride on the Bosporus. The itinerary travels up-river for one hour, under two bridges that connect Asia and Europe, with time for a one-hour stop for lunch. The whole trip cost $6, an incredible bargain.

➡ **Steve and Pat's Tip:** *Entrance to religious sites require that upper arms and legs be covered. However, most mosques will provide a skirt-like covering for men or women wearing shorts. There is no need to wear long pants on brutally hot summer days.*

Shore excursions: The cruise line's bus tour (which cost $80 per person) was identical to our independent tour. Admission to the religious sights and museum is free or of nominal price.

Mykonos, Greece

This is a quintessential Greek Island with hundreds of tiny chapels, whitewashed windmills, chic boutiques, and waterfront cafes. The narrow cobblestoned streets curve around, end, and loop back on themselves. This is a great town to explore or to stop and have a coffee at the Venice-style cafes.

Independent shore excursion: Walk through the town to the south end, and there you will find the "bus station," which consists of a mere sign! With your towel and bathing suit in hand, jump on a bus going to Plati Gialos beach, which costs only eighty cents one way. Changing rooms, showers, thatched umbrellas, and sun beds are available. For the more adventurous, take a ride on a local boat to the next beach, called Paradise. The cost for the round trip is $2.40 per person. At Paradise, the music rocks and the beach is filled with twenty- and thirty-year-olds. It's party time. The sun beds were free and music filled the air. Mykonos has beautiful, clean white beaches with sparkling water. We had a marvelous time. Retrace your route back to the cruise ship and end your cruise with lovely memories of Mykonos.

Shore excursion to Delos: This once-sacred island is uninhabited and one of the best archeological sites in Greece (if you haven't seen enough ruins by now). A quick trip by local boat from Mykonos to Delos for a two-hour guided walking tour of the island. Visit the temple of Apollo and the famed Terrace of the Lions that stands guard over the sacred lake.

Royal Olympic Cruises

Recently, two cruise lines, the Sun Line and Epirotiki, joined together and now make up Royal Olympic Cruises. Its fleet of small and medium-size recently refurbished cruise ships consist of white and blue ships. Blue ships are more formal with only four casual nights on a one-week cruise. White ships have six casual nights and no formal nights. Royal Olympic's ships have been sailing the Mediterranean and the Aegean Sea for almost one hundred years.

➡ **Steve and Pat's Tip:** *Since Royal Olympic Cruises has eight ships in service throughout the Mediterranean Sea and four are especially reserved for the Greek Isles, we feel this line offers the greatest opportunity to customize a vacation that will suit everyone's tastes.*

The company's expertise is mirrored by its native Greek officers and crew. A government-licensed guide accompanies each sailing. Meals are a delight, with everything made fresh, from pastries to potato chips. On these ships, passengers enjoy Greek specialty meals, Greek atmosphere, and a Greek crew. Expect officers and crew to entertain one evening with a Greek Night celebration. This is the closest many passengers will come to attending a full-fledged toga party! Add health spas, fitness centers, healthy entrees, special nightly cabaret-style entertainment, cinemas, and discos for a full-fledged luxury cruise experience. It also delivers a perfect Greek Isles cruise vacation. The ROC blue fleet consists of the following:

- *Stella Solaris*   The flagship of this cruise line carries 620 passengers, was completely rebuilt in 1973, and refurbished several times, most recently in 1996. There are two pools, one of which is a figure-eight design, a new 2,600-square-foot health spa, a movie theater, and air-conditioning.
- *Odysseus*   This 400-passenger ship was built in 1962 and refurbished in 1988. The ship offers all the usual amenities without the dazzle and glitz.
- *Stella Oceanis*   This ship was rebuilt in 1967 but has not been recently refurbished. The intimate 300-passenger vessel is a big plus for those who shy away from larger 1,000 to 2,000-passenger ships. The ship offers the usual amenities in smaller sizes and quantities.
- *Stella Maris*   The smallest ship in the fleet, it carries 180 passengers and offers the usual but scaled-down amenities.

The white ships consist of the following:

- *Olympic*   This 900-passenger ship was built in 1956 and refurbished in 1994. It is the largest ship in the fleet and was formerly known as Carnival's *Carnivale*. Besides the usual amenities, there are two pools and a movie theater.
- *Triton*   Formerly the Cunard *Adventurer,* this 620-passenger ship was built in 1971 and refurbished in 1991. Besides the usual amenities, the ship has a movie theater and one pool.
- *Orpheus*   Another intimate 280-passenger vessel. The ship

was built in 1952 and refurbished in 1987. The ship has the usual amenities.

- *Olympic Countess*   The newest addition to the fleet was formerly known as the *Cunard Countess*. Refurbished in 1998, the ship carries 840 passengers and has the usual amenities, including a movie theater and one pool.

Typical dinner menu entrees include grilled Kansas-city beef, sirloin steak, braised leg of lamb, broiled salmon steak, and numerous chicken and pasta dishes.

Orient Line

Orient Line offers no less than sixteen variations of Greek Isles and Mediterranean cruises using one ship! That ship is the ever-popular *Marco Polo*.

Why is the *Marco Polo* so popular? The 800-passenger ship was built in 1965, then rebuilt, refurbished, and redesigned in 1991 for cruising to exotic global destinations. Many feel the ship has a country-club atmosphere. The spacious decks have outdoor jacuzzis. No formal evenings mean no tuxedos and gowns. Alternative dining is available at Raffles restaurant for an extra charge. The multinational English-speaking cruise staff and Filipino service staff are top-notch. Low-category cabins have TVs, music consoles, phones, safes, and hair dryers. Typical Seven Seas dining room entrees include oven-baked lobster, roast pheasant, and beef Wellington.

Discount Greek Isles Land-and-Cruise Prices

There are many other cheapskate-priced Greece and Greek Isles land-and-cruise vacations. The following bargain-priced land and cruise vacations refer to off-season March and late October departures. Spring and summer departures may be priced $200 to $500 higher per person.

Homeric's "Aegean Delight"   This bargain eight-day land-and-cruise vacation includes three nights in Athens followed by a three-night Royal Olympic cruise to Mykonos, Rhodes, Patmos, and Kusadasi, Turkey. The price is $1,039, including round-trip airfare from New York.

The Homeric Delight   This ten-day land-and-cruise vacation starts with three days and nights in Athens, then a three-day tour through the Peloponnese from Delphi to Meteora and concludes with the above three-day Royal Olympic Greek Isles cruise. The price, including round-trip airfare from New York, is $1,329.

Tourlite International   This company offers a variety of low-priced Greece and Greek Isles land-and-cruise vacations. A ten-day Dorian land-and-cruise vacation is similar to the Homeric Delight tour and is priced at $1,359, including round-trip airfare from New York. Obtain a Tourlite brochure from any travel agency, or write: Tourlite, 551 Fifth Avenue, New York, NY 10176-1097.

Royal Olympic Cruises   This company advertised a seven-day Greek Isles and Turkey cruise on the ship *Stella Solaris*, with higher-priced departures in May. They priced the cruise at $1,721, including all taxes, port charges, and round-trip airfare from New York. Call Royal Olympic at (800) 872-6400 and request a Greek Isles brochure.

Orient Cruise Lines   Their "Classical Aegean" is a thirteen-day land-and-cruise vacation that includes two nights in Athens, a two-night Greek tour, a five-day Greek Isles cruise, and two days and nights in Istanbul. Prices start at $2,095 (summer departures are just $100 extra). Contact Orient at (800) 333-7300.

Orient Cruise Line's "Aegean Odyssey" is a twelve-day cruise with stops in nine ports. This includes a two-night Athens hotel stay, a full seven-night *Marco Polo* cruise and a three-night hotel stay in Istanbul. Travel of America prices this cruise as low as $1,735. Call (800) 228-8843.

Mediterranean Sea

Premier Cruises

Premier does it again! Premier advertises their seven-night Mediterranean cruise on the *Rembrandt* for $849. The discount price offered by Costco Travel is $784. Call (800) 800-8505. The cruise line's special air and cruise package, from JFK airport in New York, is priced as low as $1,199. Call Pearson Travel at (800) 336-1066 for most recent and lowest prices for Premier's cruises.

➥ **Steve and Pat's Best Deal Goal:** *Travel of America offers Orient Cruise Lines' twelve-day land-and-cruise package for $1,735.*

Premier's newest acquisition, the *Rembrandt*, was built in 1959, refurbished in 1997 and carries 1,114 passengers. This is another ship that takes us back in time with elegant chandeliers, floor-to-ceiling murals, and statuary.

Here is Premier's itinerary:

Day one: Depart from Barcelona, Spain at 4:00 P.M.
Day two: Visit Villefranche, Nice for a full day
Day three: Visit Civitavecchia, Italy for a full day
Day four: Visit Messina, Sicily for an afternoon
Day five: Visit Naples, Italy for a full day
Day six: Day at sea
Day seven: Visit Palma de Mallorca for a full day
Day eight: Disembark in Barcelona, Spain at 8:00 A.M.

Orient Cruise Line

Marco Polo strikes again with another winning itinerary. This time the *Marco Polo* sails on a twelve-day Mediterranean journey from Rome to Barcelona. Orient's innovative itinerary begins with a three-night hotel stay in Rome, continues with a seven-night cruise and concludes with a two-night hotel stay in Barcelona. Discount prices are available through Travel of America and priced at $1,750 for cabin J. Call (800) 228-8843.

14

The Yangtze River and Three Gorges Cruise: An Ultimate Adventure

Why Cruise the Yangtze River?

The Yangtze River and the Three Gorges are two of the world's greatest natural wonders. The best way to experience them and China's spectacular landscapes is to take a Yangtze River cruise. Discount San Francisco tour operator China Focus Travel calls this tour "Farewell to the Three Gorges," which refers to China's construction of the world's largest dam, on the Yangtze River. Once the dam is completed, the grandeur of the gorges will be gone forever, buried beneath a new man-made lake. However, because work is progressing slowly, tours will likely continue until 2001! In April 1998 we packed our bags, bid farewell to the pets, and headed to San Francisco International Airport, the departure point for our most exotic of cruise vacations. This was "the big one," a six-day cruise on the Yangtze River, followed by a nine-day escorted land vacation exploring the highlights of China.

> **Steve and Pat's Tip:** *Many tour companies charge $3,500 or more for this world-class all-inclusive vacation. The China Focus 1998 off-season price for their fifteen-day Yangtze River and Three Gorges extravaganza was just $1,999. Using available free travel cash or our recommended discount and rebate travel agencies would further reduce the price to about $1,800. Remember, this is a two-full-week all-inclusive cruise and escorted land tour that includes round-trip airfare to China and flights inside China! For details and a brochure, call (888) 688-1898 or (415) 788-8660.*

Getting There

The Yangtze River and Xi'an

After our arrival and day tour of Shanghai, we flew southwest to Wuhan, one of China's largest industrial river port cities.

Wuhan

Once three separate cities, Wuhan has a population of three million. The Yangtze River flows through the middle of this vibrant city. Our tour started at East Lake Park, where we mingled with hundreds of young children on school outings. We hired a boat and pilot and savored a tranquil twenty-minute ride on the lake. Others walked along the shore, hiked in lush wooded areas bordering the lake, or flew in a light plane over the lake. Next we visited the ancient Huanghe Tower, with its superb view of the city, the Yangtze River, and the famed Yangtze River Bridge.

It was time to board MS *Beidou* also known locally as the *Star Dipper*. This deluxe, four-star river cruise ship was our home for the next six days. Built in 1994, the MS *Beidou* is one of the newest cruise ships on the Yangtze and offers amenities equal or superior to most other Yangtze River cruise ships. The four-star vessel has the appearance of a Mississippi paddle wheeler, sans paddle. Its impressive amenities and specifications include:

- Five-decks with seventy-eight outside staterooms with large windows
- Intimacy by carrying only 174 passengers
- Regular cabins that measure eighteen-square meters and include central air-conditioning, a radio, closed-circuit TV, refrigerator, and bathtub
- The Hibiscus dining room, a bar and gift shop, and the Milky Way Nightclub
- Enclosed observation area with the Venus bar
- A clinic, spa with sauna and massage, fitness center, and casino.
- Private card rooms, TV, and karaoke rooms

Once onboard we unpacked, relaxed, and eagerly anticipated cruising through one of the world's greatest scenic wonders.

Chenglingji

Our first stop was the town of Chenglingji, at the confluence of Lake Dongting and the Yangtze River. A shore excursion took us to the Yue Yang Tower, Yue Yang Mansion, and Cishi Pagoda. Next to the park were many small shops that sold local arts and crafts at bargain prices.

Xiling Gorge

Our ship sailed through the night to Shashi and then on to the first of the great gorges. We awoke at 6:30 A.M. to experience the passage through Xiling Gorge, the longest of China's three gorges. Xiling Gorge stretches seventy-six kilometers (forty-seven miles) from the mouth of the Xiangxi River. It is all at once majestic, serene, and awe inspiring, with its endless gorges and shoals. As the morning mist rose, we searched for hidden waterfalls and viewed mysterious caves. Nearby peaks reached for the sky. Everywhere steep cliffs guarded the valley and river. We stared, mesmerized by the raw natural beauty all around us. Beyond the river, the region is rich in natural resources, ranging from coal to peaches tangerines. The river provides sturgeon and other varieties of fish.

Wu Gorge

The MS *Beidou* continued to the second of the great gorges, Wu Gorge. We passed through a lushly forested, zigzag valley of ethereal beauty. Again, steep cliffs and tall peaks surrounded us. The gorge extends east from the Daning River and is forty-five kilometers (twenty-eight miles) long. Every few moments the river seemed to change course as we tried to take in all the sights. The spectacular twelve peaks of Mt. Wushan were extraordinary. Many were covered with pine trees, while their peaks were shrouded in clouds.

The Lesser Gorges Boat Adventure

The greatest adventure of the river cruise was at hand. First, we walked from our boat to shore on a pontoon bridge. There we boarded buses and shortly arrived at the mouth of the Shenglongzi River. Here we departed for a six-hour, small-boat cruise through the famed Lesser Gorges. Our group of eighty split into three boats, each holding twenty-five to thirty passengers. We sat up front in the open-air section and could easily reach down to the water from our seats. This was truly a "hands-on" river adventure.

Dragon Gate Gorge

The trip started at Dragon Gate Bridge and headed through Dragon Gate Gorge, which is three kilometers (two miles) long. We viewed the famed Nine Dragon Pillars, the longest plank walkway in China, and shot the Rapids of the Silver Nest. Our oarsman maneuvered our craft through white-water rapids and then on to tranquil stretches. Again we marveled at the gorge, with its sheer cliffs and lush green mountains.

Misty Gorge

Next, we passed through lush, green terraced hillsides as we headed toward Misty Gorge. Misty Gorge is ten kilometers (six

The Yangtze River and Three Gorges Cruise

miles) long and ended before our lunch stop at Double Dragon Town. In the distance, farmers toiled on farms in open stretches. Women washed clothes the ancient way, using the rocks at the river's edge as washboards. More twists and turns loomed before us as the mountains ahead seemed truly shrouded in a soft, purple mist.

Double Dragon Town

Clinging picturesquely to the side of a mountain, this small village with a fancy name offered a brief lunch and shopping stop. Then the boats headed downstream. The rushing current made for an exciting and fast return to Dragon Gate Bridge, a fitting conclusion to an unforgettable Chinese river adventure.

Qutang Gorge

The adventure continued with day four on the Yangtze River. Early this morning our ship cruised through dramatic Qutang Gorge, the third of the Three Gorges. This eight-kilometer (five-mile) stretch was bathed in sunshine, showing off incredible peaks and cliffs in all directions. Mt. Chijia was visible in the distance. Hundreds of mountain crags altered in the ever-changing light. We cruised past Kuimen Pass, known as the most dangerous pass in the world.

Fengdu City (The Ghost City)

After lunch, our ship reached Fengdu, the legendary Ghost City, where we rode an aerial tram to the ancient hilltop city, first inhabited in 1600 B.C. and thereafter enjoyed a colorful history. Highlights of mysterious Fengdu include stunning views of the Yangtze River, larger than life demon statues from the "netherworld" that would give goose bumps to Freddy Krueger, and an ancient celestial mansion. Before leaving the city we faced the Naihe Bridge, where only good people may cross and the evil will fail. Naturally we made it across!

Cruise Entertainment

Performances ranged from audience participation in karaoke sing-alongs to an entertaining musical show by talented crew members. A modern disco is open until the very early hours of the morning. Quiet lounge areas, private karoke rooms, and TV rooms are available. All and all, the MS *Bideou* is a marvelous and comfortable ship.

➡ **Steve and Pat's Tip:** *Meals on the cruise were superb because the buffet service offered an opportunity to devour an array of tantalizing dishes. Compared to off-ship family-style dining, there was a better selection of more exotic dishes, like boneless duck tempura, delectable roast pork slices, and many superb sweet-and-sour dishes on the ship. Scrumptious!*

Chongqing

Our cruise ended all too soon at the city of Chongqing, where we embarked on a city tour which included a visit to Chiang Kai-shek's home and museum. Then we checked in to the Chongqing Hotel in the bustling center of town. After dinner, we had a carefree evening of shopping in the many stores within walking distance of the hotel.

Xi'an: Home of the Terra Cotta Warrior Army

Even before President Clinton made Xi'an the very first stop on his China trip, we knew this was the "in" place to visit!

The following morning we flew to Xi'an for an unforgettable experience touring a modern archeological wonder of the world. We checked in to the Xi'an Orient Hotel and had yet another Chinese lunch. Then we toured this industrial city of three million people that doubles as a living museum of China's ancient history. It is one of the rare cities with a well-preserved city wall.

Our tour headed to the famed Banpo Neolithic Museum. Living exhibits take visitors from China's prehistory and early dynastic period to New Stone Age settlements, some of which were 6,000 years old. Upper floors explore China's history from the Han to the Tang and Ming dynasties.

Our second day in Xi'an targeted the goal of our journey, Xi'an's terra cotta warrior army. Imagine China's first emperor, Qin Shihuang, ruling 2,000 years ago. In preparation for his death, he employed 300,000 laborers working thirty-seven years to construct his mausoleum and his army. To protect him in the afterlife, the first emperor had artisans create *life-sized* terra-cotta replicas of his entire army of 6,000 soldiers, including calvary horses, weapons, and chariots. No two figures were alike, and all the soldiers' uniforms were painted in brilliant lifelike colors. Upon his death, the first emperor and his thousands of terra-cotta warriors, plus horses and chariots, were buried in underground mausoleums. It was not until 1974 that a local farmer accidentally discovered a "soldier's" head while digging a water well. To date, excavations of the three large enclosed pits have uncovered about 2,000 of the estimated 6,000-man army.

➥ **Steve and Pat's Tip:** *Make certain to pay the few extra dollars to see the 360-degree Imax-type film just before entering the pits. Steve took an excellent video of the film, which shows the history of the first emperor's army, including pitched battles. The film continues with the artisans of the victorious first emperor creating a brilliantly painted terra-cotta army. Sadly, time has taken its toll and the colors are but a faded remnant of their original splendor.*

An enormous warehouse covers each of the three pits. Inside, visitors follow a walkway above and circling the outer perimeter of the pit, filled with the life-sized soldiers. In major pit number one, hundreds upon hundreds of soldiers stand at attention in rectangular battle formation. In some rows, infantry, archers with crossbows, and cavalry soldiers with horses stand next to one another. The infantrymen carry axes, spears, and other weapons. In each case facial features, the colors and designs of the uniforms, and hairstyles were unique for each soldier and show his rank in the army.

> **Steve's Photo Tip:** *Still photos and video are prohibited inside the pits. Naturally, museum vendors sell photos and videos galore. This really ticked me off, especially since camcorders do not use lights, so there is no possibility of damage to the exhibit. Violators will see their film confiscated. However, when the red recording light on a camcorder is covered with your finger or a piece of tape, there is no way to detect whether or not the camcorder is filming. This is equally true when filming from the hip. Not that I would suggest using this handy photo tip!*

The Xi'an experience truly offers one of the world's greatest archeological wonders and rewards visitors with vivid memories lasting a lifetime.

After leaving the pits, we enjoyed one final Xi'an attraction, the Royal Huaqing Hot Spring Park. Hundreds of children and parents reveled in the sculptured gardens, ancient buildings, and beautiful fountains. This restful stop was a most relaxing reward. We were free to walk, snack, mix with locals, or just sit and enjoy the park and surrounding mountains.

Discount China Tour Companies

China Focus Travel   As noted above, we highly recommend China Focus Travel and its "Farewell to Three Gorges" fifteen-day Yangtze River and China tour. We would be remiss not to mention our first China Focus vacation, their noncruise "Historic China" twelve-day, six-cities tour that travels from Shanghai to Beijing. Prices for this all-inclusive introduction to China journey are incredibly cheapskate priced, at $1,199! You may contact China Focus Travel at:

China Focus Travel
870 Market Street, Suite 1215
San Francisco, CA 94102
(888) 688-1898 or (415) 788-8660

Pacific Holidays   Pacific Holidays offers their fifteen-day Yangtze River all-inclusive tour. Both deluxe and first class, three-star hotels are used. Their tour price includes scheduled round-trip airfare from the East or West coasts. Pacific's itinerary seems similar to that offered by China Focus, however, there are significant differences. First, Pacific reverses the itinerary by commencing the tour in Beijing. Although Pacific describes the tour as fifteen days, it is twelve nights of actual vacation in China. By comparison, China Focus's fifteen-day Yangtze River tour includes thirteen-nights in China. Pacific Holidays includes a limited three-night Yangtze River cruise, whereas we enjoyed the China Focus itinerary with its full five-night Yangtze River cruise.

➥ **Steve and Pat's Tip:** *Always count the number of nights on any given itinerary. As you will see, two similar itineraries, each announcing a fifteen-day tour, may not include the same number of actual nights on vacation.*

Pacific's low-season March 1998 departure price was $3,440 per person. Compare this with the March 1998 China Focus price of $1,995. Add just $30 for East Coast departures. For details and a brochure, call Pacific Holidays at (800) 355-8025.

➥ **Steve and Pat's Best Deal Goal:** *China Focus continues to beat the competition with its thirteen-night "Farewell to Three Gorges—Yangtze River and China Tour," with prices starting at $1,999.*

Rim-Pac International Rim-Pac is another well-known China-specialty tour operator that offers super-bargain prices. Rim-Pac's Yangtze River cruise and tour is seventeen days, but only thirteen-nights of actual vacation in China. Their tour is also similar to our Yangtze River experience, with fully five nights cruising the Yangtze. Rim-Pac uses the cruise ship MS *Victoria*, whereas China Focus uses the four-star MS *Beidou*. A comparison of prices for similar April 1998 San Francisco departures finds Rim-Pac's tour priced at $2,869 per person, versus the China

Focus price of $2,095. Rim-Pac adds $100 for New York departures, whereas China Focus charges a $30 per person New York add-on. For details and a brochure, call Rim-Pac at: (800) 701-TOUR.

China Travel Service (CTS) This San Francisco–based China-specialty tour operator has fifteen years experience. Their bargain fifteen-day "Yangtze Dream Tour" itinerary closely resembles the China Focus fifteen-day tour. The CTS off-season March 1999 price is $2,395 per person. Add $240 for East Coast departures. Call CTS at (800) 332-2831, ext. 126, and ask for their special "China Yangtze River Cruise Tours" brochure.

15

More World-Class Bargain Cruises

Cruising the Hawaiian Islands

Many Hawaiian cruises embark from West Coast cities such as Vancouver and Los Angeles, while others cruise round-trip from Honolulu. These cruises are usually ten to fourteen days and often require a return flight home from Honolulu. Norwegian's ten-day departure from Honolulu is one example. Prices are higher for these longer itineraries, but compare very favorably to American Hawaii cruise line's much shorter and much less luxurious, seven-night cruises. Take a look at our suggestions for "extended" memorable cruise vacations to the Hawaiian islands. Current prices and itineraries are always subject to change. Use our various strategies, such as free travel cash, free air travel, and discount bookings to maximize savings on the final cruise vacation price.

Hawaiian Ports of Call and Shore Excursions

Big Island of Hawaii

Hawaii Volcanoes National Park   A tour of the Big Island begins in Hilo with a visit to Queen Liliuokalani Park and the

Japanese Yedo Garden. Next is a ride through a lush tropical forest up to Hawaii Volcanoes National Park. At the top of Kilauea, the scenic eleven-mile Crater Rim Drive traverses from rain forest to barren desert and former eruption sights, and around the steamy Halemaumau Crater, home of the goddess Pele. The tour follows the active lava flow down to Kalapana, where it pours into the sea and where the cooling lava has created the strikingly beautiful Black Sands Beach.

➥ **Steve and Pat's Pricing Tip:** *We quote at least one discount price and contact phone number for each cruise line. However, comparison shopping between rebate and discount companies like Pearson Travel and others mentioned in Chapter 4 is essential before booking the cruise. Also, save up to 33 percent by flying free to the cruise ship's departure city and, most importantly, following our advice in Chapter 2.*

Fair Wind Snorkel Cruise Kona Excursion Discover the hidden beauty of the Big Island on a cruise from Keauhou Bay to Kealakekua Bay, a spectacular natural marine reserve. Kealakekua is considered one of Hawaii's best snorkeling spots, with rainbow-striped tropical fish, extensive coral reefs, interesting underwater rock formations, and fascinating submerged lava tubes. Sail on the new *Fair Wind II*, a sixty-foot state-of-the-art catamaran complete with a fifteen-foot water slide, high-dive platform, fresh-water showers, a spacious sundeck, cabin, galley, and full bar. Snorkeling gear and instruction are provided.

The Island of Maui

Tour to Haleakala Crater This half-day excursion takes guests to the top of the world's largest dormant volcano, Haleakala. At the summit, some 10,000 feet above sea level, is a vast crater the size of Manhattan. Visitors are awestruck when viewing the eerie lunarlike landscape of cinder cones and ancient lava formations. Within the crater, see rare flora and fauna found only in Hawaii's volcanic craters, including the silversword plant and Hawaii's own nene goose. Looking out from the summit on a clear day, visitors enjoy views of Mauna Loa and Mauna Kea in the distance. The route up the volcano travels through the lush green upcountry region of farms and ranches.

> ➥ **Steve and Pat's Tip:** *Great news from American Airlines. For 35,000 program miles, an AAdvantage member can obtain two different city tickets from almost any U.S. city to either Vancouver or Los Angeles and then a return flight home from Honolulu. This is yet another reason we are enamored with the American Airlines AAdvantage program.*

Bicycle Down the Slopes of Haleakala   The adventure begins at the summit of Mt. Haleakala, more than 10,000 feet above sea level. Watch a spectacular sunrise from the top of the world, then coast more than thirty-eight miles down the mountainside at approximately twenty miles per hour. Complete safety instructions, a safety helmet, windbreaker, gloves, and foul-weather gear are provided. All of the bicycles are custom-built and come equipped with six-inch drum brakes for maximum stopping capabilities. This is a world-class adventure.

The Island of Kauai

Shoreline Bike, Hike, and Snorkel Kauai   Passengers will visit one of Kauai's most beautiful coastal areas. This tour consists of a five-mile bike trip, reef snorkeling, and a one-and-a-half mile nature hike along a spectacular wilderness coastal area of hidden beaches and sea cliffs. Along the way, the group stops at various points of interest for talks on diverse topics such as history, culture, legends, and natural history. Special emphasis is placed on local history and the identification and discussion of native plants, birds, and aquatic life.

Hanalei Sea Tours Kauai   See the towering volcanic cliffs and lush jade valleys of the magnificent Na Pali Coast and enjoy a rewarding snorkeling adventure during this delightful four-hour tour. Guests cruise through cascading waterfalls and explore giant sea caves. The captain and crew share their knowledge of this spectacular area along the way. During the one-hour snorkeling stop, passengers swim over a reef abundant with colorful tropical fish. The *Zodiac* is a twenty-three-foot inflatable rubber raft built for speed and maneuverability, and offers an exciting ride for adventure seekers.

Island of Oahu

Polynesian Cultural Center The world-famous Polynesian Cultural Center is one of Oahu's most popular attractions. The forty-two-acre complex showcases the centuries-old cultures of Samoa, Tonga, Fiji, Tahiti, New Zealand, and the Hawaiian Islands. Native-born people of each of these places have lovingly recreated authentic villages spotlighting their traditional lifestyles, customs, folklore, music, and dance. At dinnertime, passengers enjoy a lavish all-you-can-eat buffet featuring traditional dishes from each Polynesian village. Following dinner, guests are dazzled by a cast of 174 performers who present a ninety-minute extravaganza, "This is Polynesia." The show is set against a splendid backdrop of ingeniously-made waterfalls, erupting volcanoes, and wood-carved tikis.

Hawaiian Islands: Cruise Lines and Discount Prices

Norwegian Cruise Line (NCL)

Norwegian offers several ten-night Hawaiian cruises per year on their smaller eight-hundred-passenger ship, the *Dynasty*. Their cruises embark round-trip from Honolulu, on Oahu. Even better, their lowest category H cabin includes two lower beds that convert to a queen-sized bed! This ten-day cruise is almost 50 percent longer than American Hawaii's one-week cruise. The NCL itinerary includes a half-day visit to Christmas Island in the republic of Kiribati and all the luxury amenities expected on an NCL cruise.

Discount price Often, cruise lines advertise the best deals. Norwegian Cruise Line advertised their *Dynasty* cruise, priced

More World-Class Bargain Cruises 303

at $1,257. Follow our advice in chapter 4 and save even more! Golden Age Travelers offers many sailing dates from September through December 1998 priced as low as $1,287, including port charges. Call (800) 258-8880.

NCL's ten-day itinerary for its Honolulu-departure cruise that includes four days at sea and five ports of call follows:

Day One: Depart from Honolulu on (Saturday)
Day Two: Visit Kona (island of Hawaii) all day
Day Three: Day at sea
Day Four: Day at sea
Day Five: Visit Christmas Island (Kiribati) all day
Day Six: Day at sea
Day Seven: Day at sea
Day Eight: Visit Hilo (island of Hawaii)
Day Nine: Visit Lahaina (island of Maui)
Day Ten: Visit Nawiliwili (island of Kauai)
Day Eleven: Disembark in Honolulu

Royal Caribbean International (RCI)

RCI's sailings on its *Legend of the Seas* and *Rhapsody of the Seas* embark from Vancouver for ten-night Hawaiian cruises. The cruises disembark in Honolulu. RCI's itinerary includes four restful days at sea en route to Hawaii. Included are six full-day visits to ports of call on Hawaii's four major islands.

The best news, considering all the days at sea, is that the *Legend of the Seas* and its sister ship, the *Rhapsody of the Seas*, are RCI's new (1996) 1,804-passenger megaships. Both are state-of-the-art and have all the finest amenities, such as an eighteen-hole, miniature golf course that passengers enjoy during long days at sea. Both have a retractable glass canopy over the solarium spa and pool area. Also enjoy the two-story dining rooms with floor-to-ceiling windows.

Discount price CruiseMasters, a specialty agency, offers many eleven-day sailings that embark from Vancouver, discount priced at $1,704, including port charges, for a standard, category N, inside cabin. For current information, call (800) 242-9000.

⇒ **Steve and Pat's Tip:** *Whole World of Travel, a "mostly-specialty" cruise agency, is unknown outside California, but just wait. Their innovative air-and-cruise packages are cheapskate priced. Whole World advertises Royal Caribbean ten- and eleven-day Hawaiian cruises in December 1998 on the* Legend of the Seas, *embarking from Ensenada, Mexico, and disembarking in Honolulu. The cruises are super-bargain-priced at $1,532 (ten days) and $1,581 (eleven days), including port charges, taxes, and round-trip airfare from Northern or Southern California. This saves hundreds of dollars in airfare and offers a grand opportunity for a second mini-vacation in either San Francisco or Los Angeles! Regardless of your cruise destination, call Whole World of Travel for current deals at (800) 458-3636 or (916) 488-8000.*

American Hawaii Cruises

American Hawaii built the cruise ship *Independence*, in 1951 and renovated it in 1997. The ship almost makes it into the "smaller" class of vessels, since it carries only 1,021 passengers, who enjoy continental and Hawaiian food specialties at dinnertime and quiet, low-key days at sea as the ship travels between the Hawaiian Islands. The *Independence* is the only major cruise ship that sails weekly and maintains its home port in Hawaii. Its seven-day itinerary is similar to the Hawaiian Islands tour incorporated in the ten- and eleven-day cruises that embark from the West Coast. American's itinerary includes full-day ports of call stops at Nawiliwili (Kauai), two days at Kahului (Maui), Hilo (Hawaii), and Kona (Hawaii). The extra second day on Maui is a big plus.

Discount prices Travel of America offered a dozen 1998 year-round sailing dates on the *Independence* at super-discount prices. How much of a discount is available? Category F two-lower-bed economy cabins were discount-priced at $901 for the June 1998 cruise, $981 for summer cruises, and $1,141 on winter departures. Travel of America also includes a bonus $100 per couple shipboard credit! Call (800) 228-8843.

More World-Class Bargain Cruises 305

> ➥ **Steve and Pat's Tip:** *We do not recommend the* Independence *given the luxurious, reasonably priced alternatives. The* Independence *is not a "typical" cruise ship. Although the cruise line claims 87 percent passenger approval, passenger reviews are mixed. They have described the* Independence *as a floating nautical museum, a classic old liner, and an old tub. Reviews of the food range from fair to very good. Passengers may find low-end cabins unacceptable. The cruise line does emphasize the genuine Hawaiian spirit, and a* kamu *(teacher) sails on each cruise to explain the folklore, customs and dances of each island. The ship's older crowd enjoys the slow pace in the daytime and evening. Those with limited vacation days take note: Only the* Independence *does a complete Hawaiian Islands cruise in just seven days.*

Panama Canal

Since its completion in 1914, the Panama Canal has represented the ultimate of man's turn-of-the-century engineering achievements. The fifty-mile waterway that joins the Atlantic Ocean and Caribbean Sea connects forever the two diverse worlds of recreation and commerce. In one fell swoop the canal shortened by 7,900 nautical miles the distance between New York and San Francisco and created the elusive trade route explorers had sought for hundreds of years. The famed French engineer Ferdinand de Lesseps undertook the daunting task with a labor force of greater than 10,000 men. The initial project, which many predicted was an impossible task, ended in disaster when they abandoned the project, after twenty years of effort, in 1889. By that time 22,000 people had succumbed to a variety of jungle-related diseases that included malaria and yellow fever.

Construction again began in 1903. Ten years and 335 million dollars later the canal was born in the jungles of Colombia. The canal itself gave birth to the new nation of Panama. The locks of the canal are five city blocks long and higher than a six-story building, but are barely wide enough to permit passage of today's largest mega–cruise ships. A visit to the Panama Canal has at its core a firsthand viewing of intricate working locks and gates, which permit ships passage from one great ocean to another. Since its opening, more than 700,000 ships have used the marvelous shortcut.

➥ **Steve and Pat's Best Deal Goal:** *We opt for the higher-priced, luxurious, and much longer RCI ten-day cruises on the* Legend of the Seas *or* Rhapsody of the Seas. *These are an excellent choice for those who prefer the quiet time afforded by four long days at sea followed by a fabulous tour of the Hawaiian Islands.*

Panama cruise itineraries and lengths vary, but often include a visit to Costa Rica's rain forest, the Mayan ruins of Guatemala, and first-class resorts on the Mexican Riviera. The trans-canal crossing cuts across Gatun Lake, past Galliard Cut, and the ship then sails along the continental divide under the Americas Bridge.

Panama Canal—Ports of Call and Shore Excursions

The trans-canal journey is an extraordinary opportunity to experience the cultures of Mexico, the Caribbean, and South American nations.

Acapulco, Mexico

This famed resort offers colorful boutiques and restaurants, dazzling beaches, and lavish luxury hotels. Land and water sports include golf, scuba diving, snorkeling, and parasailing. We refer you to Chapter 12, "South of the Border," for our detailed discussion of this famous resort area. Cruise ships departing Acapulco travel along the Mexican coast, past crystal blue lagoons and white sand beaches, simultaneously viewing the distant Sierra Madre Mountains.

Aruba

Visit Oranjestad, the resort capital of this Dutch island. Enjoy the Dutch-colonial architecture and stroll along its quiet streets.

Explore a unique "floating" market and scores of quaint shops. The adventurous will find beach and marine activities that include scuba diving, snorkeling, and boating. Excursions outside the city visit the intriguing rock gardens of Casibari and a drive past local divi-divi trees.

Caracas, Venezuela

Passengers are invited to tour this bustling cosmopolitan Venezuelan city. Highlights include the domed capital and the Colonial Museum. Shore excursions include a four-wheel drive adventure tour, (out of the city), spending the day on a remote beach, and a trip to a Bavarian colony deep in the forest.

Cartagena, Colombia

The coastline of Venezuela and Colombia was once known as the Spanish Main. Today, Cartagena is South America's largest and best-preserved colonial city. The "old city" reflects the city's Spanish heritage, a time when pirates preyed on gold-laden ships. This Colombian city transports visitors to Old Spain. Excursions include a city tour with a visit to the old cathedral and views from a 130-foot, sky-high fortress. Here shopping turns to emeralds. Anyone wish to amass thousands more AAdvantage miles?

Cozumel, Mexico

This is Mexico's largest island, which lies off the Yucatán peninsula. The island offers world-class scuba diving, snorkeling, wonderful beaches, and the quaint and charming town of San Miguel, with its colorful shops and restaurants.

Gatun Lake

The lake provides 52,000 gallons of water per transit through the canal. This immense artificial reservoir measures 168 square miles and features scenic cruising surrounded by lush forbidding jungle.

Panama Canal Transit

On a full-transit cruise through the canal, a ship travels fifty-one miles in eight hours and passes through the Miraflores, Padro Miguel, and Gatun locks, descending eighty-five feet to the Caribbean Sea.

Puerta Caldera, Costa Rica

One thousand miles to the south of Acapulco is Costa Rica. Puerto Calder is one of the country's most picturesque ports and is sheltered by the Gulf of Nicoya. Visitors marvel at Costa Rica's raw tropical beauty. The rugged interior consists of volcanoes and rain forest. Its rain forest is home to 10 percent of the world's bird species. More than 1,000 varieties of orchids cover the landscape, and the rain forest eventually gives way to 13,000-foot mountains. The most popular shore excursion may be the drive from Puerta Caldera to the nation's capital city, San Jose, where passengers enjoy a day at the famed Carara Biological Reserve. This journey passes magnificent landscapes and takes guests through a dense rain forest. Stop and shop in the village of Sarchi, with its fine selection of local arts and crafts.

St. Thomas, U.S. Virgin Islands

Passengers flock to the duty-free shops in this U.S. Virgin Islands port of call. Anyone looking for gold, diamonds, and other assorted baubles? The many shore excursions include the following: golfing, beaches, snorkeling, hiking, sailing, scuba diving, an undersea submarine ride, and a seaplane flight. The island's main shopping area is just a short walk from the dock. See Chapter 10, "The Caribbean," for additional information.

Panama Canal—Cruise Lines and Discount Prices

Princess Cruises

This line offers more departure dates and cruise lengths than any other cruise line sailing the Panama Canal. Princess uses four of its ships for Panama Canal itineraries. The *Sun*, *Dawn*, and *Sea Princess* represent the newer vessels in the Grand Class fleet. Princess also uses the *Regal Princess* for Panama Canal cruises. Princess itineraries stretch from Mexico's top resort area of Acapulco to St. Maarten/St. Martin in the Caribbean and Cartagena and Caracas in South America. Let's look at the basic Princess Panama Canal cruise, aptly called the "Classic Panama Canal Cruise." The trip from San Juan, Puerto Rico, to Acapulco is an eleven-day cruise, and the return trip from Acapulco to San Juan is a ten-day cruise.

Princess Cruises's eleven-day "Classic Panama Canal Cruise," on the *Sun Princess*, from San Juan to Acapulco, spends four days at sea with six ports of call:

Day one: Depart from San Juan, Puerto Rico in late evening
Day two: Visit St. Thomas, USVI, for a full day
Day three: Visit Martinique (French) for a full day
Day four: Visit Grenada (British) for three-quarters of a day
Day five: Visit Caracas, Venezuela, for a full day
Day six: Visit Curaçao (Dutch) for a full day
Day seven: Day at sea
Day eight: Day at sea
Day nine: Day at sea
Day ten: Day at sea
Day eleven: Visit Acapulco, Mexico, for a half day
Day twelve: Disembark in Acapulco, Mexico.

Princess Cruises' ten-day classic Panama Canal cruise, Acapulco to San Juan, on the *Sun Princess* spends five days at sea with four ports of call:

Day one: Depart from Acapulco, Mexico, at midnight
Day two: Day at sea
Day three: Day at sea
Day four: Visit Puerta Caldera, Costa Rica, for a full day
Day five: Day at sea
Day six: Day at sea; transit the Canal
Day seven: Visit Cartagena, Colombia, for a half day

Day eight: Visit Aruba (Spanish/Dutch) for a half day
Day nine: Day at sea
Day ten: Visit St. Thomas, USVI, for a full day
Day eleven: Disembark in San Juan, Puerto Rico

➥ **Steve and Pat's Tip:** *East Coast vacationers, with access to cheap airfares to Florida, should consider the* Regal Princess's *ten-day Panama Canal cruise. It sails round-trip from Ft. Lauderdale, does a partial canal transit through the Gatun Locks, and cruises Gatun Lake. Its itinerary includes four full days followed by visits to western Caribbean ports of call that include: Grand Cayman, Cozumel, Mexico, Cartagena, Colombia, and Limon, Costa Rica. The ultramodern* Regal *offers the finest in luxury cruising.*

Discount Prices Cruise Value Center advertised:

Sun Princess: eleven-day full-transit cruise reduced to $1,439.
Regal Princess: ten-day partial-transit cruise reduced to $1,279; ten-day cruise as low as $1,179.
Crown Princess: ten-day partial-transit round-trip from Ft. Lauderdale reduced to $1,179. Call (800) 231-7447.

Costco Travel offers great deals on Panama Canal cruises. The Princess ten-night full-transit Acapulco-to-San Juan cruise was specially priced at $1,201, including port charges. Call (800) 800-8505.

Norwegian Cruise Line (NCL)

The *Norwegian Wind* does a fifteen-day Panama Canal cruise from Miami to Los Angeles. Sixteen departures are available aboard the *Norwegian Dynasty*, which sails between Montego Bay and Acapulco.

From October to March, NCL offers a ten-day Panama Canal cruise that sails from Acapulco to Montego Bay (Jamaica). The reverse route, from Montego Bay to Acapulco, is eleven days. The two itineraries are similar, except that the eleven-day cruise includes two days in Costa Rica and substitutes a port of call in Colombia for one in Guatemala. The two itineraries have five days at sea and four or five ports of call. Both routes follow, listed one after the other:

Norwegian Dynasty Ten-Day Cruise

Day one: Depart from Acapulco, Mexico
Day two: Day at sea
Day three: Visit Puerto Quetzal, Guatemala
Day four: Day at sea
Day five: Visit Caldera, Costa Rica
Day six: Day at sea
Day seven: Day at sea; transit Canal
Day eight: Visit San Blas Islands, Panama
Day nine: Cartagena, Colombia
Day ten: Day at sea
Day eleven: Disembark in Montego Bay, Jamaica

Norwegian Dynasty Eleven-Day Cruise

Day one: Depart from Montego Bay, Jamaica
Day two: Day at sea
Day three: Visit San Andres Island, Colombia
Day four: Visit San Blas Island, Panama
Day five: Day at sea; transit Canal
Day six: Day at sea
Day seven: Visit Golfito, Costa Rica
Day eight: Visit Caldera, Costa Rica
Day nine: Day at sea
Day ten: Day at sea
Day eleven: Visit Acapulco, Mexico
Day twelve: Disembark in Acapulco

Discount prices   NCL's brochure price for either the ten- or eleven-day itinerary is $2,199 for category H inside cabins with two lower beds that convert to queen size. CruiseMasters discount priced the *Norwegian Wind* cruise at $1,664. Call (800) 242-9000.

Celebrity Cruises

Ultraluxury at less than luxury prices might just be the motto of Celebrity Cruises. Celebrity's *Zenith*, built in 1992, carries 1,374 passengers. It does ten- and eleven-night trans-canal cruises that include ports of call in Acapulco, Huatulco, Puerto Caldera, Cartagena, Aruba, St. Thomas, and San Juan. The *Zenith* also does a thirteen-day sailing from New York to Acapulco.

Discount prices Travel of America offers an eleven-day full-transit cruise on Celebrity's *Zenith* priced at $1,494, including port charges. Call (800) 228-8843. CruiseMasters offers *Zenith's* thirteen-day sailing from New York, priced from $1,373, including port charges. Call (800) 242-9000. Travel of America offers November and December 1998, eleven-day sailings priced at $1,494. Call (800) 228-8843. Or try the low-priced $1,430 cruise offered by Ambassador Tours. Call (800) 989-9000. Whole World of Travel offers special April and May 1999 repositioning fifteen-day cruises on the *Mercury* and *Galaxy* that include port fees, taxes, *and* round-trip airfare from Los Angeles, priced at $1,898 (*Galaxy*) and $1,799 (*Mercury*). Call Whole World at (800) 458-3636 for these and other more current deals.

Holland America Line (HAL)

HAL is a major player in the Panama Canal cruise market. In fact, HAL claims that their *Maasdam* is the only award-winning ship offering regular Panama Canal sailings. A *Travel and Leisure* magazine poll listed the *Maasdam* as one of the ten best cruise ships in the world. Holland America is known for quality, value, and luxury. The *Maasdam* sails on ten-day canal cruises with full daylight transit. HAL's itinerary is unique. The cruise travels from Ft. Lauderdale to Acapulco. Here is the itinerary:

Day one: Depart from Ft. Lauderdale, Florida at 5:00 P.M.
Day two: Visit Half Moon Cay, Bahamas, for a full day
Day three: Day at sea
Day four: Day at sea
Day five: Day at sea; transit the Panama Canal
Day six: Day at sea

Day seven: Visit Puerta Caldera, Costa Rica, for a full day
Day eight: Day at sea
Day nine: Visit Puerto Quetzal, Guatemala, for a full day
Day ten: Visit Santa Cruz Huatulco, Mexico, in the afternoon
Day eleven: Disembark at Acapulco, Mexico, at 8:00 A.M.

Discount prices We have seen this cruise advertised at a discounted price of $2,234. Much better, by far, is Costco Travel's advertised price of $1,578 for the November 8, 1998, departure! During the December holiday season, they price identical routes at $2,143. Call (800) 800-8505.

Premier Cruises

Premier's *Ocean Breeze* is an older classic cruise ship built in 1955 and most recently refurbished in 1997. It is a vessel that reminds passengers of earlier, less crowded sailing days. Its 776 passengers will find the teak decks, wooden deck chairs, polished brass, and etched glass delightful.

➥ **Steve and Pat's Tip:** *Premier is the only cruise line that offers a seven-night partial transit of the Panama Canal. It is also the only cruise line that disembarks passengers at the Panama Canal for up-close shore excursions, starting at $25, that capture the sights, sounds, and flavor of this special place.*

Here is Premier's unique round-trip Montego Bay itinerary. One of the best reasons to take this cruise is that it has two days at sea and four ports of call.

Day one: Depart from Montego Bay, Jamaica, in early evening
Day two: Day at sea
Day three: Visit Cartagena, Colombia, for a full day
Day four: Visit the San Blas Islands for a full day
Day five: Visit the Panama Canal and Gatun Lake for a full day
Day six: Visit Puerto Limon, Costa Rica, for a full day
Day seven: Day at sea
Day eight: Disembark in Montego Bay, Jamaica

The itinerary includes the following ports of call:

Montego Bay, Jamaica A recreational playground with beaches, countless beachfront resorts, nearby mountains and rivers.

Cartagena, Colombia Experience the history and culture of Colombia's big and bustling port city.

Partial Transit to Gatun Lake The only cruise that permits passengers to disembark for exciting shore excursions, including incredible close-up views of the locks.

San Blas Islands (owned by Panama) Cuna Indians in traditional dugout canoes greet passengers. These "untouched" islands are a throwback in time.

Puerto Limon, Costa Rica Take the rain forest and shore excursion to get close to the country's best asset, its natural beauty.

Here is a sample of Premier's Panama Canal area shore excursions:

Chagres River Tour Guests travel across the Gatun locks for a riverboat adventure on the Chagres River.

Panama Canal Aerial Tour Guests board a twin-engine sightseeing plane for a one-hour tour of the canal area, Chagres River, Gatun Lake, and Panama City.

Forest and Forts This is a fabulous jungle sightseeing adventure that highlights the country's tropical flora and fauna. Then on to Fort San Lorenzo, built by the Spanish in the 1500s to protect the city from pirates. Guests enjoy a walking tour of the ruins.

➥ **Steve and Pat's Tip:** *Because the itinerary has unique ports of call, generally no other cruise ship comes into view at the ports, nor do thousands of passengers disembark from other ships. Amenities are scaled to ship size but are of high quality. Passengers with a sense of adventure and who do not crave all the amenities and hordes of the megaships should consider this innovative package.*

Gatun Yacht Club This joint venture of Panama and Premier Cruises exists for the sole purpose of sponsoring weekly lakeside *Ocean Breeze* parties. For just $20 passengers party with unlimited food, alcoholic and nonalcoholic drinks, and entertainment provided by local musicians and dancers.

Discount prices Why pay thousands of dollars more? Costco Travel advertises Premier Cruises's seven-night, partial-transit canal cruise for just $615! Premier itself advertises cruises-only prices as low as $629 for category K cabins. There are only two category K cabins on the *Ocean Breeze*, and one of these offers a double bed. Upgrades are available to category J, which includes both inside and ocean-view staterooms, for about $50.

➥ **Steve and Pat's Canary Island Tip:** *Premier's seven-night Canary Islands cruise: How about something different, exotic, fun, and exciting, like a combination of tropical islands and Casablanca in one cruise package? Premier's one-week Canary Islands and Casablanca cruise is priced at just $579, including port charges. Call Premier for a brochure, its latest schedule, and price information at (800) 373-2654.*

Premier's Air and Cruise Packages Premier loves to innovate. They often advertise air-and-cruise packages from the East and West coasts. Air-and-cruise packages from San Francisco are priced at $1,049, and from New York at $899!

Royal Caribbean International (RCI)

RCI offers super quality, luxury amenities, and multiple itineraries that depart from San Juan and Ft. Lauderdale and disembark in Los Angeles and San Diego. Reverse itineraries depart from Los Angeles and San Diego and disembark in Miami and Ft. Lauderdale.

Discount prices Whole World of Travel offers great deals that include port fees *and* round-trip airfare from select cities for thirteen- and fourteen-day cruises on the *Song of the Seas* and *Legend of the Seas*. Several departures from November 1998 through March 1999 are priced from $1,665. Call Whole Word at (800) 458-3636.

Time to Travel offers a ten-night San Juan-to-Acapulco cruise at $1,294 per person, and an eleven-night Acapulco-to-San Juan cruise at $1,329 per person. Call (800) 524-3300. Travel of America offers both the *Legend of the Seas* and *Vision of the Seas* ten-day cruises priced at $1,449. Call (800) 228-8843.

➥ **Steve and Pat's Best Deal Goal:** *Costco Travel advertises Premier Cruises's seven-night, partial-transit canal cruise for just $615! Upgrades are available to category J, which includes both inside and ocean-view staterooms, for about $50.*

Russia

Russia is now available for exciting cruising to major cities on their extensive river systems. A fifteen-day river cruise offers passengers an incredible visual contrast between cosmopolitan cities like St. Petersburg and the rural countryside.

FOS Tours and Travel

Fifteen-Day Russian River Cruises These comprehensive fifteen-day cruise-tours sail along the Volga River, lakes Onega and Ladoga, and through the Belomorsko-Baltiisky Canal. Three cruise ships, the M/S *Lenin*, *Litvinov*, or *Andropov*, are used. All staterooms are outside, affording fantastic views. All cabins are air-conditioned with private bath and shower. Shipboard amenities include shops, a music salon, dining room, theater, and sundeck. The cruise ship doubles as the hotel throughout the tour. Major tour features include the following: round-trip air travel from New York to St. Petersburg on Finnair, all transfers, a fourteen-night cruise in an outside cabin, all daily meals, a welcome-to-the-ship cocktail reception, all daily sightseeing, nightly entertainment, English-speaking guides and cruise director, and all entrance fees. Here is the exciting itinerary for this two-week river-cruise adventure:

Day one: Depart from New York and arrive in St. Petersburg via Finnair
Day two: Day cruising

Day three: Visit Moscow. Spend three days exploring Moscow, including a city tour, St. Basil's Cathedral, the Kremlin, the Armory, and the Pushkin Fine Arts Museum.
Day six: Visit Uglich, an old-world town built in 1148
Day seven: Visit Kosstroma, a city that retains its eighteenth-century charm and has lovely streets that fan out from the central square. Tourists visit the outdoor museum village Berengevka and the museum at the former Ipatyevsky Monastery.
Day eight: Visit Yaroslavl, a Volga River port city founded in the eleventh century
Day nine: Visit Irma. Enjoy a quiet walk through this tiny village and an outdoor *shashlyk* barbecue.
Day ten: Day at sea
Day eleven: Visit Kizhi Island, at the northern end of Lake Onega. Its famed open-air Museum of Architecture offers a rare glimpse into Russia's past. Also visit Petrozavodsk, the largest city in the Karelian Republic.
Day twelve: Day at sea
Day thirteen: Visit St. Petersburg for three days of sightseeing. The ultimate highlight of any visit to Russia is a trip to this famous capital, created by Peter the Great to rival Venice. The city has 101 islands, 66 canals, and hundreds of bridges. Visit the world-famous Hermitage Museum, formerly the Winter Palace, home of the last six czars. Enjoy an excursion to Pushkin, summer palace of Catherine the Great. Explore the city's shops, cafes, and theaters, and then fly home.

Discount prices Considering the two-week length of this world-class cruise vacation, the price is definitely right. This tour, offered by FOS Tours and Travel, is priced at $2,329 from New York. Because this is a fourteen-night cruise-and-air package, available free travel cash may be used. Add $300 for West Coast departures. Additional savings is available by following our advice for discount bookings. Remember, the 40,000-mile American AAdvantage award qualifies for free round-trip air travel to Moscow and St. Petersburg. With free air travel, a cruise-only package costs $1,595, and discount booking can reduce it even more. For more information contact FOS Tours and Travel at (516) 466-5651, or fax (516) 466-5899.

GT Cruises

This is another Russian-specialty cruise tour operator. Their Moscow-to-St. Petersburg river tours mimic the above FOS Tours itinerary. GT uses nonstop Finnair flights from New York or San Francisco to Helsinki. These flights earn Delta Skymiles. The sixteen-day air-and-cruise tour uses the MS *Russ*, a newly built German river cruiser.

➥ **Steve and Pat's Tip:** *The quality of food, services, and amenities on Russia cruise-tours is inferior to that found on the ships of mass-market cruise lines. Russian cruise brochures talk in terms of "The food is . . . the best available." One brochure's testimonial notes, "The food was good (for Russian cuisine) . . . " Do your homework on this one. Review sample menus and ask for testimonials and references.*

Discount prices Prices for double cabins in low seasons are $2,298 from New York and $2,398 from San Francisco. Call GT Cruises for their latest bargain Russia cruise packages at (800) 828-7970 or (718) 934-4100.

Appendix A
Steve and Pat's Essential Contacts

Cruise Lines

American Hawaii Cruises
1380 Port of New Orleans Place
New Orleans, LA 70130
(504) 586-0631

Carnival Cruise Line
3655 NW 87th Avenue
Miami, FL 33178
(800) 227-6482

Celebrity Cruises
5201 Blue Lagoon Drive
Miami, FL 33126
(305) 262-6677; (800) 437-3111

Commodore Cruise Line
4000 Hollywood Blvd.
South Tower, Suite 385
Hollywood, FL 33021
(954) 967-2100; (800) 237-5361

Costa Cruises
80 Southwest 8th Street
Miami, FL 33130
(305) 358-7325; (800) 462-6782

Disney Cruise Line
210 Celebration Place, Suite 400
Celebration, FL 34747
(407) 566-7000; (800) 939-2784

Holland America Line
300 Elliott Avenue West
Seattle, WA 98119
(206) 281-3535; (800) 426-0327

Norwegian Cruise Line
7665 Corporate Center Drive
Miami, FL 33126
(305) 436-0866; (800) 327-7030

Orient Lines
1510 Southeast 17th Street, Suite 400
Fort Lauderdale, FL 33316
(954) 527-6660; (800) 333-7300

Premier Cruises
P.O. Box 573
Cape Canaveral, FL 32920
(800) 990-7770

Princess Cruises
10100 Santa Monica Blvd.
Los Angeles, CA 90067
(310) 553-1770; (800) PRINCESS

Renaissance Cruises
1800 Eller Drive
Fort Lauderdale, FL 33335
(800) 525-5350; (954) 463-0982

Royal Caribbean International
1050 Caribbean Way
Miami, FL 33132
(305) 539-6000; (800) 659-7225

Royal Olympic Cruises
1 Rockefeller Plaza, Suite 315
New York, NY 10020
(212) 397-6400; (800) 872-6400

China Cruise Tour Operators

China Focus Travel
870 Market Street, Suite 1215
San Francisco, CA 94102
(888) 688-1898; (415) 788-8660

China Travel Service (CTS)
(800) 332-2831, ext. 126

Pacific Holidays (800) 355-8025

Rim-Pac International (800) 701-TOUR.

Cruise-Only Agencies

Ambassador Tours (800) 989-9000

Costco Travel (800) 800-8505

CruiseMasters (800) 242-9000

CruiseOne (888) 703-7245 (516) 872-1466

Cruise Value Centers (800) 231-7447

Cruise World (800) 442-9278

Golden Bear Travel (800) 551-1000

Time to Travel (800) 524-3300

Travel of America (800) 228-8843

Whole Word of Travel (800) 458-3636

Free Airline Travel Program

American Airlines AAdvantage
(800) 882-8880

Citibank AAdvantage (800) 359-4444

Diners Club (800) 234-6377

Appendix A

Free Companion Ticket

United Airlines (800) 767-9839
Apply for the United Mileage First Plus Visa or MasterCard: (800) 421-4655

Greece Cruise Tour Operators

Homeric Tours, NY
55 E. 55th Street
New York, NY 10022
(800) 223-5570

Tourlite International
551 Fifth Avenue
New York, NY 10176
(800) 272-7600

Magazines, Catalogues

Brookstone (800) 926-7000

International Travel News
2120 28th Street
Sacramento, CA 95181
(800) 366-9192

Magellan's Travel Catalogue
P.O. Box 5485
Santa Barbara, CA 93150
(800) 962-4943

Miscellaneous

Travisa (800) 222-2589
(Emergency passport and visa service)

Phone Cards

American Travel Network
10211 North 32nd Street, Suite A5
Phoenix, AZ 85028
(800) 477-9692

World Link
3399 Peachtree Road, NE
Lenox Building, Suite 400
Atlanta, GA 30326
(800) 432-6169

Rebate and Discount Agencies

Discover Wholesale Travel
New Zealand/Australia South Pacific
(800) 576-7770; (949) 833-1136
Fax: (949) 833-1176
(Noncruise consolidator)

Golden Age Travelers (GAT)
Pier 27
The Embarcadero
San Francisco, CA 94111
(San Francisco)
(800) 258-8880

Pearson Travel
93 Dyer Street
Providence, RI 02903
(800) 336-1066; (401) 274-2900
Fax: (401) 831-5328

Pennsylvania Travel
(800) 331-0947; (610) 251-9944
Fax: (610) 644-215
(Rebate agency)

Travel Avenue
(800) 333-3335
Fax: (312) 876-1254
(Rebate agency)

Travelers Advantage
Box C32123
Richmond, VA 23261
(800) 843-7777; (800) 482-2964
(Rebate program)

Russia Cruises

FOS Tours and Travel
15 Great Neck Road
Great Neck, NY 11021
(516) 466-5651
Fax: (516) 466-5899

GT Cruises World Trade
  Center
2610 E. 16th Street
Brooklyn, NY 11235
(800) 828-7970; (718) 934-4100
Fax: (718) 934-9419

Travel Cash Giveaways

International Travel House
789 Route 202 North
Bridgewater, NJ 08807
(908) 685-7644

Travel Discounts

Entertainment Publications
P.O. Box 1068
Trumball, CT 06611
(800) 374-4464

Travel Insurance

Traveler's Travel Pak
  Insurance
Downtown Travel
1609 Locust Street
Walnut Creek, CA 94596
(510) 945-8004
Fax: (510) 945-8081

Travel Insured International
National Distributor for
  Travel Pak
(800) 243-3174

Travel Guard International
(Travel Guard Policy)
(800) 826-1300
Fax: (800) 955-8785

Appendix B
Cyberspace—Great Web Sites

Travel Resource for the Year 2000

You have heard about it, read about, talked about it, and perhaps spend your life dabbling in it. The Web, also known as the World Wide Web, WWW, the Internet, and the Net are now commonplace terms.

Assume one Sunday morning, several inviting cruise advertisements are in the *New York Times* Travel Section. Each offers a similar Caribbean itinerary. Which cruise line and ship is right for you? Helpful information beyond that found in brochures may often be found on the Web.

Helpful Categories

A New Window to Recreation   For any port of call, the Web provides instant access to all available recreational activities from commercial sources or government travel agencies.

Maps   Amazingly, find a color map of any city in the world and print it in minutes. The same is true for a subway or "underground" systems.

Transportation   Most passengers need transportation to their cruise ship's departure city and from the airport to their cruise ships. Details on all facets of transportation are found on the Web.

Ports of Call, Sightseeing   Want information on shopping, recreation, museums, flea markets, castles, beaches, or any of a hundred other topics? All this and more are easily available on the Web.

➥ **Steve and Pat's Cyberspace Travel Connections Tip:**
The following list contains Web sites for all major cruise lines, and that is just the beginning. Want to check out the latest deals from cruise-specialty travel agencies? Boldfaced Web sites carry our special-interest recommendation.

Steve and Pat's Great Websites

Steve and Pat's sites: nextfx.com/CheapskateGuide and CheapTravel.net

Airlink (link to all airlines on the Web)	airlink.net/airlines.htm
Albermarle of London (show tickets)	albermarle-london.com/news2.html
Ambassador Tours (specialty agency)	**ambassadortours.com**
American Airlines (AAdvantage)	americanair.com/
American Hawaiian Cruises	**cruisehawaii.com**
Australia	australia-online.com/austravel
Barry House (London show tickets)	traveling.com/london/barryhouse/theatre.htm
Beach Camera	beachcamera.com
Best air fares	bestfare.com
Bizmiles (tracks frequent-flyer accounts)	**bizmiles.biztravel.com**
British Airways	britishairways.com/regional/usa/offers/details2.shtml
British Rail	railtrack.co.uk/travel or accessworldwide.com/tours_travels/britrail/ or britpass.html
British train schedules	timetables.railtrack.co.uk/cgi-bin/devtt,fcgi
Carnival Cruise Line	**carnival.com**

Appendix B

Celebrity Cruises	**celebrity-cruises.com**
Central Holidays (global travel)	centralholidays.com
Cheap Tickets, Inc.	cheaptickets.com
Cities (5,000 worldwide)	city.net
Club Med Cruises	clubmed.com
Commodore Cruise Line	**commodorecruise.com**
Costa Cruises	**costacruises.com**
Costco Travel	**costcotravel.com**
Cruise Holidays (specialty agency)	3000.com/cruise
Cruise News (newsletter)	safari.net/~marketc/cruisenewsmenu.html
Cruise Ship Center (Mexico)	cruiseshipcenter.com
Cruise Value Center (cruise-only)	cruisevalue.com/main.html
Cruise World Specials (ten cruise lines)	cruiseworld.com/specials.htm
Currency converter	**xe.net/cgi-bin/ucc/convert**
Diners Club	dinersclub.com
Disney Cruise Line	disneycruise.com
Egypt (Homeric Tours)	homerictours.com
Entertainment Publications	entertainment-gold.com
France Vacations	france-vacations.com
French Experience (N.Y.)	frenchexperience.com
Greece (Homeric Tours)	**homerictours.com**
Greece (Tourlite International)	tourlite.com
Holland America Line	**hollandamerica.com**
Homeric Tours	homerictours.com
Ireland (Shamrock Airlines)	shamrock.org
Israel Tourist Office	teletel.co.il/infotour or Infotour.co.il
Israel (Egged Tours)	eggedtlalim.co.il
International Cruise Association (100 members with links)	cruising.org
Internet Travel Network (general travel)	itn.com
Italiatour (Alitalia Airlines)	italiatour.com

Italy (Perillo Tours)	perillotours.com
London: Albermarle of London (tickets)	**demon.co.uk/albermarle london2/index.html**
London sightseeing	netlondon.com/e-places.html
Low air fares	lowestfare.com
Magellan's Travel Catalogue	**magellans.com**
Mapquest (U.S. maps with directions)	**mapquest.com**
Maps (global)	maps.com
Maui: *Aloha* magazine (discounts and deals)	travelwithaloha.com
Maui Visitors Bureau	visitmaui.com
Morocco (Homeric Tours)	homerictours.com
New Zealand (Kelly Tarlton)	tgint.com/pages/nz/attrac/ kelly/kelly001.html
New Zealand (Rotorua)	rotorua.co.nz/stylesheet.html
New Zealand (Queenstown)	atoz-nz.com/Queenstown
New Zealand campgrounds	holidayguide.com/ cam-nz/index.html
New Zealand camper-van rentals (Kea)	dmd.co.nz/kea
New Zealand maps	us.discovernz.co.nz/ discovernz/maps.html
Norwegian Cruise Line	**ncl.com**
Paris information	city.net/countries/france/ paris/info
Pennsylvania Travel	**patravel.com**
Pearson Travel	**pearsontravel@edgenet.net**
Perillo Tours (Italy)	perillotours.com
Pleasant Hawaiian Holidays	pleasant.net or pleasantholidays.com
Poland	amta.com
Portugal (Homeric Tours)	homerictours.com
Portugal (Skyline Travel)	skylinetravel.com
Portugal (Sun Holidays)	sun-holidays.com
Premier Cruises	**premiercruises.com**
Princess Cruises	**princesscruises.com**
Regal Cruises	regalcruises.com

Appendix B

Royal Caribbean International	**royalcaribbean.com**
Royal Olympic Cruises	**royalolympiccruises.com**
Sea Letter (cruise newsletter)	sealetter.com
Shamrock Airlines	shamrock.org
Skyline Travel (Spain and Portugal)	skylinetravel.com
Spain (Homeric Tours)	homerictours.com
Sun Holidays	sun-holiday.com
Tahiti (information and travel)	tahiti.com
Tahiti Vacations	tahitivacation.com
Tom Barefoot's Cash Back Tours (Maui)	tombarefoot.com/activities.html
Top twenty cruise ships	**oceancruisenews.com/top20.htm**
Travel Guard Insurance	**noelgroup.com**
Travelers Advantage	**cuc.com**
The Trip	thetrip.com
Travisa Passport and Visa Service	**travisa.com**
Travelocity (general travel)	travelocity.com
Turkey	keytours.com/keytours
Turkey (Homeric Tours)	homerictours.com
TWA Airlines	twa.com
United Airlines Mileage Plus	**ual.com**

Index

Acapulco, Mexico, 258–59, 306
Airline travel programs
See specific airlines
Alaska cruises, 179–204
  Anchorage, 194
  Cordova, 192–93
  discount prices, 180, 195–204
  Glacier Bay National Park, 179, 187, 189
  Gulf of Alaska cruises, 179–80, 191–95
  Haines, 190
  Hubbard Glacier, 187
  Inside Passage-only cruises, 179, 182–90
  Juneau, 185–86
  Ketchikan, 183–84
  Prince William Sound, 192
  Sawyer Glacier, 188
  Seward, 194
  shore excursions, 180–82
  Sitka, 186
  Skagway, 188
    Valdez, 193
    Vancouver, B.C., 182–83, 192
    Wrangell, 191
All-inclusive service, 5–8
Ambassador Tours, 67, 235–38, 247–48, 312

American Airlines, 29–38, 39–41, 42
  AAdvantage Program, 29–38, 74, 203
  Citibank AAdvantage, *see* Citibank Aadvantage
  companion awards (free), 40
  first class upgrades, 42
  newsletter, 34
  travel awards, 34–37, 41
  two-city ticket awards, 37, 301
American Hawaii Cruises, 304–305
Anchorage, Alaska, 195–96
Aruba, 306–07

Babysitting services, 25–27
Bahama Islands, 219–22
Barbados, 230–31
Bermuda cruises, 239–48
  discount prices, 246–48
  golf, 244–45
  Hamilton, 241–42
  King's Wharf, 242–43
  shore excursions, 240
  St. George, 243–44
Books on Tape, 141
British Airways Program, 33
Brookstone, 140, 142

Cabin selection, 74–77, 101, 115–22, 148
Cabo San Lucas, Mexico, 256–57
Cancellation fees, in general, 102
Caracas, Venezuela, 307
Caribbean cruises, 205–38
  Bahama Islands, 219–22
  Barbados, 230–31
  Cozumel, Mexico, 213–15
  discount prices, 234–38
  Eastern cruises, 205, 219–27, 235–36
  Grand Cayman Island, 218
  Jamaica, 216–18
  Key West, Florida, 222–23
  Martinique, 231–32
  Playa del Carmen or Calica, Mexico, 216
  San Juan, Puerto Rico, 223–24, 227–29, 236
  seasonal discounts, 208–209
  shore excursions, 209–11
  Southern cruises, 207–208, 227–34, 236–38
  St. Croix, USVI, 224, 228
  St. John, USVI, 225–26, 228
  St. Maarten/St. Martin, 233–34
  St. Thomas, USVI, 226–27, 228
  Western cruises, 206, 211–18, 235
Carnival Cruise Lines
  Alaska cruises, 196–97
  Caribbean cruises, 212–13, 219–20, 235–38
  diets, special, 109–11
  dining, 151, 160
  disabled persons' facilities, 107
  discount rates, kids', 24
  fire safety, 79
  in general, 13, 28, 115
  kids' programs, 19, 20, 24, 26, 30
  medical facilities, 87
  Mexican Riviera cruises, 259–61
  vacation guarantee, 102
Cartagena, Columbia, 307
Catalina Island, California, 252
Celebrity Cruises
  Alaska cruises, 197–98
  Bermuda cruises, 246–47
  cabins, 116, 148,
  Caribbean cruises, 235, 220
  diets, special, 109–13
  dining, 152
  disabled persons' facilities, 108
  discount rates, kids', 24
  in general, 116
  kids' programs, 20, 26, 30
  Kosher meals, 111–13
  medical facilities, 87
  medical insurance policy, 90
  Panama Canal cruises, 312
China Focus Travel, 296–97
China, Yangtze River cruises, 289–98
  Chenglingi, 291
  Chongqing, 294
  discount prices, 296–98
  Dragon Gate Gorge, 292
  Fendu (ghost city), 293
  Misty Gorge, 292
  Qutang Gorge, 293
  tour operators, 296–98
  Wu Gorge,
  Wuhan, 290–91
  Xi'an, terra cotta warriors, 294–96
  Xiling Gorge, 291
Citibank AAdvantage, 29–38, 40, 74
  companion awards (free), 40
  program miles (free), 34–36
Commodore Cruise Line
  diets, special, 111–13
  dining, 153–54
  discount rates, kids', 24
  in general, 13, 17, 116
  Kosher meals, 111–13
  medical facilities, 87

Index 331

Companion airline tickets (free)
   MCI, 44
   Worldlink, 38
   See specific airlines
Cordova, Alaska, 192–93
Costa Cruise Lines, 117
   Caribbean cruises, 213, 220, 235–36
   diets, special, 109–13
   dining, 153–54
   in general, 117
   kids' programs, 21, 26, 30
   medical facilities, 87
   medical insurance policy, 90
Costco Travel, 59–60, 200, 235–37, 261, 310, 315–16
Cozumel, Mexico, 213–15, 307
Cruise-ad jargon, 70–73
Cruise participation quiz, 12–13
Cruise-only agencies,
   Ambassador Tours, 67, 235–38, 247–48, 312
   Costco Travel, 59–60, 200, 235–37, 261, 310, 315–16
   Cruise Master, 66, 303, 311, 312
   Cruise One, 67, 204, 247
   Cruises Inc., 235, 237–38
   Cruise Value Center, 67, 203
   Cruise World, 66, 198, 200, 235, 237–38, 247
   Time to Travel, 67, 198, 236–38, 315
   Travel of America, 67, 197, 201, 204, 237–38, 304, 312
   Whole Word of Travel, 65–66, 198, 200, 262, 304, 312, 315
Cruise terminology, 98–102

Delos, Greece, 284
Delta Airlines
   American Express card, companion award (free), 39–40
   Sky Mile Program, 39–40, 318

Diets, special, 109–13
Diners Club card, 36–37, 38
   topping-off travel awards, 36
Dining and seating
   alternative dining, 115, 118, 120–122, 159–60
   attire, formal, and informal, 16–17
   diets, special, 109–13
   kids' meals, 23–24
   Kosher meals, 111–13
   meals, 148–60
   seating selection, 76–78
Disabled persons' facilities, 106–109
   Carnival Cruise Lines, 107–109
   Celebrity Cruises, 108
   Princess Cruises, 107–109
Disney Cruise Line
   Caribbean cruises, 219
   diets, special, 111–13
   in general, 19
   kids' programs, 21
   Kosher meals, 111–13
   medical facilities, 87

Electricity, foreign, 144–45
Emergency medical evacuation, 89–90
Ensenada, Mexico, 251
Entertainment, in general, 161–64
Entertainment Publications, 61–62
Exercise facilities/programs, 168–71

Family vacations, 18–27
   activities and programs, 19, 20–24, 26, 30
   babysitting services, 25–27
   discount rates, 24–25
   kids' meals, 23–24

Gambling, casinos 16
Gatun Lake, Panama, 307

Glacier Bay National Park, Alaska, 179, 187, 189
Grand Cayman Island, 218
Greek Isles' cruises, 263–88
    Athens, 272–73
    cruise itineraries, 267–71
    Delos, 284
    discount prices, 286–87
    Heraklion, Crete, 278
    Homeric classical land tour, 274–75, 286–87
    Istanbul, Turkey, 281–83
    Kusadasi, Turkey (Ephesus), 281
    land tours, 265–66, 274–75
    Mediterranean cruise, 287–88
    Mykonos, 283–84
    Patmos, 281
    Rhodes, 278–80
    Santorini, 277
    tour operators, 271–72, 286–87
Golf courses, miniature, 121
Golf cruises, *see* Bermuda cruises
Guarantee, vacation, 102–103

Haines, Alaska, 190
Hawaiian Islands cruises, 299–305
    discount prices, 302–304
    Hawaii Island, 299–300
    Kauai, 301–302
    Maui, 300–301
    Oahu, 302
Heraklion, Crete, 278
Holland America Line
    Alaska cruises, 199–200
    Caribbean cruises, 213, 236
    diets, special, 109–13
    discount rates, kids', 25
    in general, 117–18
    kids' programs, 19, 20, 24, 26, 30
    Kosher meals, 111–13
    medical facilities, 87
    Panama Canal cruises, 312–13

Homeric Tours, Greece, 274–75, 286–87
Hubbard Glacier, Alaska, 187

Infirmaries, ship, 87
Insurance, travel 79–91
    camera coverage, 80–82
    cancellation, 15, 83–84
    claims, 86–87
    medical, 15, 84–91
    Travelers Travel Insurance Pak, 80, 82–85
    Travel Guard International, 15, 85
International Travel House (ITH), 46–47, 52–53
Istanbul, Turkey, 281–83

Jamaica, 216–18
Juneau, Alaska, 185–86
Junk mail, 34, 36, 39, 43–44

Kauai, Hawaii, 301–302
Ketchikan, Alaska, 183–85
Key West, Florida, 222–23
Kids at sea, *see* Family vacations
Kusadasi, Turkey (Ephesus), 281

London vacation package, 32–33

Magellan's Travel Catalogue, 128, 140, 142, 144
Manzanilla, Mexico, 259
Martinique, 231–32
Maui, Hawaii, 300–301
Mazatlan, Mexico, 255–56
MCI (free airline ticket), 43–44
Meals, *see* Dining and
Meals, kosher, 111–13
Medical evacuation at sea, 88–89
Medical facilities, 87–89
Medical tips, 126, 130–32, 143–44

Index

Mediterranean cruises, 287–88
  discount prices, 287–88
  itineraries, 288
Mexican Riviera cruises, 249–63
  Acapulco, 258–259
  Cabo San Lucas, 256–57
  Catalina Island, 252
  discount prices, 260–62
  Ensenada, 251
  Manzanilla, 259
  Mazatlan, 255–56
  Puerto Vallarta, 252–55
  shopping tips, 250–51
  Zihuatanejo and Ixtapa, 257–58
Mykonos, Greece, 283–84

Newsletter, Steve and Pat's Cheap Travel, 53–55
New Zealand land vacation, 95–96
Norwegian Cruise Line
  Alaska cruise, 200–201
  Bermuda cruises, 247
  Caribbean cruises, 213, 220, 235, 237
  diets, special, 109–13
  dining, 118, 155–56, 160
    alternative dining, 118
  discount rates, kids', 25
  Hawaiian Islands' cruises, 302–303
  in general, 13, 118–19, 302
  kids' programs, 22, 26, 30
  Kosher meals, 111–13
  medical consent form, kids', 88
  medical facilities, 87–88
  medical insurance policy, 91
  Panama Canal cruises, 310–11
  vacation guarantee, 102

Oahu, Hawaii, 302
Onboard activities, 100, 122–23, 164–71
  exercise programs, 168–71
  kids' programs, 20–23
  Port of call talks, 172–75
Orient Lines, Inc.
  Alaska cruise, 200–201
  Bermuda cruises, 247
  Caribbean cruises, 213, 220, 235, 237
  diets, special, 109–13
  dining, 118, 155–56, 160
    alternative dining, 118
  discount rates, kids', 25
  Hawaiian Islands' cruises, 302–303
  in general, 13, 118–19
  kids' programs, 20–24, 26, 30
  Kosher meals, 111–13
  medical facilities, 87–88
  medical insurance policy, 91
  Panama Canal cruises, 313–16
  vacation guarantee, 102

Packing tips, 128–32
Panama Canal cruises, 305–16
  Acapulco, Mexico, 306
  Aruba, 306–307
  Caracas, Venezuela, 307
  Cartagena, Columbia, 307
  Cozumel, Mexico, 307
  discount prices, 308–16
  Gatun Lake, Panama, 307
  Panama Canal, 308
  Puerta Caldera, Costa Rica, 308
  St. Thomas, USVI, 308
Patmos, Greece, 281
Pearson Travel, 30, 56–7, 123, 200, 207
Pharmacy, *see* Princess Cruises
Phone cards, discount, 38, 43
Photography, mail-orders, 136–139
Photography tips, 132–139
Playa del Carmen or Calica, Mexico, 216

Premier Cruises
  Canary Islands' cruises, 315
  Caribbean cruises, 222, 229, 235, 237
  diets, special, 111–13
  dining, 156
  disabled persons' facilities, 119
  discount rates, kids', 25
  fire safety, 79
  in general, 119
  kids' programs, 22, 26, 30
  Kosher meals, 109–13
  medical facilities, 87
  medical insurance policy, 91
  Mediterranean cruises, 287–88
  Panama Canal cruises, 313–16
Princess Cruises
  Alaska cruises, 201–204
  cancellation fee, 102
  Caribbean cruises, 213, 220, 229, 235–36
  diets, special, 109–13
  dining, 149–50, 151–58, 160
  disabled persons' facilities, 107–109
  discount rates, kids', 25
  fire safety, 79
  Greek Isles cruises, 266
  in general, 10–11, 13, 16, 119–20
  kids' programs, 22–23, 26, 30
  Kosher meals, 111–13
  meals, 149–50
  medical facilities, 88–89
  Panama Canal, 308–10
  pharmacy, 88
Prince William Sound, Alaska, 192
Puerto Caldera, Costa Rica, 308
Puerto Vallarta, Mexico, 252–55

Rebate and discount agencies,
  Costco Travel, 59–60, 200, 235–37, 261, 310, 315–16
  Discover Wholesale Travel, 95
  Golden Age Travelers, 303
  Pearson Travel, 30, 56–7, 123, 200, 207
  Pennsylvania Travel, 60
  Sears Discount Travel, 59
  Travel Avenue (Chicago), 60, 197
  Travelers Advantage, 57–59, 200
Recreational discounts, 61–62
Regal Cruises
  Bermuda cruises, 247
  discount rates, kids', 24
  kids' programs, 26, 30
Renaissance Cruises
  cancellation fee, 103
  vacation guarantee, 102–103
Rhodes, Greece, 278–80
Room service, 122, 160–61
Royal Caribbean International
  Alaska cruises, 203–204
  Bermuda cruises, 247–48
  Caribbean cruises, 213, 220, 299, 234–37
  diets, special, 109–13
  dining, 158, 160
  discount rates, kids', 25
  golf course, miniature, 121–22
  Greek Isles cruises, 266, 270–71
  Hawaiian Islands cruises, 303–304
  in general, 17, 121–22, 303
  kids' programs, 23, 26, 30
  Kosher meals, 111–13
  medical facilities, 87
  medical insurance policy, 91
  Mexican Riviera cruises, 261–62
  Panama Canal cruises, 306, 315–16
Royal Olympic Cruises
  diets, special, 111–13
  Greek Isles' cruises, 266–69, 271–72, 275–86
  medical facilities, 87
Russian river cruises, 316–18
  discount prices, 317–18
  tour operators, 316–18

Index

Safety at sea (SOLAS), 78–79
San Juan, Puerto Rico, 223–24, 227–29, 236
Sawyer Glacier, Alaska, 188
Seniors, 14–16
Seward, Alaska, 194
Shore excursions, in general, 180–82, 209–11
Singles, 13, 41, 104–106
   activities, 104–106
   cabins, 103
   companion airline awards, 41
Sitka, Alaska, 186–87
Skagway, Alaska, 188–89
Southwest Airlines
   companion award (free), 44
St. Croix, USVI, 224, 228
St. John, USVI, 225–26, 228
St. Maarten/St. Martin, 233–34
St. Thomas, USVI, 226–27, 228, 308

Terra-cotta warriors, Xi'an, *see* China
Time to Travel, 67, 198, 236–38, 315
Tipping, 175–76
Travel accessories, 127–28, 139–40
   safety items, 127–28
Travel Avenue (Chicago), 60, 197
Travel awards (free), 34–37, 41
Travel cash (free), 45–54
   future programs, 51–52
Travel documents, 88, 124–26
   medical consent form, kid's, 88

Travelers Advantage, 57–59, 200
Travelers Travel Insurance Pak, 80, 82–85
Travel Guard International, 15, 85
Travel insurance *see* Insurance, travel
Travel of America, 67, 197, 201, 204, 237–38, 304, 312
Travisa, 143

United Airlines
   companion award (free), 35, 39, 41
   Mileage Plus First card, 35–36

Valdez, Alaska, 193–94
Vancouver, B.C., 182–83
Video photography tips, 135–36

Websites 68–70, 323–27
   cruise sites, 70, 324–27
Whole Word of Travel, 65–66, 198, 200, 262, 304, 312, 315
Worldlink, discount phone card travel award program, 38, 43
Wrangell, Alaska, 191

Yangtze River and Three Gorges river cruise, *see* China

Zihuatanejo and Ixtapa, Mexico 257–58